Commissioned Spirits

Commissioned Spirits

The Shaping of Social Motion in Dickens, Carlyle, Melville, and Hawthorne

Jonathan Arac

COLUMBIA UNIVERSITY PRESS
NEW YORK

Columbia University Press Morningside Edition 1989
COLUMBIA UNIVERSITY PRESS
New York Oxford

Library of Congress Cataloging-in-Publication Data

Arac, Jonathan, 1945–
Commissioned spirits : the shaping of social motion in Dickens, Carlyle, Melville, and Hawthorne / Jonathan Arac.
p. cm.
Reprint with new pref. Originally published: New Brunswick, N.J.: Rutgers University Press, c1979.
Includes bibliographical references.
ISBN 0-231-07116-7 (alk. paper).—ISBN 0-231-07117-5 (pbk. : alk. paper)
1. English prose literature—19th century—History and criticism.
2. American fiction—19th century—History and criticism.
3. Literature and society—History—19th century.
4. Dickens, Charles, 1812–1870—Political and social views.
5. Social history in literature. I. Title.
PR788.S46A7 1989 89-22060
828′.80809—dc20 CIP

Casebound editions of Columbia University Press books are Smyth-sewn and printed on permanent and durable acid-free paper

Printed in the United States of America
c 10 9 8 7 6 5 4 3 2 1
p 10 9 8 7 6 5 4 3 2 1

To my parents

Contents

Preface to the Morningside Edition

WHAT IS A LITERARY EVENT? When a tremendous new formal possibility has been achieved in writing, how can we explain it? If we invoke literary tradition, we isolate culture from other human activities, and the biographical account of "genius" similarly isolates an individual from the rest of humanity; even "influence" does no more than connect genius to genius or to tradition. *Commissioned Spirits* began as part of the widely shared search in the early 1970s to resolve these problems by developing a "new literary history." I wanted to understand what had made possible the totalized organization shared by the greatest mid-nineteenth-century novels in English—*Moby-Dick* and *Bleak House.* My attempt required overcoming entrenched scholarly boundaries and forging new links between areas of investigation that had been segregated from one another. To connect England and America required overcoming the split of novel versus romance; to connect the practices of history-writing and novel-writing, overcoming the split of fact versus fiction; to connect fictional shaping and nonfictional forms of social knowledge, overcoming the split of writing as end versus writing as means.

What is a critical intervention? In attempting to work out these connections, *Commissioned Spirits* posed problems that have become more timely now than when the work first appeared a decade ago. By 1979, the project of new literary history had turned into the controversies over "literary theory": it was the year of Paul de Man's *Allegories of Reading,* the Yale critics' collective volume *Deconstruction and Criticism,* and the anthology *Textual Strategies.* "Theory" was then widely understood as what we might now call a negative formalism. That is to say, the structure of a particular masterwork defined the focus of a critical argument, as in New Criticism, but in the work of the new theory, this structure would be shown not to hold. Theory thus qualified the most extravagant claims for aesthetic form, while at the same time honoring their centrality; in working out its arguments, theory typically related the work to nothing more local or contingent than "western metaphysics," or "language itself," and thus I found it historically imprecise.

As against this theoretical strategy, *Commissioned Spirits* understood the form of nineteenth-century fiction as a process, "the shaping of social motion," and it displaced the centrality of aesthetic form by studying this process in relation to other contingent historical forms, such as the shape of a writer's career, changes in the institutions of publication, and the organization of social knowledge in medicine, economics, and historiography. My procedure, thus, was contextualization, taking one text, not necessarily literary, along with *(con)* another. In this textual collation, the two (or more) texts are discussed together, but there is no presumption that one necessarily determines the other, in the sense of predictively circumscribing it. They are mutually determining: each sets limits and exerts pressure on the other. This formulation echoes the redefinition posed by Raymond Williams in "Base and Superstructure in Marxist Cultural Theory" *(New Left Review,* 1973) but the general point joins *Commissioned Spirits* with most varieties of the renewed historical, contextual emphasis that has characterized literary study in the 1980s.

Commissioned Spirits argues that in the process of shaping social motion, *Bleak House* and *Moby-Dick* succeeded in acts of totalization. In these acts, Dickens and Melville worked from and extended a new definition of the writer's role in England and America that Thomas Carlyle had exemplified. In my account here, as in the book itself, there is a problem, however. What is "total" takes in everything, but what is "defined" is limited, and thus excludes much. I understood this problem in Carlyle to mean that "as his universal significance increases, the relation of the writer to the communal life of his time diminishes" (p. 152).

Since *Commissioned Spirits* appeared, much new work has familiarized us with this kind of problem, without solving it. The strongest attempt to put the problem behind us has been by Bruce Robbins in a series of essays on professionalism. He argues that the professions, classic instances of specialization and segregation, in fact rely on a rhetoric of public service that continually forces them to negotiate their claims in a larger arena than the enclosure in which they are understood to be confined. Much important work, however, has instead redefined the problem's terms. A decade's elaboration of feminist studies highlights the problem in the gender restriction of the supposedly universal "his." For the problematic of Marxism as developed in the 1980s, the problem would be phrased in a different way, which requires us to negotiate between two distinct claims: the force of capital is for the first time bringing humanity into a fully shared single world (thus "universal"); but also, the force of capital repeatedly, continually restricts and damages humanity by a process of segregation and isolation, most evidently in the ever-refined division of labor. In the work of Michel Foucault, yet another version of the problem demands negotiation: between such synoptic models as the *episteme* or the panopticon, and the fine-meshed analytic of differentiation that produces innumerable, incommensurable "local" practices.

These instances demonstrate that the problem is not the same as that of part and whole, which may be figured as synecdoche and called "mediation." Instead, I have been using the term "negotiation"—derived from a Latin term that basically means un-ease, trouble, busyness or business. In this usage, I am rephrasing the key idea of "social motion" in *Commissioned Spirits* and bending it toward what is now known as "new historicism." Beyond what has become the trade name for a publisher's series, however, I am trying to convey the problematic in which Edward Said's work has most instructed me: the give and take between the system of a cultural work and the systematic work of culture.

Among the contemporary perspectives that I have been surveying, it was Foucault's work that most deeply engaged me while I was completing *Commissioned Spirits.* I found in his *Discipline and Punish* resources that helped me to relate my concern with novelists' technique of "overview" to the social history that I had begun exploring as part of Victorian Studies. *Commissioned Spiritis* integrates technique with history by claiming that overview joined the novelist, as subject, to the Benthamite panoptic agencies of inspection and centralization, which made their objects the potentially deviant environments in which disease (damaged bodies) and delinquency (broken homes) might arise. Diseases are known by their symptoms, criminals by their actions; together they suggest the strategies by which the spatializing moment of overview could elaborate a full novelistic fiction. The rhetorical figure of synecdoche joins part and whole, as does a symptom; and the sequential narrative of plot structures an action. From the conjunction of these elements emerges totalization, the literary event that Foucault's "toolkit" helped me specify as it came into possibility and then changed.

In analyzing overview, I understood my work as helping to develop the uses of Foucault for cultural study; "realism" is also important in the book, but I was less aware of the links between my undertaking and major lines of Marxist analysis. It now seems evident, however, as I reread *Commissioned Spirits*, that my narrative construction of Dickens's career is modeled on Georg Lukács's characterization, in "Narrate or Describe," of the shift from realism to naturalism in European literature. For Lukács, realism has the totalizing power to face the challenges of history; naturalism, in contrast, reifies the integrated world of realism into overelaborated description that is not effectively related to the work's human action. My argument for the "segregation of orientations" in *Our Mutual Friend* (p. 165) replays this analytic gesture. In *Our Mutual Friend*, plot, psychology, setting, and figurative language no longer work together as they had in *Bleak House* but instead pull in differing directions, each relatively independent of the others.

I called this new technique "modernism," however, rather than naturalism. In Anglo-American literary history, unlike in Lukács's European perspective, the "modern" is understood as the rival-successor to the "Victorian," which I took as the term for Dickens's mode in *Bleak House*. More particularly, as part of my argument concerning the shape of Dickens's career, I attributed to his continuing novelistic practice a self-aware, critical renunciation of already perfected and thus incipiently conventionalized forms, even if those forms had been his own. Flaubert, James, and Joyce are among the models by which critics have come to understand such a career, and the American academy of the 1970s drew on the writings of Wallace Stevens to theorize the pressures of such rejectionist, reconstructive modernity. In contrast, naturalism understood itself as inheriting realism to complete it, not to overthrow it.

As I reread *Commissioned Spirits*, the interplay of period concepts becomes even more entangled. In Lukács's historical studies of the 1930s, to chart the fate of nineteenth-century realism had important meaning for his own times. His critique of naturalism stood in for a politically impermissible critique of party-line socialist realism. I now find in the discussion of *Our Mutual Friend* that my terms of description clearly correlate Dickens's novel with a particular conception of the "postmodern." Thus my analysis speaks of "free play," a "dispersed world," "unfixed circulation of figurative language" (p. 184). Here I deploy the language of the *Tel quel* avant-garde, more neutrally than enthusiastically, taking care to indicate its historical place rather than transhistorical virtue. As a communist intellectual in Moscow, Lukács had his life on the line. My situation as an assistant professor in the 1970s carried a different rhetorical imperative: the need to find a discursive mode that would enable me to continue an academic career while telling the truth as I saw it.

These considerations on the circumstances of critical writing bear out one of the prime emphases in *Commissioned Spirits:* no person works "save under conditions" (p. 13). One condition that provoked my concern with the literary event of nineteenth-century novelistic totalization was the belief that the most vital fiction of my own time was still working through the aftermath of that event. This belief, in turn, arose not only from a formal judgment about literary means and achievements, but also from a further judgment that such writing was making a difference in the contemporary world. So the first version of this project that I circulated to presses had an introduction treating Martha Quest's initial apprehension of London in Doris Lessing's *The Four-Gated City* (1969) and the construction of the rocket as a means of overview in Thomas Pynchon's *Gravity's Rainbow* (1973).

It soon became clear that this presentist, genealogical procedure, searching the past to find a starting-point for current concerns, made my work unpublishable in the judgment of the academic authorities of the time. My choices were already cross-grained enough in other respects. My stance toward Dickens's shift from realism did not condemn him, as Lukács would; I adapted Foucault's analysis of panopticism, while praising Dickens's progressive human achievement. Above all, I think this book was a troubling intervention because it refused to choose sides in the polemics between "theory" and the establishment. What could it mean to develop the argument for a "Victorian mode of writing" by combining M. H. Abrams and Roland Barthes (pp. 117–118)? Or to document a claim about the newly emerging importance of economic crime by a footnote citing an English Marxist historian, Michel Foucault, and Lionel Trilling (p. 77)? So I recomposed the work into what was more recognizably a historical period-study, and therefore certain of its initial concerns appeared only as transposed and displaced. Even then an editor much involved in "post-structuralism" did not see how his press could handle a study that devoted so much energy to problems of plot. It was not yet the commonplace it has become that plot is crucial among what Fredric Jameson calls "strategies of containment," the techniques of restriction, sometimes conventional and sometimes innovative, that make possible the effect of totality.

These remarks on "conditions" point to one respect in which *Commissioned Spirits* differs from the work that I have done in the decade since. The experiences of the 1960s gave some basis for my positive tone toward Victorian "anti-politics" (p. 137*n*), yet as the 1980s come to an end, I am no longer so sure about the possibilities of oppositional or progressive power that holds aloof from politics. These changes in my thought have been aided by discussions with Carol Kay, especially in conjunction with her *Political Constructions* (1988), but they also come from the public life of our time. I have been chastened through witnessing the impact in the United States and Great Britain of programmatic right-wing occupation of the seats of national executive power, and I am moved by the current renewals of political hope in China, the Soviet Union, and Poland.

The wish to trace more finely the connections between politics and writing has led me, along with my associates at *boundary 2*, including W. V. Spanos, Paul Bové, Daniel O'Hara, and Donald Pease, to explore not only the institution of literature but also the institutions of criticism, in particular the ways in which "literature" as we know it now has been constructed by criticism as its appropriate object of knowledge. It now seems to me important, for instance, that the term "totalized," on which *Commissioned Spirits* hangs so much weight, is first cited in the *OED* from Coleridge's lecture "On Poesy or Art." This in turn suggests that in English, at least, the heritages of New Criticism and Hegelian Marxism may be harder to untangle than has been assumed, or wished.

Such issues focus my *Critical Genealogies* (1987). Most important for *Commissioned Spirits,* I find there problems in the position of F. O. Matthiessen, whose *American Renaissance* (1941) has exerted great influence on nearly fifty years of the American study of American literature, including my discussion of heroism in chapter 6. In the last few years, I have been at work on part of the new *Cambridge History of American Literature*, and in treating Hawthorne and Melville, I have found it necessary to pay more attention to political and economic history than I chose, or was able, to bring to bear in *Commissioned Spirits*. Thus my concerns in "The Politics of *The Scarlet Letter*" (*Ideology and Classic American Literature*, ed. S. Bercovitch and M. Jehlen, 1986) are related to the Compromise of 1850 and the incipient crisis of the party system; and in "A Romantic Book" (*boundary 2,* 1990), I show that the railroad counts for *Moby-Dick* not only as an emblem of Ahab's will (as on p. 109 below), but also as an organization of employment that forced a new understanding of human responsibility. My own current projects thus remain in dialogue with this book; I hope, then, that the new readership which this edition makes possible will also find in *Commissioned Spirits* the power of engagement.

Preface

I HAVE TRIED TO COMPACT into my title and subtitle a sense of Dickens, Carlyle, Melville, and Hawthorne as "commissioned spirits," writers with an imaginative mission to reveal and transform through their powers of knowledge and vision the brute circumstances of the changing world in which they and their readers lived. Such a mission involves a stance of overview, a positioning toward the materials of the world that brings both privilege and guilt, and with this special technique of narrative are further involved special techniques of plotmaking and linguistic organization. The combination of stance, plot, and rhetoric defines the shape that is achieved for the social motion with which any work grapples, but every such shaping fails to be definitive, for the motion continues, at least in part impelled by the disturbance that this new activity of shaping has brought about; a literary form that has worked once will not be adequate a second time.

My project in defining the shapes of social motion that Dickens, Carlyle, Melville, and Hawthorne achieved in their work as "commissioned spirits" is fundamentally historical. I am trying to define a field that thus far has a journal, *Nineteenth-Century Fiction,* but very few books; that field is the novel in England and America, limited for the purposes of this work to the mid-nineteenth century, though I try to suggest something of the extension backward to romanticism and forward toward Henry James. Worthwhile literary history requires serious literary criticism, and I hope that I contribute to the specific criticism of the individual works I study. Nonetheless, literary history requires more than stringing together in chronological order a series of readings, and in every instance I have tried to exercise a stringent self-discipline in limiting my criticism to the relevances of my overall argument. Thus, even in the case of *Martin Chuzzlewit,* the single work I read most fully (in part because it has received less satisfactory criticism than the others I treat), I could not make place for any extended commentary on Mrs. Gamp.

I should observe further that my history is more a survey than a teleology; I devote some attention to changes over time, but my major goal is to define a system of interrelated elements that makes up a moment of literary possibility. In both my historical construction and my readings I try to exploit the innovations that have recently begun to transform the study of language, texts, and discourse. Nonetheless, I avoid matters of pure theory and methodology in the interests of application, in order to specify concrete achievements and limitations.

As a study in literary history, this work may seem unusual in choosing to focus on a few major figures. I take heart from Ian Watt's *The Rise of the Novel,* and like Watt I do not intend to deracinate the figures I attend to. They are emphasized over their background, but I strive to include a sense of that background, both of the writers whom I do not treat at length and of the works that are not explored. My work establishes an outline; it is more an essay than a treatise, and it leaves many spaces open that may be developed at length elsewhere. I hope to do some of that developing, but I hope that others will find themselves encouraged to join me. The many fine books on each of the individual writers I treat testify to our sense of the idiosyncratic in their work, but there is a community of achievement as well in the fiction of the mid-nineteenth century, such as is suggested by rare books like F. O. Matthiessen's *American Renaissance* and Kathleen Tillotson's *Novels of the Eighteen-Forties.* In trying to bridge the Atlantic, I want to add an important further extension to that community.

As I reflect on the institutions and individuals whose aid has contributed to my work over the years, this book itself almost feels a communal project. Of institutions I particularly thank Roxbury Latin School; Harvard University, especially the department of English, Dudley House, Leverett House, the Committee on Degrees in History and Literature, the Harvard Victorians, and the Society of Fellows; Princeton University, especially the department of English, the University Committee on Research in the Humanities and Social Sciences, and the Literary Criticism Discussion Group. An earlier version of Chapter V appeared in the *New England Quarterly* (March 1978) and an earlier version of Chapter VI in *Nine-*

teenth-Century Fiction (June 1977), and the editors of these journals have generously allowed me to reuse these materials. For splendid typing, I am grateful to Geraldine DiCicco and Helen S. Wright. Of my teachers I wish particularly to remember two now deceased: Van Courtland Elliott and Reuben A. Brower. I thank Harry Levin and Monroe Engel, in whose seminars I formed the first ideas of this study and who supervised my dissertation. At a later stage the responsive scrutiny of Edward W. Said and of Daniel T. O'Hara has greatly aided my work. I feel special gratitude to Bruce Robbins and Chaviva Hošek. The insight, interest, love, and criticism of Carol Kay have accompanied this project from its beginnings. Even before that, my parents were there for me.

Note on Abbreviations

In my text I refer parenthetically to the following frequently cited works.

By volume and page, e.g. (1:1)

NH *The Centenary Edition of the Works of Nathaniel Hawthorne,* ed. William Charvat et al. (Columbus, Ohio: Ohio State University Press, 1962–). In Chapter V, however, references to *The House of the Seven Gables* (vol. 2) will specify page alone.

TC *The Complete Works of Thomas Carlyle in Thirty Volumes: Centenary Edition* (1896–1899; rpt. New York: AMS, 1969).

By chapter, e.g. (1)

BH Charles Dickens, *Bleak House,* ed. Norman Page (Harmondsworth: Penguin, 1971).

DS Charles Dickens, *Dombey and Son,* ed. Alan Horsman (Oxford: Clarendon, 1974).

MC Charles Dickens, *Martin Chuzzlewit,* ed. P. N. Furbank (Baltimore: Penguin, 1968).

MD Herman Melville, *Moby-Dick,* ed. Harrison Hayford and Hershel Parker (New York: W. W. Norton, 1967). This volume also contains Melville's essay "Hawthorne and His Mosses" (pp. 535–551), to which I refer by page.

By book and chapter, e.g. (I, 1)

LD Charles Dickens, *Little Dorrit,* ed. John Holloway (Harmondsworth: Penguin, 1967).

OMF Charles Dickens, *Our Mutual Friend,* ed. Stephen Gill (Harmondsworth: Penguin, 1971).

Whenever the context makes clear the work or author being cited, the abbreviation will be omitted.

Commissioned Spirits

Introduction

Commissioned Spirits: An Overview

I take my title from a moment in Wordsworth's *Prelude* that brings together many of the elements with which I am most concerned in this study. During his time in London, Wordsworth went to displays of the arts to observe:

> those sights that ape
> The absolute presence of reality,
> Expressing, as in mirror, sea and land,
> And what earth is, and what she has to shew.

These sights were not works of high culture but a more popular art:

> I do not here allude to subtlest craft,
> By means refined attaining purest ends,
> But imitations, fondly made in plain
> Confession of man's weakness and his loves.

In particular, Wordsworth observed panoramic spectacles, either painted or modeled in three dimensions:

> Whether the painter, whose ambitious skill
> Submits to nothing less than taking in
> A whole horizon's circuit, do with power,
> Like that of angels or commissioned spirits,
> Fix us upon some lofty pinnacle,
> Or in a ship on waters, with a world
> Of Life, and life-like mockery, beneath,

Above, behind, far stretching and before;
Or more mechanic artist represent
. . . .
In microscopic vision, Rome herself.[1]

The condition of the novelist in the mid-nineteenth century significantly echoed that of Wordsworth's earlier visual craftsmen. Despite working in a mode that did not enjoy high cultural prestige, that was not a pure or refined art but aimed instead at satisfying the "weakness" and "loves" of mankind, the novelist nonetheless possessed an extraordinary ambition, to grasp and encompass the "whole horizon" of "what earth is" and "has to shew," to allow readers to experience something like the "absolute presence of reality" in the pages of a book. In undertaking this project, these novelists arrogated the power of "commissioned spirits" to set their readers, along with themselves, in a position of overview, as if pinnacled high above the world they viewed. Thus, when Henry Wadsworth Longfellow wished to define Hawthorne's "point of view" as an author, he concluded his analysis, "Set the imagination free, like another Bottle-imp, and bid it lift for you the roofs of the city, street by street, and after a single night's observation you shall sit you down and write . . . for the rest of your life."[2] This technique of narrative overview and its consequences for the organization of fiction comprise one of my major recurrent concerns in this work.

Strangely enough, for the novelists, as for Wordsworth and Longfellow, this position of overview resonates with a spiritual tremor. The technique brings with it a ghostly uneasiness, as if it were a meddling with extraordinary powers. Such comprehensive overview achieves a return to a wholeness of perception, an integral view of the world, common in early life but typically lost in adulthood. To regain such a view, even if through intellectual orga-

1. William Wordsworth, *The Prelude*, ed. Ernest de Selincourt (2nd ed., revised by Helen Darbishire; Oxford: Clarendon, 1959), 1850 text, bk. VII, ll. 232–253. For the context of such displays, see Richard Altick, *The Shows of London* (Cambridge: Harvard University Press, 1978), pp. 129–133.

2. Review of *Twice-Told Tales, North American Review* (July 1837), rpt. in *Hawthorne: The Critical Heritage*, ed. J. Donald Crowley (London: Routledge and Kegan Paul, 1970), p. 57.

nization of concrete knowledge, brings us back to an infantile perception. Freud argues that the sensation of the "uncanny" arises whenever such a return to lost infantile perceptions occurs; even if the perception itself was a pleasure in infancy and is positively charged in adulthood, it has been estranged from us by an intervening repression and thus seems unsettlingly eerie.[3] Such an analysis accounts for the recurrence in Dickens, Carlyle, Melville, and Hawthorne, as in Wordsworth and Longfellow, of a curiously supernaturalizing rhetoric that colors the experience of narrative overview and haunts the world seen from this perspective. This conjunction of the uncanny—in action, image, and language—with the narrative overview forms another continuing concern of my work.[4]

It is appropriate that Wordsworth confronted the arts of overview in the city, for the metropolis suggestively condenses all those forces of the nineteenth century, already present in Wordsworth's time but growing greater every year as the century wore on, that made it so difficult for writers to achieve a total, integral, coherent view of their worlds, that made it seem as if only a magical power could organize an incomprehensible, ungraspable world. Whether the content of a work were "Rome herself" or a "ship on waters," a world like Dickens's city or Melville's sea, the chaos of urban experience fostered a wish for a clarifying overview. The complex of capital, democracy, and industry seemed to tear the world apart, simultaneously unsettling from its old place all that had existed and bringing into being ever fresh novelties. To capture a sense of this sheer force felt as transforming the social world, I use the materialist term "motion," because the changes were not perceived as resulting from the "action" of traditional humanism or from the "vision" of an idealistic renovation.

This social motion, the mobile thrusts and counterthrusts of energy, shook things loose, forming an ever shifting set of circumstances around the members of this society. Writers understood

3. See Sigmund Freud, "The Uncanny" (1919), trans. Alix Strachey, in *Studies in Parapsychology*, ed. Philip Rieff (New York: Crowell-Collier, 1963), p. 55.

4. For the fullest treatment of Dickens and the uncanny, see Robert Newsom, *Dickens on the Romantic Side of Familiar Things* (New York: Columbia University Press, 1977), chap. 3. Newsom moves less toward social issues than toward acute biographical speculation.

their task as a process of shaping, of giving a direction to this motion, a form to this force, to create a vision from which action might follow.[5] Against the weight of circumstances an imaginative effort was demanded, new techniques of plotting and language that would make the world comprehensible and allow people to engage with it more readily. Throughout this study I focus both upon the organization of action—the techniques of plotting that integrate the worlds of my chosen books—and upon the linguistic strategies, the characteristic figures of speech that add another dimension to the shape of a plot.

Despite their great ambitions, the writers of midcentury shared the skepticism of Wordsworth rather than the naïve hopes that he attributes to the popular craftsmen. Like Wordsworth, these writers recognized that finally the "absolute presence of reality" was unavailable in their texts, that they could only "ape" such a plenitude, that any hope of "expressing as in a mirror" the shape of the world's motion could only yield, as in the sea's mirroring of what floats on it, a "life-like mockery."[6] A consequent discomfort and impatience with the forms of representation available to them marked these writers. Even as they try to find more effective techniques of getting the world into their books, they must criticize past techniques that have channeled and shaped the world into mock-realities and must recognize their own enterprises as tentative. My chapters note repeatedly the writers' concerns with their medium, their self-consciousness as artists.

Not the least disturbing aspect of their work for the writers of the mid-nineteenth century was the extent to which writing itself as a force was not only trying to form the world, to shape the energetic chaos, but was also transforming the world, itself actively joining in the motion it was trying to chart. A final recurrent topic of my study is therefore the place of the institution of literature within society, and the powers and responsibilities of the writers within this institution.

In this study as a whole my critical intention aims both at specific

5. On the function of vision in "periods of crisis," see Sheldon S. Wolin, *Politics and Vision* (Boston: Little, Brown, 1960), p. 294.

6. On such problems of representation, see J. Hillis Miller, *The Form of Victorian Fiction* (Notre Dame: University of Notre Dame Press, 1968), chap. 2; and John Romano, *Dickens and Reality* (New York: Columbia University Press, 1978), especially chap. 1.

illuminations of particular works and at more general clarifications of literary history. As Carlyle once lamented, however, narrative is linear, while the objects of its description are solid. Inevitably, then, I have had to do one thing at a time, yet I have tried to solidify my work by suggesting a spiral movement, circling round one problem with increasingly heightened understanding. Although I end with *Our Mutual Friend,* it contains the problem from which I started.

In beginning this project, my point of departure was a few panoramic passages in Dickens's later novels.[7] In his role as commissioned spirit, surveying from above, the narrator turns to his audience and reflects at once on the world he has created within the novel and on the shared world he claims to be representing, and he asserts that the movements, the fates, of his everyday fictional characters tell us something important about the movement of the whole society in which we are living and thus about our own fates. In their combination of general and specific, their attempt at organized knowledge that bears on individual concerns, such passages focus a crucial aspect of nineteenth-century culture: "the really human, the communicative, side of that vivid show of a society trying to build itself, with every elaboration, into some coherent sense *of* itself, and literally putting forth interrogative feelers, as it goes, into the ambient air; literally reaching out (to the charmed beholder, say) for some measure and some test of its success."[8]

These passages defined for me the right place to begin a literary study of the novel's relation to society, that is, a study that does not investigate novels primarily as products of social causes and that does not view novels primarily as causes of social effects.[9] While not neglecting the historical experience that precedes the act of writing and succeeds the act of reading, I have tried to

7. For "point of departure" (*Ansatzpunkt*), see Erich Auerbach, "Philology and *Weltliteratur,*" trans. M. Said and E. W. Said, *Centennial Review* 13 (1969):1–17.

8. Henry James, *The American Scene* (New York: Harper and Brothers, 1907), p. 154. James here defines that process of "the imagination of society" with which Steven Marcus concerns himself in *Representations* (New York: Random House, 1975), pp. xiii–xiv.

9. My emphasis thus differs from that in the important work by Patrick Brantlinger, *The Spirit of Reform* (Cambridge: Harvard University Press, 1977).

demonstrate the significance within selected, specific novels of a particular sense of society, a particular way of imagining social motion.

The resonance of my chosen passages could not be contained within a study of Dickens alone. Carlyle's literary forms and definition of the writer's role came together in a mode of writing that was the first to articulate such concerns. Analysis of Carlyle's *French Revolution* shows that this exemplary Victorian history projects in its writing a sense of society like Dickens's at its most comprehensively integrated, in *Bleak House*. Not just Victorians are illuminated by Carlyle, but Americans also. Despite the idiosyncrasies and intense nationalism of the "American Renaissance," there was no sudden rupture in Anglo-American literary relations. No more than in the previous generation of Cooper and Irving, no more than in the following generations of James, Pound and Eliot, and Auden, is this generation of American writers isolated from England. Like Dickens, Melville began his career as an easy entertainer but became a serious and difficult writer, and in this movement Melville's goals and methods also resembled those of Carlyle. Even Melville's American exemplar, Hawthorne, shared with England elements of social vision that were "in the air," as a comparison of *The House of the Seven Gables* with Dickens's *Dombey and Son* reveals.[10]

These three novelists thus bear a complex relation to romanticism, for Carlyle was by birth a romantic of the second generation, who by his long life and slow development became the major revisionary of the romantic heritage. Carlyle kept alive and usable for the next generation both the apocalyptic excitement of the French Revolution and the Burkean critique of it; not only the rebellious individualism of Byron but also Scott's sense of society's historical transformation. Carlyle's social vision thickened the sense of "atmosphere" and strengthened the force of "circumstances" through brilliant, new metaphoric specifications of the "environment" that connected people to each other; yet both his writing and his life emphasized the power of human imaginative energies

10. A significant complement to my social emphasis is Edwin M. Eigner, *The Metaphysical Novel in England and America: Dickens, Bulwer, Hawthorne, Melville* (Berkeley and Los Angeles: University of California Press, 1978).

to transform, even to negate, circumstances. The writer's commission is not merely to survey the city, scanning its enclosing surfaces; he must "lift . . . the roofs" to lay bare the human agents within their circumstantial shell. The writer must not only *see* society but also see *through* it, thus at once recognizing and embodying the human forces that have made society and will change it.

THE ARGUMENT

AS WRITERS, Dickens, Carlyle, Melville, and Hawthorne were closely involved with the forces at work in the world around them. Their relations to the conditions under which they worked follow a dialectic of understanding and transformation, totalizing and mobilizing. In seeking to achieve an "imaginative sense of society," these four authors join the writers of journalism and social polemic in establishing a discourse crucial for the new social sciences. In building up "systems of vision and knowledge," their writings parallel the activity of the centralizing agencies of government that were studying and shaping the new human problems of a society much larger and more mobile than had ever before been known. If airborne disease threatened the public health of a city, then techniques of aerial observation were required to combat that danger by gathering and organizing information. The narrative overview in fiction accompanies the new techniques of inspection and centralization worked out by a growing interventionist bureaucracy.

Like such governmental agencies, the writers' tool of overview is not detached from the world it surveys, nor does it achieve a frozen stasis. For writing was part of a literary "career," a public relationship to readers, and a new narrative stance affected that relation. It raised fresh questions of what claims the novelist was making, how seriously he was to be taken, and what effects he might work on his readers. The new understanding achieved through the fictional technique of the overview, and its associated organization of plot and language, transformed the writer's role. In totalizing his perspective, it mobilized new powers. To many readers—whether eagerly or hostilely—the age's powerful new forms of journalistic, periodical, and fictional publication were associated with the revolutionary power that had changed so much of the world already and threatened to leave nothing in the economy, polity, or society as it had been. Even the way writers managed their prose could seem part of a new movement that was disrupting the established regularities and conventions of an older way of writing and living.

Yet if narrative prose seemed innovative and disruptive, an agency of mobility and transformation, it also worked toward a totalizing understanding. Through the interplay of "metaphor and metonymy," local stylistic effects combined to build up the coherence of a book's world, as in the case of *Little Dorrit*. The search for continuity involved in trying to see society as a whole extended to the search for figurative techniques to integrate a book. What would be the point of arguing for an integrally related society in a book that fractured itself into formlessness in trying to bear the weight of that argument? These issues of coherence and continuity are also at stake, but more negatively, in the "rhetoric of character" that makes the human figures of a book. Not the smoothness of a harmonious development, but the fragmentation and repetition of "grotesquerie and the uncanny" typify the fictional characters of Dickens and Melville. Such problems of character—of human life in literature—point back again to the historical interplay of "the family and the city" that defined the overall conditions of intimate life.

To understand how this complex of social and literary forces worked together requires not only a synoptic overview but also a more narrative, chronological study. Dickens's career spans the total period of my concern, the thirty-odd years from the mid-1830s to the mid-1860s. The year of Victoria's ascension, 1837, marks the beginning, since it also saw the publication of Dickens's first novel, *The Pickwick Papers;* Hawthorne's first book, *Twice-Told Tales;* and the work of Carlyle that made his reputation, *The French Revolution.* An ending is firmly marked by Hawthorne's death in 1864 and the publication in 1865 of Dicken's last completed novel, *Our Mutual Friend.* Within this period falls the crucial decade (1843–1853) in which Dickens created his characteristic social novel through a series of experiments running from *Martin Chuzzlewit* to *Dombey and Son* and *Bleak House,* which itself is contemporary with *Moby-Dick* (1851) and *The House of the Seven Gables* (1851).

To follow Dickens's career, with constant awareness of the relevance of Hawthorne, Carlyle, and Melville, illuminates a crucial historical problem: how is the institution of literature related to the other forms and forces of the age, whether those disrupting the age, those building it, or—most typically—those doing both? To achieve and define its new external relations, its place in the world, literature had to undergo much internal reorientation. The novel had to discard old forms and techniques; it had to appropriate smaller forms and borrow from adjacent practices of discourse to make new forms in order to contain the mobility of its age in a new totality. To "contain" new forces is not only to check and perhaps neutralize them, but also to be invigorated by them, and, most importantly, to use and direct them.

For Dickens in *Martin Chuzzlewit,* then, the disruption of family life, in a society felt to be more drastically commercial and urban than ever before, renders inadequate the picaresque and allegorical models that were available for providing fiction with shape and significance. "Society" comes to predominate over "story" and "morality" in giving energy to the book. Through initial "techniques of dislocation" the novel begins to establish its new form by satirically purging away old ones. Even in finally getting underway and introducing significant agents and settings—finding a "modern heroism" to replace old types and "activating London" to replace a static countryside—Dickens continues to work negatively. Only late in the novel and then only briefly does he begin to join the city to a detective plot organized through powers of overview. This positive construction, the "yes of the realist" who ventures a model of his own to replace those discarded, points forward to the much greater achievements to follow through the newly comprehensive "understanding" that the plotting techniques associated with "overview" permit.

Dickens was not alone in moving toward a new fictional mode adequate to the complexity of the times. Like Dickens, Hawthorne began his career as a writer of short pieces for periodicals, and as novelists, they both drew upon newly important journalistic forms to aid in constructing a new kind of novel. Their new literary techniques gave them a grasp on the new content of their society. If the city—both too densely packed and too widely sprawling—symbolizes the threat of chaos that makes modern life difficult to apprehend, the railroad, with its speed and power, condenses and increases such problems. Moving to bind cities ever closer together, integrating nations in a newly effective way, the railroad also worked dispersively, promoting all forms of geographical mobility. A product of the heavy industry of the second phase of the industrial revolution, the railroad hit the areas through which it passed with tremendous impact. Like a bomb it blew apart whole neighborhoods to make its way. Thus both Dickens in *Dombey and Son* and Hawthorne in *The House of the Seven Gables* seize upon the railroad as a figure for the impact of modernity upon family life (symbolized in the stability of a house). Drawing upon the literary resources of the Gothic tale to explore the interplay of "past and self" in the house, Dickens and Hawthorne exploit the rhetorical figure of synecdoche to work out relations of part and whole, inhabitant and house. Joined to the Gothic within a newly comprehensive novelistic whole, the sketch of contemporary life is adapted as a means for coming to terms with the railroad's force, which challenges the complacencies of domesticity. Through his powerful use of these techniques to understand and improve society, the writer emerges in both books as a seer, though of a somewhat different kind in each.

The private emphasis of *Dombey and Son* yields in *Bleak House* to a greater public ambition. England as a whole becomes the house that must be set in new order. In the earlier nineteenth century England had suffered social and economic changes so massive and unsettling that they seemed to revolutionize life, even though the fundamental political structure remained the same. To deal with such social transformation, Carlyle's *History of the French Revolution* offered both an intellectual and a literary model in its devaluation of the political-constitutional in favor of what bore more directly on human life in society. The "Victorian mode of writing" first articulated in Carlyle and exemplified in *Bleak House* as well, through its plotting and narrative stance, combined a broad clarity of vision—associated with the "theory" of philosophical essay writing—with the human "experience" in which the novel as a form had long excelled. The worlds that Carlyle and Dickens portray are threatened by "something in the air," an ominous "atmosphere" registered in two "cultural codes": both through the Gothic motif of haunting spirits and through the scientific discourse that investigated the dangers miasmic infection posed for public health. As ghosts threaten the household that has left important obligations unfulfilled, so disease threatens a society that has not taken care of all its members, and revolution threatens a neglectful polity. In working through these analogies, both writers draw upon the figure of synecdoche even more extensively than had been done in *Dombey and Son* and *The House of the Seven Gables*. Furthermore, both Dickens and Carlyle confront in their works a characteristic fear: many members of the new society perceived change as so profound and drastic that it seemed the end of the world. People yearn for apocalypse to show a meaning and direction in events that seem too chaotic to bear any human form, but Dickens and Carlyle show that their worlds are not controlled from the outside by powers inaccessible to mankind. Instead they reveal the human activity that is producing these changes and hope through their writing to guide that change.

From the seer of *Dombey and Son* and *The House of the Seven Gables* to the guide for a lost society offered by *Bleak House* and *The French Revolution*, the role of the writer grows greater and the work of writing more ambitious. The institution of literature itself seems one of the transforming forces of the age, along with the city, railroad, epidemic, and revolution. The question of what force the writer may wield and what place he may occupy in society was answered for many in the mid-nineteenth century through the life and work of Carlyle. He embodied a "portrait" of the writer, he offered a specific analysis of the writer's troubled position, and he held out the hope that the modern man of letters could be a "hero" like kings, priests, and prophets of old. This analysis not only directly inspired Melville with a sense of his own potential as a writer; it also gave him a new relation to the literary past and liberated him to find a new way of reading Shakespeare that was crucial to his achievement in *Moby-Dick*. Both through his manipulation of Ishmael as narrator and through the language of the book, Melville's programmatic self-consciousness of himself as a writer is crucial to the total effect of *Moby-Dick*, and it is felt largely as exuberance.

Self-consciousness may open out joyful prospects, but it poses as well many problems for the writer. For a few years, the stance of overview allowed a working distance from society, from which a writer could readily return with fresh knowledge and intervene in the world. But a growing sense of distance shadowed the writer's relation to society, making the return more difficult. Professionalization and specialization began once again to segregate the elements that had come together briefly to make possible the social novel of the early 1850s. "Experience" no longer was something easily shared in a public work through an apprehensible shape of action; instead, it became an obscure private domain only to be hinted at with a language itself contaminated by convention.

The writing of *Our Mutual Friend* suggests the transition of the greatest English social novelist into a much more private writer. Just as Dickens in his early work had turned critically against previous forms of fiction, in *Our Mutual Friend* he turns against his own previous accomplishments as outworn constraints. He undoes his old mystery-plot organization and its relation to London; he criticizes the use of synecdoche for social representation and develops new figurative techniques that emphasize personal transformation more than social totality. In *Our Mutual Friend* a "new economy of writing" marks the end of a fiction of "social motion." The spirits have abandoned their commission and are reduced to their sole selves. It remains, however, to explore this history in detail.

I

The Conditions of Work

Of Shakespeare, Carlyle observed that despite his immortal genius his writing bore the imprint of his age and was thus placed in history, for "no man works save under conditions" (TC 5:110). Not only did Dickens, Melville, and Hawthorne share this position with Carlyle; it guides my method as well. In this chapter I try to specify a set of problems that these writers faced at their moment in history and to indicate the opportunities they had to forge tools for solving the problems. The new forces and mobility of the 1830s and 1840s in England and America posed a challenge to comprehension that the writers met in forming their "imaginative sense of society" through the technique of overview that established "systems of vision and knowledge." Yet this apparently stabilizing literary mission launched the writers on the trajectories of their careers and enmeshed them in the institution of literature, which was itself part of the age's transforming energy. Emerson might try to distinguish between the "Establishment" and the "Movement,"[1] but these writers found that the forms they established, the institutional niches in which they were established, only increased the movement of which they were a part.

The Imaginative Sense of Society

In the early and middle nineteenth century, imaginative writers and journalists joined politicians and those whom we now consider the founders of the social sciences in a common effort to comprehend the disturbances of their age and to organize them in

1. "Historic Notes of Life and Letters in New England," in *Emerson's Complete Works*, Riverside Edition (Cambridge, Mass., 1883), 10:307.

a useful model.[2] The writings of Dickens and Mayhew epitomize the sharing that went on across the borders of what are now separate domains. Mayhew's findings, for example, made available to Dickens material on "mud-larks," Thames-side scavengers, for *Our Mutual Friend,* but Mayhew's initial inquiries followed the interest Dickens's early writings had awakened in exploring the life of the poor and outcast, and Dickens's literary methods helped to establish the canons of verisimilitude by which Mayhew's accounts could seem plausible because so fantastic.[3] In *Oliver Twist* (1837–1838) Dickens first brought the London slum of Jacob's Island into the writing of his time, and when cholera broke out there a decade later, Mayhew covered the scene in language that looks back for local color to *Oliver Twist* but also looks forward to the sociomedical idiom of *Bleak House* (1852–1853).[4] If I choose then to speak of the "imaginative sense of society" in Dickens, Melville, Hawthorne, and Carlyle, it is not so much to differentiate them from Tocqueville, Disraeli, or Mayhew as to indicate that I will not be primarily concerned to test this vision against other records of nineteenth-century social reality but rather to analyze the internal relations among the elements of vision.[5]

The "sense" of society includes consciously developed as well as intuitive understanding, but rather more what is expressed by story and plot arrangement, by narrative perspective and tone, and by imagery than by any elaborate form of explicit "scientific" analysis. Nonetheless, such scientifically derived nineteenth-century commonplaces as "environment" and "circumstances" are important,

2. Cf. Hayden White, "The Burden of History," *History and Theory* 5 (1966):125.

3. See H. S. Nelson, "*Our Mutual Friend* and Mayhew's *London Labour and the London Poor,*" *Nineteenth-Century Fiction* 20 (1965): 207–222; and Gertrude Himmelfarb, "The Culture of Poverty," in *The Victorian City,* ed. H. J. Dyos and Michael Wolff (Boston: Routledge and Kegan Paul, 1973), 2:714. For a similar process of "de-novelizing" in Spain, see Claudio Guillén, *Literature as System* (Princeton: Princeton University Press, 1971), p. 76n.

4. *Morning Chronicle,* 24 September 1849; rpt. in Henry Mayhew, *Voices of the Poor,* ed. Anne Humphreys (London: Cass, 1971), pp. 3–4.

5. In this sense my work resembles that of Robert Nisbet, *Sociology as an Art Form* (New York: Oxford University Press, 1976) and differs from that of Morroe Berger, *Real and Imagined Worlds: The Novel and Social Science* (Cambridge: Harvard University Press, 1977).

both as emotive counters of the writer's attitude to his society and as pointers to some of the more concrete representations of these attitudes.

The "society" that these writers portray comprises not only the other men and women with or among whom, knowingly or unknowingly, an individual lives, but also the humanized nonhuman around him, those elements of nature or material culture with which an individual is involved, such as possessions, dwelling place, or area of economic activity. Furthermore, "society" encompasses the customs and laws that regulate the individual's relations with these people and things.

In the early nineteenth century great changes unsettled old social arrangements and demanded new efforts of coherence on the part of a writer who wished to represent the life of his times in some comprehensible yet inclusive form. From a given, society became a problem. In earlier picaresque fiction the picaro is an anomalously rootless figure investigating the niches of a relatively fixed social order, but in the nineteenth century the "young man from the provinces"[6]—Melville's Ishmael, Hawthorne's Holgrave, Dickens's Pip—is just one moving figure in a shifting world. Politically the democratic revolutions in America and France and the ensuing wars, demographically the great growth of cities, economically the industrial revolution, ideologically such forms of individualism as utilitarian ethics and laissez-faire economics, no less than the accelerating improvements in transportation, all meant more mobility for more people: "Every age may be called an age of transition—the passage . . . from one state to another never ceases; but in our age the transition is *visible*."[7]

As a beneficent freedom from immemorial oppression under old regimes, old dogmas, and the "idiocy of rural life," these new developments allowed new men to search to become something in life; but at the same time they allowed for a new proliferation of vices, such as hypocrisy, the pretense of being what you have not yet become, or of having always been what you've just become. The desperately earnest façades of bourgeois respectability pro-

6. See Lionel Trilling, *The Liberal Imagination* (New York: Viking, 1950), p. 64.

7. Edward Lytton Bulwer, *England and the English* (1833), ed. Standish Meacham (Chicago: University of Chicago Press, 1970), p. 318.

voked the wish to take off the roof and see what was really inside. Yet once exposed, the pathetic sights solicited sympathetic understanding rather than the lash of the satirist. A world in which "people have no exact and fixed position" but experience only "mystic, shifting, and various shades of graduation" makes society shimmer with "shot-silk colours" and breeds in people a "lust of imitation" based on their "horror of descending."[8] More massive methods of working, fighting, or living together made it apparent that private destinies had come to depend "more visibly than ever before on all-encompassing public events."[9] Thackeray's connection of the Napoleonic Wars with Sedley's financial ruin in *Vanity Fair* (1848) is very different from Fielding's use of the Jacobite uprising in *Tom Jones* (1749).

In direct confrontation with these energies, Burke and Scott produced a stabilizing view of historical continuity as the guarantee of coherence. Carlyle's adaptation of this romantic social thought was the crucial example for many of the novelists, politicians, and social thinkers in England of the 1840s—for Engels and Disraeli as well as for Dickens. Carlyle's significance is not only ideological but more strictly literary. He helped define what it meant to be a writer in society and how to write about society, as well as how to understand society.

Melville's path to Carlyle differed greatly from Dickens's. Since the United States was born of the Revolution and never had a counterrevolution, its relation with the Enlightenment was continuous. Jefferson was a *philosophe* as was neither Burke nor Scott despite their links to Enlightenment thought. Melville's first two works, *Typee* (1846) and *Omoo* (1847), carry on eighteenth-century cultural criticism, exposing Western civilization by contrast with an untouched Polynesian island and by showing the grim effects colonization had on the natives (one of our earliest fictional views of the "third world"). In *Mardi* (1849) a different kind of social satire, although Swiftian in technique, shows in its substance Melville's contact with Carlyle's thought, and in *Redburn* (1849) Melville addresses the topics of nineteenth-century social criticism on their exemplary ground of industrial England. *White-Jacket* (1850)

8. Ibid., pp. 31–32, 77; René Girard illuminates this problematic in *Mensonge romantique et vérité romanesque* (Paris: Grasset, 1961).

9. Peter Demetz, *Marx, Engels, and the Poets* (revised ed.; Chicago: University of Chicago Press, 1967), p. 1.

presents a synecdochic view of "The World in a Man-of-War": one "total institution" representing the totality of society.[10] Melville characteristically takes a part in detail to link it metaphorically with a whole, while Dickens proliferates examples within his work that he links metaphorically with each other. Both exemplify the "desire for the enormous and for totality" that led Zola to proclaim, "When I attack a subject, I would like to force the whole universe into it."[11] Even in his much slighter works, Hawthorne too finds figural strategies for achieving comprehensiveness.

SYSTEMS OF VISION AND KNOWLEDGE

THE MAJOR MID-NINETEENTH-CENTURY WRITERS with whom I am concerned participated in one of the great enterprises of their age, the production of knowledge from the observation of disorder and disruption, thereby transforming that disorder into the basis for a newly conceived order. In literary tradition satire had been the antiformal form established from gazing on chaos, but satire looks back to a previous order, and if it has a hope, it is not for innovation but restoration. Traditionally, too, the ambition to gain usable power from observation had satanic overtones, as in the temptations of *Paradise Regained,* III and IV. Satire and Satan combined in Asmodeus, the "Limping Devil" of Lesage's *Diable boiteux* (1707, 1726), who snatches up a young man, carries him through the air to the highest steeple in Madrid, and lifts off the rooftops of the city's houses to reveal in satiric vignettes the moral disorder within.

By the late eighteenth century, however, the study of physical disorder through pathological anatomy had become a major new source of medical knowledge, and its discoverers transformed the whole science of health through their observations of death and the diseased.[12] Yet such activity was still connected in the popular imagination with transgression, as the stories of "resurrection men" or—in an extreme instance—*Frankenstein* suggest. Around the same time a new popular amusement coined for modern times an indis-

10. For "total institution" see Erving Goffman, *Asylums* (New York: Doubleday, 1961), pp. 1–125.

11. Cited in F. W. J. Hemmings, *Emile Zola* (Oxford: Clarendon, 1953), p. 36.

12. See Michel Foucault, *The Birth of the Clinic* (1963), trans. A. M. Sheridan Smith (New York: Random House, 1973).

pensable word. From the late 1780s Barker's "Panorama" allowed the curious for a small price to assume over the painted simulacrum of a city a position like that to which Milton's Satan had led Jesus.[13] At this time, too, a more serious version of this toy was projected in Bentham's *Panopticon* (1791).[14] This architectural machine also began from the pathological, for Bentham devised it as a prison, but in his later plans it became adaptable for factory design as well, or for any institution that had to organize large numbers of individuals. The principle involved a central watchtower around which were deployed in a circle the cells of the individual criminals. As opposed to the recently razed Bastille, which had hidden its inmates away from any view, the inmates here would be constantly susceptible to observation, although they would never know whether they were actually being seen at any moment. This device created a secular version of the "specular mount" Satan offered, from which his "optic skill" served as an "airy microscope" to peer into dwellings (*P.R.*, bk. IV, ll. 236, 57–58).

This system of unseen observation, destroying the reciprocity of seer and seen,[15] allowed both for knowledge of individuals as cases and for aggregating such cases into knowledge of populations as statistical wholes. Satire, in contrast, had typically focused on the individual and used mob scenes simply for the force of destructive chaos within them. Although no Panopticon was built, the same principle governed the management of the new workhouses in which the English poor were institutionalized in the 1830s. Criminals and paupers began to be the individuals in society about whom most was known, the objects of an increasing body of writing in all the new records and registers that accumulated the facts from which decisions about social policy would be made.

This systematic organization of the medical, the panoramic, and

13. For panoramic moments in English literature from 1640 to the Romantics, considered more metaphysically than socially, see W. B. Carnochan, *Confinement and Flight* (Berkeley and Los Angeles: University of California Press, 1977), pp. 102–119.

14. See Gertrude Himmelfarb, "The Haunted House of Jeremy Bentham," in *Victorian Minds* (New York: Alfred A. Knopf, 1968), chap. 2; and Michel Foucault, *Surveiller et punir* (Paris: Gallimard, 1975), pp. 197–229.

15. For the dangers classical thought found in unseen observation, see Marc Shell, *The Economy of Literature* (Baltimore: Johns Hopkins University Press, 1978), pp. 30–31.

the satanic emerges clearly from a moment in Dickens's *Household Words,* written around the time of *Bleak House,* which shares similar images and concerns. The writers are considering the interrelations of conditions in prisons with those of the poor outside prison. The medical analogy is drawn on: just as "Political economy . . . is the physiology of the civil constitution," so is the study of crime and poverty its "morbid anatomy."[16] The governor is to his jail as the physician is to his hospital. Knowledge must be coherently organized by "classification" in order for proper action to be taken. Prisons must be seen not as "so many disconnected undertakings" but as "all parts of one great whole." In order to know this totality, "we must mount with the aid of a good spirit to the highest tower in the jails"; we must let this beneficent Asmodeus unroof the houses for us and show us "how the people live, and toil, and die." For "without a just consideration for every humble figure in the great panorama" we will not properly know how to administer prisons.[17]

The administrative methods of centralization and inspection that made possible such comprehensive vision were strongly defended by Dickens in his speeches on public health around this same time.[18] Indeed, epidemic disease, as well as crime and poverty, was one of the major forms of disorder from which the age made new knowledge in the service of new order. Even in earlier times, plague had provided occasion for a more stringent ordering of the city, keeping everyone in his proper place, subject to roll call and a daily review of the living and the dead,[19] in a strange echo of apocalypse. Dickens's use of epidemic disease in the organization of *Bleak House* and *Little Dorrit* and the analogy between the useful knowl-

16. The prevalence of this metaphoric system is suggested by Balzac's self-definition as "doctor of social medicine" in his preface to *Les Parents pauvres.* See *La Comédie humaine,* ed. Marcel Bouteron (Paris: Gallimard, 1950–1965), 6:133.

17. "In and Out of Jail" (1853), rpt. in *Charles Dickens' Uncollected Writings from "Household Words,"* ed. Harry Stone (Bloomington: Indiana University Press, 1968), 2:478–488.

18. On centralization and inspection see David Roberts, *Victorian Origins of the British Welfare State* (New Haven: Yale University Press, 1960), especially chap. 3. For Dickens on centralization in 1851, see *The Speeches of Charles Dickens,* ed. K. J. Fielding (Oxford: Clarendon, 1960), p. 130.

19. Foucault, *Surveiller et punir,* pp. 197–200.

edge about the whole of society that he presented in his books and the new inquiries on behalf of public health provoked by outbreaks of disease explain the strange conjunction in the contemporary comment that "the novels of Mr. Dickens" and "the cholera" were two of "the great social agencies . . . at work among us."[20]

Crime, disease, and poverty were all to be found in the same areas. Another disrupting, transformative power of the age, the railroad, typically ran through these areas as well, both because the inhabitants lacked the organized political power to block this destruction and because of the hope—from above—that destroying slums would improve conditions. Destroying housing without adequate provision for new housing, however, only produces further overcrowding. Railroads exacerbated crowding not only through those they displaced but also through those they transported. Train stations were jammed with passengers, those seeing them off, those waiting to receive them, those serving the travelers or spectators, and many more. This necessitated crowd control, for which the railroads employed personnel in uniforms modeled after those of Peel's new (1829), centralized Metropolitan Police.[21] At the same time, therefore, that they compressed England as a whole, by reducing the time of intercity travel, the railroads also acted as forces of compression within each city.[22] This compression increased the "knowability" of the city, both by condensing certain districts right along the railroad into epitomes of social problems and by clearing a space from which an observer could survey the scene, as Engels did in Manchester.[23] Dickens's brother-in-law Henry Austin first

20. Cited in G. M. Young, *Victorian England* (2nd ed.; London: Oxford University Press, 1953), p. 55.

21. Jacques Barzun, "The Imagination of the Real, or Ideas and Their Environment," in *Art, Politics, and Will,* ed. Quentin Anderson et al. (New York: Basic Books, 1977), p. 18. The formation of Peel's police, the "Bobbies," owed much to the English experience of controlling the rebellious Irish. See Norman Gash, *Mr. Secretary Peel* (Cambridge: Harvard University Press, 1961), p. 498.

22. John R. Kellett, *The Impact of Railways on Victorian Cities* (London: Routledge and Kegan Paul, 1969), p. 342.

23. Friedrich Engels, *The Condition of the Working Class in England* (1845), trans. and ed. W. O. Henderson and W. H. Chaloner (1958; rpt. Stanford: Stanford University Press, 1968), p. 61. See also Steven Marcus, *Engels, Manchester, and the Working Class* (New York: Random House, 1974), pp. 188–190.

became interested in the problems of public health while a surveyor for a new railway. "Appalled by seeing the conditions of the working-class homes," he went on to work with the Association for promoting the Improvement of the Dwellings of the Labouring Classes and from there became first (1848) Secretary of the General Board of Health.[24]

While all these new developments gave an unparalleled "publicity" to the working classes,[25] analytic knowledge was less quick to develop about the higher reaches of society, even where their effacement was not so great as in the Panopticon or in the omniscient narrator of a novel. In their reviews, the cultivated class of opinion-makers praised Dickens's revelation of the lives of the poor but questioned the accuracy, validity, and use of his inquiry when it reached into the spheres of business, production, administration, or leisure. Dickens couldn't paint a gentleman, went the cry. The classes that were underrepresented politically and overrepresented in the new documentation, however, recognized the political overtones in observation. When, for purposes of sanitary survey (public health, we say), "crows' nests" were erected "on the pinnacles of Westminster and above the cross of St. Paul's," the *Examiner* mocked the "consternation of many Chartist agitators" who saw only a "gigantic machinery of espionage," a "bird's-eye watch" over imagined treason.[26] But this new supervisory apparatus indeed aimed at building up records for the purpose of protecting the state's interests as defined by those who were surveying, rather than the surveyed.

In conceiving of various individuals as an integral population with specific characteristics that related them to other populations in the workings of the city, bureaucratic demography carried out an act as "foreign and external" to those individuals as was the capitalist's action of organization to the factory workers whom it united into "one single productive body" by establishing a "con-

24. K. J. Fielding and A. W. Brice, "*Bleak House* and The Graveyard," in *Dickens the Craftsman*, ed. Robert B. Partlow, Jr. (Carbondale: Southern Illinois University Press, 1970), p. 119.

25. See Donald J. Olsen, "Victorian London: Specialization, Segregation, and Privacy," *Victorian Studies* 17 (1974):271.

26. *Examiner*, 14 July 1849, cited in Fielding and Brice, "*Bleak House* and The Graveyard," p. 122. Note the symptomatic appropriateness of the title "Examiner."

nexion between their individual functions." Thus, for the workers that enforced connection appeared "in the shape of the authority of the . . . capitalist";[27] for the neighborhood it appeared in the menacing shape of state authority. Within a novel, that enforced connection gives shape to the writer's authority.

In an anecdote recounted by his reading manager, Dickens emblematizes his power to organize material in a panoptical image: "He would decide on the various heads to be dealt with. These being arranged in their proper order, he would in his 'mind's eye' liken the whole subject to the tire of a cart wheel—he being the hub. From the hub to the tire he would run as many spokes as there were subjects."[28] Such a spatializing power to locate and relate the peripheral to the central was needed to integrate an imaginative view of the city, and the assumption of this centralizing, panoramic, privileged view is a gesture of essential concern to all the writers I am treating. Carlyle takes "an Asmodeus' Flight" (3:291) to see Paris from the rooftops at a crisis in the Revolution; Hawthorne in "Sights from a Steeple" worries over the powers of a "spiritualized Paul Pry" (9:192); Melville meditates on the seductions and dangers of observation from "The Mast-Head," and Ishmael's terrifying totalized vision of the ship at the climax of "The Try-Works" at once provokes as a counterimage the soaring "Catskill eagle." Even Bulwer responded journalistically to the crises of 1832 with a series called *Asmodeus at Large,* a prelude to his more serious survey of the age in *England and the English.*

To a contemporary reviewer of *Bleak House,* it was crucial to consider whether a novelist had the power "of looking right through his story, and marshalling his characters and incidents in their proper order." He warned of the danger of finding so much interest and pleasure in every individual part as to "forget the relation it bears to others." The image of city-top survey culminated this meditation. A novelist must do better than "some short-sighted persons" who could read the Ten Commandments off a sixpence

27. Karl Marx, *Capital* (vol. 1, 1867), trans. from 3rd German ed. by Samuel Moore and Edward Aveling (1887; rpt. New York: International Publishers, 1967), p. 331. On the widespread belief in early industrial England that successful enterprise required direct surveillance by the owner, see Sidney Pollard, *The Genesis of Modern Management* (Cambridge: Harvard University Press, 1965), pp. 12–13.

28. *Speeches of Charles Dickens,* p. xxi.

but would "be at a loss to point from the top of St. Paul's to the exact localities of the Post Office, the Mansion House, or the Exchange."[29] Dickens himself echoes these terms in his 1867 preface to *Martin Chuzzlewit*: "What is exaggeration to one class of minds and perception is plain truth to another. That which is commonly called a long-sight, perceives in a prospect innumerable features and bearings non-existent to a short-sighted person." The capacity to organize a "prospect" and yet to discern innumerable details within it characterizes his works as well as those of Melville and Carlyle, while Hawthorne achieves a similar effect with somewhat different technique.

THE PROBLEMATICS OF CAREER

BEFORE I CAN PROCEED into my substantive explorations, I must further clarify the notion of a literary "career," an institutional bearing that is crucial to the conjunction of writers and techniques I am concerned with. The very notion of a career as we know it, a course of professional activity, only comes into English in the nineteenth century,[30] and the first uses are for action with wide and obvious public consequence—in politics especially. The earliest *OED* citation for an artistic career appears in 1834, and this shift from the political to the aesthetic corresponds to the direction of much else in the post-Napoleonic world. Thus the term "movement" in France after 1830 referred to politics and society, as in the contrast of a "party of movement" and a "party of resistance," but it soon came to include in addition what we call intellectual or artistic "movements."[31] Etymologically, and with a force still felt in many of the metaphors that attend the term (to launch, to be diverted from)

29. *Eclectic Review*, December 1853, in *Dickens' "Bleak House,"* ed. A. E. Dyson (London: Macmillan, 1969), p. 81. For a view from St. Paul's, see the opening of Mayhew's *Morning Chronicle* survey of "Labour and the Poor" (1849), rpt. in *The Unknown Mayhew*, ed. Eileen Yeo and E. P. Thompson (New York: Random House, 1971), pp. 97–98.

30. On the new notion of career in mid-nineteenth-century America, see Burton J. Bledstein, *The Culture of Professionalism* (New York: W. W. Norton, 1976), pp. 171–178.

31. Ernst Robert Curtius, *Essays on European Literature* (1949), trans. Michael Kowal (Princeton: Princeton University Press, 1973), p. 438.

"career" is a word of motion and of competition. Chariot racing is its original context. This issue of the force and rightness of the writer's motion in relation to his public will inevitably affect in complex ways the writer's own work of getting into his texts the motion that he sees the public as a whole engaged in. Indeed, the larger issue implicated in this, the interplay between the reading public and the *res publica*—the sense that especially in the new circumstances of periodical and book production and distribution of the earlier nineteenth century, one may have to offend, ignore, or evade the reading public in order to reach the real public—is one of the issues first fully posed by the Romantics and continuously at stake ever since. Coleridge's use of the term "reading public" is the first cited in the *OED*, and as early as 1843 Ruskin wrote, "There is a separate public for every picture, and every book" (*OED*). The problem of the career then is deeply involved with the problem of social motion.

For poets there had once been a clear ideal course to follow, the Virgilian progress from pastoral to epic, but by the early nineteenth century even such traditionally oriented poets as Wordsworth and Keats found this model problematic. It was worse for the novelists, for there were no examples of a novelistic career. Cervantes's masterpiece seems almost accidental, and the great novels of the eighteenth century were only episodes in the lives and works of their authors. Marivaux, Lesage, and Defoe produced their important novelistic works intermixed among a wide variety of other productions; Fielding and Richardson came too late in their lives to fiction to achieve more than one masterpiece each; Rousseau and Goethe are perhaps the two greatest novelists whose greatness in no way depends upon their having written novels. After the "Rise of the Novel" in the 1740s, it has difficulty continuing itself as a genre and keeps threatening to disappear again into the subliterary commerce from which it rose. Novelists did not understand well enough or value highly enough what they were doing to discern the productive principles of their art. The growth in the nineteenth century of what Henry James called "appreciation"—a set of terms for proper descriptive and analytic criticism of the novel—is a story that we cannot follow here to its culmination in James and overflow into Proust, Woolf, Lawrence, Ortega, Lukács, and Benjamin.

The case of Jane Austen shows what might have been an exemplary career halted by the brute mechanics of the publishing market, emblematically in the gap between the purchase of *Susan* and the appearance of *Sense and Sensibility* (1803–1811). Austen's story was not as well known to the early Victorians as it is to us, however. In contrast, the case of Scott was unavoidable. As the most popular poet of his time, who shifted into prose and renewed the grand practice of the novel, bringing it to heights of respectability and acceptability that it had never before known, Scott might well have made an exemplary career, had it not been for his bankruptcy and degeneration into exhausted self-repetition. Scott is nonetheless symptomatic, for the relation between financial and artistic solvency remains a great complexity through the nineteenth century. Balzac imitated Scott, as in so many other things, in his attempts to combine writing and printing, but he managed to keep afloat, although adrift, and for Henry James, Balzac's career formed the first really usable lesson that the history of fiction had to offer. James could add Flaubert too as a counterinstance of the private career, but this category begins to move decisively toward the modern,[32] and it is with the strange middle ground of the 1840s that we are now concerned, with Dickens who was making his own career before the full contours of Balzac had become visible (even if Dickens had, like Thackeray, been looking in that direction).

For Hawthorne and Melville, matters of career are equally crucial. *Moby-Dick* and *The House of the Seven Gables* mark moments of crisis in the careers of their authors. The success of *The Scarlet Letter*—both as an act of writing for Hawthorne and as a fact of the market for his publisher—gave Hawthorne for the first time the real opportunity, the security and respectability, that made it seem possible to become a professional novelist: "As long as people will buy, I shall keep at work." His publishers write of his prospects in language that relates the career to the great agent of social mobility of the age: "We intend to push yr. books a-la-Steam Engine. . . . We shall apply the publishing steam to this new volume with the confident assurance that it will run like a locomotive" (*NH* 2:xv). But the "new volume," *The House of the Seven Gables*, did not go like steam for Hawthorne. Although he hoped that it was more "natural and healthy," more "characteristic" and "proper," for him than *The Scarlet Letter*, he found nonetheless that the actual composition took more "care and thought" than had *The Scarlet Letter*

32. For analysis of the modern literary career, see Edward W. Said, *Beginnings* (New York: Basic Books, 1975), pp. 224–261.

because it was not "all in one tone" (2:xvi–xviii). Hawthorne here faces the problems of career: the need to avoid mere self-repetition; the need gradually to replace inspiration with craft, care, and thought; and the wish that somehow still the work be naturally like oneself. Hawthorne failed to reconcile these imperatives, perhaps because he failed adequately to recognize what his own nature was. *The House of the Seven Gables* repeats textually the railroad that had been so ready an image for the publisher and seriously questions the value of its force and modernity. Hawthorne felt ill at ease with the power necessary to keep a career in motion, to keep the wheels of publication turning.

Melville also finds ambivalent the power that he locates in *Moby-Dick,* but the work exults in the mobility of its subject, form, and language; only in *Pierre, The Confidence-Man,* and "Bartleby" do tortured immobility, drifting, and apathy characterize Melville. After the accident of *Typee,* Melville had shown himself a skilled professional in continuing to find ways to vary the store of his experience into one fiction after another; but such writing did not suffice for him, and first in *Mardi* and then in *Moby-Dick* he attempted to do something else and thereby brought himself to the crisis of modernity. Carlyle's place in Melville's attempt to become a modern writer forms a major concern in my treatment of *Moby-Dick.*

A full comparative study of Anglo-American fiction in the mid-nineteenth century would demand further inquiry into why the careers of Melville and Hawthorne are such failures, why their writing could not maintain its level of accomplishment while maintaining a challenging but workable relation to the public. Overemphasis on this pattern of interruption, however, and the consequent search for uniquely national, or biographical, explanations, have tended to obscure the extent to which the initial posing of the question of career for these two exemplary American writers resembles that of their greatest English contemporary. Dickens himself by the end of his career has become a much more private writer than he was at first, and in investigating the full span of his career, patterns emerge that may be fruitful for further Anglo-American comparison.

Those of Dickens's own English contemporaries who came to prominence just before him in the 1830s also exemplify the problems of a career, though the problems are inverse: their careers are not fractured but stagnant. Although Bulwer continued to produce even longer than Dickens, he was never again a figure of the first importance, as he had briefly seemed. He did competent work in all the available forms of fiction but brought to none anything distinctive enough to efface the new names that were springing up around him. Ainsworth is a more interesting example, because we see him driven by market pressures into constant repetition of the type of novel that had won him his most characteristic early success. So a series of formulaic, topographically oriented historical fiction (e.g., *The Tower of London*, 1840; *Old St. Paul's*, 1841; *Windsor Castle*, 1843) goes on until he has run himself into the ground, both in inner resources and in market value.[33]

PUBLICATION AND REVOLUTION

IN LAUNCHING A LITERARY CAREER, English and American writers from the 1820s through the 1840s were joining themselves to one of the major new mobilizing forces of their age. Bulwer saw "the Press" as the only "antagonist power" strong enough in the early 1830s to act as a "formidable check" to the force of aristocracy in England.[34] The word "journalism" itself had originated in French in the last years of Enlightenment polemics against the Old Regime (1778), and Carlyle devoted a chapter to journalism as one of the characteristic phenomena of the French Revolution (*TC* 3:25–29). The term entered English first in the *Westminster Review* (1833), the organ of the philosophical radicals who had just prevailed in the agitation for Reform. In that campaign to effect a bloodless English Revolution—by first organizing the "out of doors" political activity of unrepresented industrial workers and then publicizing that activity to frighten the House of Parliament—James Mill made strategic use of "*the* Engine—the Press" to give "the mob" leverage against the immobile establishment. When Joseph Parkes, political manager of Birmingham radicalism, said of a related campaign that "steam alone could do the business," he meant by steam "the pressure of public opinion, as expressed through petitions, public meetings, and especially the press."[35] The major organ of middle-class reform propaganda, the *Times*, had actually been founded to adver-

33. See J. A. Sutherland, *Victorian Novelists and Publishers* (Chicago: University of Chicago Press, 1976), pp. 152–162.

34. Bulwer, *England*, p. 232.

35. Joseph Hamburger, *James Mill and the Art of Revolution* (New Haven: Yale University Press, 1963), pp. 1–2.

tise a technical advance in printing and came to its position of prominence, earning its nickname "The Thunderer," in the period after 1814 when it was printed on the world's first steam printing press.[36]

This "revolution . . . effected by Periodical Literature" in the fourth estate,[37] harnessing the advances of the industrial revolution to further the democratic revolution, offered new opportunities as well for literary activity. The early nineteenth century saw not only the growth of newspapers but also the establishment of the great quarterly reviews and a proliferation of other magazines. Outsiders, new men like Carlyle and Macaulay, could earn a living and come to prominence in the periodicals long before their major historical works appeared to cement their popularity. Their American contemporary William Prescott similarly served a literary apprenticeship to the *North American Review* before his series of histories appeared. Not only did Dickens and Hawthorne, like Thackeray and George Eliot, begin as periodical writers, but Dickens transformed the market and public for the novel by his exploitation of monthly part publication.

My later chapters will say more about the particular importance of periodical writing for the larger forms of fiction and history; for now I want to emphasize the social transformation that was felt in this new surge of publication and the techniques and perspectives that accompanied it. The definition Hazlitt offered of the work of the "Lake Poets" in relation to the French Revolution applies as well to the innovative city sketches of "Elia" that Charles Lamb began to publish in *London Magazine* (1820). Like the early Wordsworth, Coleridge, and Southey, Lamb found his subject matter in the "meanest and most unpromising" topics, which "grew like mushrooms out of the ground." Like them he embellished such material with his own "unbounded stores of thought and fancy" in a way that threatened to become a self-displaying "egotism." "Sheer humanity," "the commonest of people," fill his pages, and his task was somehow to make them memorable.[38]

Just as the Lake Poets had done in poetry, the new periodical literature was radically changing the relation of a writer to his

36. Raymond Williams, *The Long Revolution* (New York: Columbia University Press, 1961), pp. 188–189.

37. Bulwer, *England*, p. 262.

38. "On the Living Poets," in *The Complete Works of William Hazlitt*, ed. P. P. Howe (London: J. M. Dent and Sons, 1931), 5:161–163.

subject matter and his audience, a change most notably manifest at the level of style, syntax, and diction. Thus Carlyle's writing posed a constant challenge to the cultivated standards of even his strongest supporters. After *Sartor Resartus* had appeared in *Fraser's Magazine* (1833), while Carlyle was trying unsuccessfully to place it as a book, John Sterling questioned the propriety of its style. Carlyle replied, "Do you reckon this really a time for purism of style, or that style (mere dictionary style) has much to do with the worth . . . of a book? I do not. With whole ragged battalions of Scott's novel Scotch, with Irish, German, French, and even newspaper Cockney (where literature is little other than a newspaper) storming in on us, and the whole structure of our Johnsonian English breaking up from its foundations, revolution *there* is visible as everywhere else."[39] Carlyle thus wishes to ally himself with the irruptive force of the outsiders who are giving new voice to the meaning of the age.

Nearly twenty-five years later James Fitzjames Stephen looked over Dickens's career and saw the triumph of what Carlyle had called "newspaper Cockney": "Dickens's writings are the apotheosis of what has been called newspaper English. . . . He makes points everywhere, gives unfamiliar names to the commonest objects, and lavishes a marvellous quantity of language on the most ordinary incidents." Stephen finds such a style one "in which it is very hard for people to think soberly of others, and almost impossible for them not to think a great deal too much about themselves and the effect which they are producing." Although his description of the manner and its implications closely matches Hazlitt on the Lake Poets, Stephen does not link Dickens to Wordsworth, Coleridge, and Lamb, who by midcentury were all felt as safely socially conservative. Instead, he names Cobbett as the first exemplar of Dickens's style. He even misdates the beginnings of Dickens's novelistic career to fix more closely its revolutionary spiritual affinities: "*Pickwick* was first published . . . [in] 1832 or 1833, when the Reform Bill had just been passed. . . . We should be at a loss to mention anyone who reflected the temper of the time in which he rose to eminence more strongly. . . . One principal cause of his popularity is the spirit of revolt against all established rules which pervades every one of his books."[40] Such testimony does not present the whole

39. James Anthony Froude, *Thomas Carlyle: A History of His Life in London* (New York: Harper and Brothers, 1885), 1:21.

40. [James Fitzjames Stephen], "Mr. Dickens," *Saturday Review* 5

truth, but it valuably reminds us that Dickens the rebel is not merely a creature of modern criticism, and that this rebellion was felt to begin in the manner of publication and writing, not just in the content of the works.

Although the American writers did not have the same possibility of an antagonistic relation to their established national institutions—since so little was yet culturally established—the predominant sense that a new nation required a new literature made by a new kind of writer pushed them too toward a variety of stylistic transgressions. The very attempt, furthermore, to deviate from ordinary British literary norms often meant writing like the British rebels. As part of the American writer's obligation to "carry Republican progressiveness into literature," Melville proclaimed in his manifesto on Hawthorne, "Let us boldly contemn all imitation, though it comes to us graceful and fragrant as the morning, and foster all originality, though, at first, it be crabbed and ugly as our own pine knots" (*MD* 546, 550). Even from his fellow literary nationalists the knotty originality of Melville's prose in *Moby-Dick* was to suffer reproach that questioned its social and moral principles. Duyckinck condemned its alliance with "the conceited indifferentism of Emerson" and the "run-a-muck style of Carlyle."[41]

Melville singled out as a type of the new writer the obscure figure in Hawthorne's "A Select Party," "a young man of poor attire, with no insignia of rank or acknowledged eminence," who was nonetheless to become "Master Genius" of the age. Like most of Hawthorne's work of the 1840s, this piece had been published in the *Democratic Review*, and the turn to writing for this organ, rather than for the gift-annuals, was part of Hawthorne's increased concern with the problematic realities of his times that led him to such larger works as *The House of the Seven Gables* and *The Blithedale Romance*. In his self-portrait as M. de Aubépine, Haw-

---

(1858):474–475. See also Anthony Trollope's link between Dickens and Carlyle for their self-creation of a style "in defiance of rules," in *An Autobiography* (1883; rpt. New York: Dodd, Mead, 1916), p. 216.

41. [Evert A. Duyckinck], New York *Literary World*, 22 November 1851, rpt. in *"Moby-Dick" as Doubloon*, ed. Hershel Parker and Harrison Hayford (New York: W. W. Norton, 1970), p. 51. See the valuable analyses of Melville's relation to his readership by William Charvat, *The Profession of Authorship in America, 1800–1870*, ed. Matthew J. Bruccoli (Columbus: Ohio State University Press, 1968), pp. 204–282.

thorne praises the *Democratic Review* for its "defense of liberal principles and popular rights" and sees its title in the mirror of French as "*La Revue Anti-Aristocratique*" (*NH* 10:93). In describing himself as a foreigner, Hawthorne recognized that he was not truly a popular writer in his age's response to him, and Melville went so far as to find Hawthorne exemplary for being one to "deem the plaudits of the public . . . strong presumptive evidence of mediocrity" (*MD* 548).[42] This nascent sense that the truly revolutionary (and therefore American) position for an American writer was unpopularity was to color Melville's later career strongly, but for now it is enough to note the association for all of our writers between their new literary forms and the social innovations of the age.

42. The most recent study of Hawthorne's career provocatively reverses Melville's emphasis, finding instead a search for "intimacy" with readers. See Kenneth Dauber, *Rediscovering Hawthorne* (Princeton: Princeton University Press, 1977).

II

Dickens and Melville

DICKENS AND MELVILLE present many grounds for comparison.[1] Thematically one might work from the specific resemblances in mood and milieu between the worlds of law in *Bleak House* and "Bartleby the Scrivener," or between the satire of the American scenes of *Martin Chuzzlewit* and *The Confidence-Man.* The alternation of idyll and nightmare characterizes much of the writing of the two authors, especially in the early works like *Typee* and *The Pickwick Papers* and *Oliver Twist.* Furthermore, *Pierre* and *Little Dorrit* both redefine the tradition of *Bildung* fiction by going back to the example of Shakespeare's Hamlet that was so crucial for Goethe in *Wilhelm Meister.*[2] The Hamletism of Pierre is well known, but in *Little Dorrit* too the injunction of the dead Hamlet, "Do not forget," provides a mystery that acts as a structural principle for the story of Arthur Clennam, torn between the wrongs of time past and the paralyzed hope for a future that will set things right.

In particular, the excitement in their use of language, the constant creativity that despite dangers and lapses holds us enthralled not only to what they represent but to their act of representation,

1. For an extensive program of suggestions, see Lauriat Lane, Jr., "Dickens and Melville: Our Mutual Friends," *Dalhousie Review* 51 (1971):315–331; a study that emphasizes the historical and biographical aspects more exclusively than I do (and in highlighting the divergence of England and America neglects Carlyle) is Pearl Chesler Solomon, *Dickens and Melville in Their Time* (New York: Columbia University Press, 1975).

2. I develop this suggestion further in "*Hamlet*, *Little Dorrit*, and the History of Character," *South Atlantic Quarterly* 87 (1988):311–28. As in this book, I again take my bearings from Lukács and Foucault.

first led me to associate Dickens with Melville, and both with Carlyle. These writers are representative men, heightened types, of an age that loved eloquence. In *American Renaissance* Matthiessen has charted the concern with expression that led Melville and his great contemporaries beyond the notorious American political rhetoric to a style, no less the product of artifice, that could carry a great intellectual weight, or that touched more closely the things and talk of everyday work, or that combined these two achievements in a recovery of "metaphysical" style. Given the decade Thackeray spent lampooning Bulwer's attempts to demonstrate that "Fiction . . . is the oratory of literature,"[3] we may suspect, however, that the great Victorians reacted so sharply against romantic eloquence as to seek only a genteelly modest plainness. Yet Macaulay's achievement and popularity were based on his rhetorical ability to elevate the commonplaces of thought; the neoromanticism of the "Spasmodic" poets had a significant impact on the major writers; and an emphasis on emotion, imagination, and the eloquent speaker continued to dominate popular religious and political discourse.[4] Witness the great success that Carlyle's friend Edward Irving achieved as an apocalyptic preacher in London around 1830. All the great writers of the mid-nineteenth century sought techniques to transform eloquence into writing, while maintaining a cruel eye for others' failures to achieve this task.

In treating Carlyle in later chapters, I explore the relations between eloquence and writing. Here I intend, however, to take a tack that directly addresses the formal difference most strongly felt between the works of Dickens and Melville. I then go on to consider issues of characterization and rhetoric, before concluding with some speculation on the biographical and historical ground the two writers share, which helps to explain the striking similarities I discern through their differences.

3. Edward Lytton Bulwer, *England and the English* (1833), ed. Standish Meacham (Chicago: University of Chicago Press, 1970), p. 298.

4. For popular materials see G. Kitson Clark, "The Romantic Element: 1830–1850," in *Studies in Social History*, ed. J. H. Plumb (London: Longmans, 1955), pp. 211–239. The best treatment of Dickens's relation to this tradition is Garrett Stewart, *Dickens and the Trials of Imagination* (Cambridge: Harvard University Press, 1974), especially pp. 1–29. On the Spasmodics see Jerome Hamilton Buckley, *The Victorian Temper* (Cambridge: Harvard University Press, 1951), chap. 3.

METAPHOR AND METONYMY: THE CASE OF *Little Dorrit*

I EARLIER DREW ATTENTION to one fundamental respect in which the fiction of Dickens and Melville seems to differ: Melville typically focuses on one specific setting that is related by narrative metaphor to the larger world outside that sphere of action, while Dickens proliferates instances within a work that he links to each other. Melville's work, we usually say, is symbolic in that the represented world of fictional action calls out for completion by being related to a larger whole of which it is a part. In contrast, we call Dickens's work realistic, presenting a fictional whole that mirrors in miniature the larger world of which it is a model. Roman Jakobson tried linguistically to formalize such a distinction between symbolism and realism by drawing attention to the metaphoric and metonymic poles of language and the contrasting principles of similarity and contiguity. In distinction to the metaphoric, symbolic procedure, "The predominance of metonymy . . . underlies and actually predetermines the so-called 'realistic' trend. . . . Following the path of contiguous relations, the realistic author metonymically digresses from the plot to the atmosphere and from the characters to the setting."[5]

Jakobson's distinctions break down, however, since neither pole can by itself constitute a complete text, for each without the other makes a case of aphasia, of the failure of language. Instead, his terms allow us to see that the work of both Dickens and Melville is based on the synecdochic relation of part to whole, and that in giving continuity and coherence to his novels—that is, in linking character to setting or plot to atmosphere—Melville for all his metaphoric proclivities relies on metonymy, just as Dickens must employ the principle of metaphor to generate meaning from his myriad details and stories, to keep them from being an eccentrically linked chain of fragments.[6] So the metaphor of imprisonment links the various plot lines of *Little Dorrit*.

5. "Two Aspects of Language and Two Types of Aphasic Disturbances," in Roman Jakobson and Morris Halle, *Fundamentals of Language* (The Hague: Mouton, 1956), p. 78.

6. For reflection on the "means of condensation" in the novelistic "enterprise of totalization," see J. Hillis Miller, "Optic and Semiotic in *Middlemarch*," in *The Worlds of Victorian Fiction*, ed. Jerome H. Buckley (Cambridge: Harvard University Press, 1975), pp. 125–126.

Melville begins from the ship's totality and metonymizes it into its parts. Recall such chapter titles as "The Mast-Head," "The Line," "The Crotch," "The Doubloon," and "The Quadrant." He does the same with his agents. Ahab appears in chapters like "The Pipe," "The Hat," and the whale is sometimes only "The Tail." To work through one instance, in "The Line" (60) Ishmael takes this part, joined by contiguity to the rest of the ship, and follows it through its threadings to specify the further, contiguous parts of the whale-boat. But from this partialization a new whole reemerges, for the line "folds . . . in its complicated coils" the whole boat, and "all the oarsmen are involved" in it. From this metonymy new metaphors develop: the boat embraced by the line endangers its occupants as much as "the manifold whizzings of a steam-engine in full play" endanger factory workers. This metaphoric relation between two conditions of labor then opens through the view of a "philosopher" to the whole human condition: "All men live enveloped in whale-lines. . . . All are born with halters round their necks." Metaphor and metonymy interact to form a whole, a synecdochic cosmos of interlinked parts like the city atmosphere in which Dickens's people "live enveloped."

Let me develop further the theoretical issue. The limited length of a lyric poem makes it easy for us to memorize it and to imagine it spatially, all parts simultaneously coexisting, as is indeed often the case typographically on the page. In contrast, a novel is so long that to read it inevitably involves us in an experience of time, in which we meet, one after another, new people, places, or situations. At an immediate first level a novel exists as story, a series of "what next's?": a metonymic sequence of combinatory links. The more analytic, less immediate, plot is similarly a metonymic chain of cause and effect. If we consider, however, the actual ordering of material presented, the aesthetic deformation imposed on the sequence of event and causality, we see how the metaphoric principle enters the experience of novel reading. If in the second chapter of *Bleak House* Dickens connects Chesney Wold to Chancery syntactically by use of the present tense and metonymically by physical proximity "as the crow flies," he also relates the two by calling them "Rip van Winkles" and "sleeping beauties." Metaphoric allusion justifies an otherwise jarring conjunction. As is typical of a novelist, however, Dickens further binds these two realms together by developing metonymic plot connections between them, rather than relying exclusively on metaphoric analogy to join them. In this respect even *Our Mutual Friend,* Dickens's most "symbolic" novel, differs from a poem like *The Waste Land.* In the novel, characters do meet each other, while Eliot's people "meet" only as images in the eyes of Tiresias or the mind of the reader. Similarly, even such novels as *Mrs. Dalloway* or *Ulysses,* which resemble Eliot more closely than Dickens in their analogical procedures, impose a basic metonymic unity of time and place—a day in London or Dublin.

The opening installment of *Little Dorrit* further illustrates these issues. The remarkable first chapter of *Little Dorrit* at once demands of us that we read it allegorically, that we make metaphoric translations in order to interpret the reality that it presents.[7] In any case, the end of the chapter makes this demand, for the narrator there himself allegorizes the fireflies. Their lights mimic the stars "as men may feebly imitate the goodness of a better order of beings" (I, 1). But I say "at once" not just because the image of "Babel" on the first page anticipates, negatively, the relation of the fireflies to the stars, but because the very rhythm of insistent repetition of the sun's "stare" in the first pages arouses an expectation of heightened significance: "the studiously paratactic rhythm sets off a number of compartmented elements, all of which are seen simultaneously, in a timeless cross-section whose static order is *prima facie* emblematic."[8] The anaphoric repetition of "fog" and the succession of present participles that open *Bleak House* also fit this characterization and help to confirm it, for the narrator himself begins to decipher the emblem by locating Chancery, which had begun the series, at the center of the fog and then proceeding to describe and analyze Chancery. The opening of *Little Dorrit* operates on the same principle, the "staring" light of the sun dominating it as the fog did the opening of *Bleak House*.

The first pages of *Little Dorrit* make present a moment that reveals a universe of hierarchy and distinctions within a fixed moral frame: "There was no wind to make a ripple on the foul water within the harbor, or on the beautiful sea without. The line of demarcation between the two colours, black and blue, showed the

7. See Morton W. Bloomfield, "Allegory as Interpretation," *New Literary History* 3 (1972):301–319; and also, on Dickens's pushing the reader to interpret, John M. Robson, "*Our Mutual Friend:* A Rhetorical Approach to the First Number," *Dickens Studies Annual* 3 (1974):246.

8. Angus Fletcher, *Allegory* (Ithaca: Cornell University Press, 1964), p. 173 (describing the opening of Kafka's "The Hunter Gracchus").

point which the pure sea would not pass, but it lay as quiet as the abominable pool, with which it never mixed." In this view of the world the only possible mixing is not nearby but far off, and not horizontal but vertical: "Towards the distant line of the Italian coast, indeed, it was a little relieved by light clouds of mist, slowly rising from the evaporation of the sea, but it softened nowhere else." The reference to "Babel" that follows alludes to a premature, impious human attempt to bridge a gap whose closure apparently lies beyond man's control, at least until the time when the sea "shall give up its dead," bringing the depths to surface and darkness into light.

The "universal stare" dominates not only the represented world of Marseilles, but also the language by which it is represented. Metonymically, at the level of the signified a stare requires an object to stare at, but it is by analogy of the pattern of signifiers that the "staring white houses, staring white walls, staring white streets" generate "strangers" as their object. The consonants of "staring" are graphically reduplicated in "strangers," through the basic poetic process, projecting "the principle of equivalence from the axis of selection into the axis of combination."[9] Similarly assonance identifies the "stare" with "the atmosphere . . . the air" which is its medium.

Under the staring light of judgment in the first pages of *Little Dorrit* we meet the three institutions, family, religion, and state, that form the book's central concern, and we see their characteristic edifices: houses, churches, and a prison. People cannot build the right sort of building to keep the "stare" out. Houses are scarcely adequate: "Blinds, shutters, curtains, awnings, were all closed and drawn to keep out the stare. Grant it but a chink or keyhole, and it shot in like a white-hot arrow." Although "the churches were freest from it," they offer only a dreamy "twilight" which Dickens paints disapprovingly. He condemns the churches for shutting men out from the light that until this point has "made the eyes ache" and been inhumanly oppressive.

The prison is "so repulsive a place that even the obtrusive stare blinked at it and left it to such refuse of reflected light as it could find." Paradoxically, although one is glad to avoid the "obtrusive stare," any other light is mere "refuse." "Like a well, like a vault,

9. Roman Jakobson, "Linguistics and Poetics," in *Style in Language*, ed. Thomas A. Sebeok (Cambridge: The M.I.T. Press, 1960), p. 358.

like a tomb, the prison had no knowledge of the brightness outside, and would have kept its polluted atmosphere intact in one of the spice islands of the Indian Ocean." Dickens's attitude pivots, and the "stare" becomes a desirable "brightness" with which the prison can no more mix than could the foul harbor water with the pure sea. In the twilight anarchy of the church, only "shadows" were visible, but the prison has a window "by means of which it could be always inspected," like a Panopticon. Human surveillance replaces the "universal stare," as if the technique of representation through narrative overview were contaminating the represented world.

This constant vulnerability to observation underlies Rigaud's determination always to act, as if on stage, the "gentleman," to "play it out" wherever he goes; and it warrants the ambiguity by which we understand his "posture" to be a pose as well as a position. Here we encounter the false appearance, a "pretense" that is both "pretentiousness" and "pretending," which recurs importantly throughout the book, usually associated with prisons, real or metaphorical. In the Marshalsea Mr. Dorrit enforces upon Amy the "genteel fiction" of idleness (I, 7), and she must live with the "family fiction" that she is a "plain . . . little creature" (I, 20). Closed up in her father's home, Flora puts on a "caricature" of her girlish manner, and Arthur sees her as "going through all the old performances—now, when the stage was dusty, when the scenery was faded, when the youthful actors were dead" (I, 13). Accompanied by her parrot, Mrs. Merdle explains that "Society suppresses us and dominates us" so that we cannot show our natural selves (I, 20), and Mr. Merdle, who lives on a street of grim "staring" houses, must give parties where the people stare at each other as houses do. He does nothing for himself but "everything for society," to placate that "expressionless uniform" stare (I, 21).

If the "universal stare" of Marseilles is like a "white-hot arrow," the human stare is no less acute. Rigaud's eyes are "sharp . . . pointed weapons." A variation of this metaphor relates the second chapter analogically to the first, to which it is already linked metonymically by contiguity in Marseilles. Not only is the party of travelers shut up against their will in quarantine, as Rigaud and Cavalletto are in prison, but in both cases the enclosure ensures observation. The carceral and medical systems of vision work alike. Meagles thinks the situation is worse than having "a spit put through" him in order to be "stuck upon a card in a collection of beetles" (I, 2). In the first chapter the "stare" carried ominous overtones of voyeurism: "Something quivered in the atmosphere as if the air itself were panting." Miss Wade's relation in the second chapter to Tattycoram realizes this suggestion in action. Going up the stairs, Miss Wade "heard an angry sound. . . . A door stood open, and within she saw the attendant upon the girl she had just left. . . . She stood still to look at this maid. A sullen passionate girl! Her rich black hair was all about her face, her face was flushed and hot, and as she sobbed and raged, she plucked at her lips with an unsparing hand" (I, 2). Tattycoram does not welcome but fears this intrusive attention. She imagines that Miss Wade has come like her own anger, her own malice, as if her feelings could be personified outside her and could then watch her struggle under their power. Indeed, Miss Wade observes Tattycoram as she might a "dissection." Phiz's illustration of this scene is entitled "under the microscope." Once again hostility, sharpness, and staring are identified. Like the first chapter, the second ends at night, as "again the wide stare stared itself out," and again the narrator engages in allegorical reflections, this time on "the pilgrimage of life."

The third chapter suddenly brings us to London, apparently with no connection to what has gone before, but metaphor relates the two cities even before we learn that we have followed Arthur Clennam on his "pilgrimage" from Marseilles to London. "Gloomy, close, and stale," London appears just opposite to the dazzling sun, sea, and sky of Marseilles, and its exterior, where everything is "bolted and barred" (I, 3), is more like the prison within Marseilles than like the city itself. The plague that literally terrified Marseilles metaphorically fills London's moral atmosphere: "In every thoroughfare, up almost every alley, and down almost every turning, some doleful bell was throbbing, jerking, tolling, as if the Plague were in the city and the dead-carts were going round." As in Marseilles, plague and suspicion go together. Meagles exclaimed, "To suspect me of the plague is to give me the plague," and in London the appearance of plague derives from the rulers' suspicious fear of what the people might do if allowed the freedom to enjoy themselves. Instead, the people are allowed "nothing but a stringent policeman" to oversee them. Dickens condemns as irrational the rulers' behavior by comparing it to Polynesian "taboo."[10] This gen-

10. Dickens here reverses and thereby satirizes the comparison, common in Victorian social theorists, between the working classes and

eral social attitude prevails also in specific personal contexts. Mrs. Clennam's punitive moralism reflects the general atmosphere which it helps to produce: "The plagues of Egypt, much the dimmer for the fly and smoke plagues of London, were framed and glazed upon the walls." Mrs. Clennam has made her own house a prison within the larger prison of London.

In these chapters the plague, which travels by contagion and so is the metonymic malady par excellence, is used metaphorically. The plague in *Bleak House* has a firmer literal grounding, for the disease he carries dramatically illustrates Jo's connection to all society, but here plague metaphorically relates Marseilles to London and later in the book will metaphorically characterize the spread through all of society of Merdle's financial fraud. The same mixed procedure occurs in *Moby-Dick,* when to express the metonymic relation of ruler to ruled, Ahab says metaphorically that his "cog" turns the "wheels" of his men (37).

If the opening of *Little Dorrit* presents a moment in which hierarchy, order, and distinction are all visible, the following chapters begin to blur such lines, and the whole book will chart a further confusion of borders. Prisons and plague are everywhere. Church bells, which should bring hope to the human condition, seem to Arthur Clennam to cause "the death" of "many sick people" (I, 3). Mrs. Clennam in her enclosure is "beyond the reach of the seasons," expecting snow in September. Sexual relations are also disordered. Affery's wedding could as well have been a "smothering." But there is a way out. At the end of the third chapter, as a third night has fallen, the sight of Pet's pretty face has reawakened old memories in Arthur, and with a gaze that reverses the sun's downward beam of intrusiveness he looks up and out the window to dream: "It had been the tendency of this man's life—so much was wanting in it to think about . . . to make him a dreamer after all." Even raised as Arthur was, an individual has the imaginative power to negate the environment and dream of a different world. Since this description of Arthur occupies the same chapter-ending position as Dickens's allegorizing overviews in the first two chapters, perhaps the narrator in these earlier chapters was enjoying the same privilege as Arthur, dreaming of an order that does not really exist. The fourth chapter, the last chapter of the first installment,

---

"primitives." See J. D. Y. Peel, *Herbert Spencer* (New York: Basic Books, 1971), p. 203.

throws this problem wide open by presenting a "dream" that proves in fact to be reality, as Affery observes Flintwinch and his twin brother.

In *Little Dorrit* Dickens brings two major dreams to reality, for characteristically he shows a nightmare as well as a good dream.[11] The hard, staring world and uncrossable barriers of Marseilles first present the nightmare that much of the rest of the book realizes—the world of Mrs. Clennam's jealous God. Appropriately, Blandois comes from Marseilles to plague her in the book's later parts, for her view of the world creates men like him. The second world of the book, the good dream of love as contrasted to grimly suspicious justice, is most fully embodied in Little Dorrit herself, who is prefigured in Marseilles by the jailer's daughter. Like a human reincarnation of the beneficiently overviewing "commissioned spirit," the daughter looks in on Rigaud and Cavalletto, "touched with divine compassion . . . like an angel's" (I, 1), a look free of any sadism. We first see Arthur Clennam between these two worlds, "a half smile breaking through the gravity of his dark face" (I, 1), and the book charts his course from the one world to the other, from enclosure in his mother's house to walking down the streets with Little Dorrit.

Nonetheless, Arthur's good fortune does not show that Dickens has wholly committed himself to his good dream. The other fates in the book tell a different story. In a play like *King Lear* the secondary plot of Gloucester only heightens the sense of necessity in what befalls Lear, but in a novel multiple plots typically stress the individuality of the central characters' fates. Thus in *Anna Karenina*, for instance, Anna's disastrous ending "reveals the inner contradictions of modern bourgeois marriage in the most powerful terms. But what is also shown is first, that these contradictions do not always necessarily take this particular path . . . and, secondly, that similar kinds of conflict will only lead to Anna's tragic fate in very specific social and individual conditions."[12] Dickens differs from Tolstoy in *Anna Karenina* or from the major French realists

11. On Dickens's double vision see John Carey, *Here Comes Dickens* (New York: Schocken, 1974), p. 15.

12. Georg Lukács, *The Historical Novel* (1937), trans. Hannah and Stanley Mitchell (London: Merlin, 1962), p. 142. See also Peter K. Garrett, "Double Plot and Dialogical Form in Victorian Fiction," *Nineteenth-Century Fiction* 32 (1977):1–17.

in presenting his happy story centrally, but the qualifying function of parallel plots still holds. In this respect *Moby-Dick,* in contrasting the fate of the *Pequod* with the fates of the boats that the *Pequod* encounters, follows the practice of Dickens and the novel more than that of Shakespearean drama.

These observations suggest an important fact about novel reading. We do, at the end, add up significances. The novel, different as it is from pure storytelling, incorporates the earlier and simpler form into itself and, although much more, is also a collection of stories whose lessons concern us. Considering *Little Dorrit* in this light, we can see how the two axes of language must always work together in practice. We can establish a basic sentence pattern along the axis of combination and see how the multiple stories of the book vary this pattern along the axis of selection.[13] For example:

a) By evil Mrs. Clennam metamorphoses her house into a prison.
b) From incompetence Old Dorrit must exchange his house for prison.

A third fate slightly varies the pattern by reducing to equivalence the complementarity of house and prison that marks a) and b):

c) For evil Blandois is imprisoned (buried) in a falling house.

In the second chapter Mr. Meagles speaks of "all the influences and experiences that have formed us" as we have lived our lives, and we begin to compare Arthur, Pet, Tattycoram, and Miss Wade with regard to these factors. The book as a whole continually returns to this concern and introduces further characters whose responses to "influences and experiences" we must also consider, notably Little Dorrit and her siblings, Flora, and Henry Gowan—those major characters who appear as children of parents, rather than as full adults on their own. The book asks how it is possible to grow up in a society such as it portrays. To grow up properly, one must avoid a traumatic break with one's past, the sort of vain denial that Old Dorrit encourages all his children to make once they are rich; but one must also avoid merely repeating the past in a "grotesque revival," as Flora does with Arthur. Flora lives in a house that is the "Patriarchal" equivalent to Mrs. Clennam's matriarchy. It too is a capitalist, dissenting, "quaker-like" household

13. On narrative as the expansion of a sentence, see Gérard Genette, *Figures III* (Paris: Editions du Seuil, 1972), p. 75.

where life is "stifled" and which is "unchanged . . . by the influence of the varying seasons" (I, 13). The reference to the "seasons" contrasts nature to an unnatural human will, organic growth to mechanical repetition. Ideally Dickens seeks continuity with change, that is, development. The following chart summarizes this topic:

a) Despite environmental disadvantages Amy grows up responsible.
b) Despite environmental disadvantages Arthur grows up loving.
c) Because of environmental disadvantages Flora stagnates frustrated.
d) Because of environmental disadvantages Miss Wade stagnates tormented.
e) Despite environmental advantages Gowan stagnates nasty.
f) Despite environmental advantages Pet stagnates unhappy.
(The novel does not actualize all combinations of beginnings and ends. The common romance pattern of ending happily after beginning advantageously would not have suited Dickens's purposes.)

Even if various readers of *Little Dorrit* may prefer different adjectives, I think that the large point holds: the stories, the contrasting object lessons, that make up *Little Dorrit* are metaphorically analogous to each other and metonymically connected, as Dickens joins these various threads in a plot.

THE RHETORIC OF CHARACTER: GROTESQUERIE AND THE UNCANNY

MELVILLE IS NO LESS CONCERNED than Dickens with growth, its dangers and failures, and in common with Dickens embodies this problem in three major types of characters. A traumatic break with the past defines the first type, often some single event or moment that cancels the whole life up until then and determines the mechanical repetition that will comprise the life to follow. Not only Ahab, but even so minor a character as the blacksmith in *Moby-Dick* exemplifies this type. Although the break in his life is somewhat more gradual than Ahab's, it also takes the form of literal and metaphoric amputation. Dickens's Miss Havisham (in *Great Expectations*) is the great example of this type, but Old Dorrit is hardly less so. Cast into prison, at first he does all he can to deny the reality of the present, to pretend a smooth continuity with his past, but once he is freed and made rich, he denies his whole past, refusing to acknowledge that he was ever not what he has just become.

This general character type is common in romantic and post-romantic literature, from Oswald in Wordsworth's *The Borderers* and Coleridge's Mariner, Byron's Manfred, and Hawthorne's Hester and Dimmesdale (in *The Scarlet Letter*) and Clifford (in *The House of the Seven Gables*) to Conrad's Lord Jim and many modern instances. Some of these characters are still visibly chained to the crucial moment, but others are apparently cut loose in an uneasy weightlessness, which Freudians associate with the typically hysterical defense of repression. This psychoanalytic perspective suggests that the repressed past still specifically determines the present, as proves the case with Old Dorrit, Lady Dedlock, Wordsworth's Oswald, and many others.

This character type is especially important for Dickens, because—even if frequently represented only in the unchanging aftermath—it can also provide a convention for showing character change. In early Dickens there are no such changes. When Jonas Chuzzlewit kills Tigg, he only makes visible what he has always been, for he already intended to kill his father. His change is no more essential than that of Spenser's Malbecco, who was always jealous but only after the traumatic loss of Hellenore visibly becomes "Gealosie." Bradley Headstone, however, undergoes a real change in *Our Mutual Friend,* even though only of this two-step variety.[14] A passage from Carlyle's *French Revolution* illustrates this psychological convention:

> From the purpose of crime to the act of crime there is an abyss; wonderful to think of. The finger lies on the pistol, but the man is not yet a murderer; nay, his whole nature staggering at such consummation, is there not a confused pause rather—one last instant of possibility for him? Not yet a murderer. It is at the mercy of light trifles whether the fixed idea may not yet become unfixed. One slight twitch of a muscle, the deathflash bursts, and he is it, and will for Eternity

14. For a contrast of Jonas and Bradley wholly opposed to mine, see Albert J. Guerard, *The Triumph of the Novel* (New York: Oxford University Press, 1976), pp. 252–253. Such disagreements alert us to the uncertainty of our ideas about character, both in life and in literature.

> be it;—and Earth has become a penal Tartarus for him; his horizon girdled now not with golden hope, but with red flames of remorse; voices from the depths of Nature sounding. Wo, wo on him!
>
> [*TC* 4:25–26]

This sense of the moment of crisis, in which the "twitch of a muscle" may totally and permanently transform an individual, haunts the nineteenth century. At the same time that industrial technology was making more and more mechanical power available in response to ever-decreasing human input, and that daily life saw more and more devices activated by a mere flick—the match, the camera, the electric switch—writers brooded on this feared experience of shocking change.[15] In Wordsworth's early tragedy *The Borderers* (1797), which Carlyle may be echoing, Oswald reflects,

> Action is transitory—a step, a blow,
> The motion of a muscle—this way or that—
> 'Tis done, and in the after-vacancy
> We wonder at ourselves like men betrayed
>
> [ll. 1539–1542]

In Conrad we find not only Jim's leap and the sudden bursting of Haldin into the life of Razumov (in *Under Western Eyes*) but particularly the Professor in *The Secret Agent*, carrying with him at all times the explosive device that need only be squeezed to trigger an explosion that will totally transform both himself and whoever encounters him at that moment into brute matter.

A second type is the character who has no significant past but always performs in the present flexible variations on a set role. Such characters are not so rigid and seclusive as the first type. We get some sense of their trying to mold the circumstances of the real world to fit themselves, even if their molding is largely verbal and they have little understanding of either circumstances or themselves. Flask and Stubb, Micawber and Skimpole, Pecksniff and Mrs. Gamp are all of this type. We marvel that they so inventively vary their repetitive routines.

15. See Walter Benjamin, "On Some Motifs in Baudelaire" (1939), trans. Harry Zohn, in *Illuminations* (1968: rpt. New York: Schocken, 1969), pp. 174–175.

The third type is more common in Dickens than in Melville. These characters are eternally oblivious both to themselves and to the world around them. Their behavior seems neither determined by a specific past nor directed toward any goal, although its ritual quality encourages our interpretive filling in of the outlines. Mr. F.'s Aunt in *Little Dorrit* is the purest example of this type, but in *Bleak House* old Smallweed's routine with his wife also shows it well. The carpenter in *Moby-Dick* approaches this type, since even if purposeful, a "pure manipulator" of his material, he is apparently all mechanism:

> His brain, if he had ever had one, must have early oozed along into the muscles of his fingers. He was like one of those . . . highly useful . . . Sheffield contrivances, assuming the exterior —though a little swelled—of a common pocket knife, but containing, not only blades of various sizes, but also screw-drivers, corkscrews, tweezers, awls, pens, rulers, nail-filers, countersinkers. So if his superiors wanted to use the carpenter for a screw-driver, all they had to do was to open that part of him, and the screw was fast: or if for tweezers, take him up by the legs, and there they were.
>
> [*MD* 107]

Yet Ishmael insists that the carpenter is "after all, no mere machine of an automaton" but contains "a subtle something," an "unaccountable life-principle." Thus Ishmael himself begins to interpret for us a character type whose essence in Dickens is to be baldly there.

This third class of characters clearly exemplifies the pure grotesque, but even in the relatively comic second class and relatively tragic first class grotesque elements are important. If the carpenter is like a machine, the comic Stubb is "fearless as fire, and as mechanical." If the carpenter soliloquizes "only like an unreasoning wheel, which also hummingly soliloquizes," he resembles the tragic Ahab, who while preparing to nail up the doubloon rubs it on his clothing, "meanwhile lowly humming to himself, producing a sound so strangely muffled and inarticulate that it seemed the mechanical humming of the wheels of his vitality in him" (36). The mixture, or reversal, of the vital and mechanical—the repetitive, "driven," behavior that suggests the action of some unknown power of which the characters are mere puppets—centrally defines the grotesque.[16]

The crucial proclamation of the grotesque as the major innovative type in modern art prefaces Victor Hugo's play on Cromwell (1827), the hero whose depiction by Carlyle was to be so important to Melville. Furthermore, the same artist who would so impress Melville in Carlyle's version is the hero of Hugo's preface: Shakespeare. For Hugo, the grotesque enables humanity to express the dualism that since Christianity's advent has been felt in the relation of body to soul, earth to heaven. The grotesque type not only underlies comedy but also creates the dualism typical of modern tragedy by providing a contrast to the sublime. Hugo judges that by use of the grotesque, the ugly, shapeless, and deformed, an artist can create a larger, more complex design than with the simple harmony and symmetry of beauty. The Hunchback of Notre Dame anticipates the city of Dickens.[17] So the landscape of romantic art will include the ocean at dusk, rather than the river at noon that typifies classical art, or the lake at dawn of archaic art. Not level plains and mirror-like lakes, but lofty mountains and deep precipices and eagles symbolize the modern imagination. Recall Melville's image of the soaring and swooping Catskill eagle. Much of what Melville responded to in Carlyle embodied a general romantic sense of the grotesque.

As Hugo suggests, the comic and the grotesque share much common ground. Thus Baudelaire's essay on laughter begins from the same point of Christian dualism as does Hugo's preface. The list of comic devices and techniques in Bergson's essay on laughter shares with the grotesque such basic categories as "the mechanical," "doubling," and "equivocal meaning." In modern mixed modes, criticism struggles to define the conditions that make a given passage comic or grotesque.[18] Today we are much more likely to see the comic as grotesque than vice versa, perhaps because we are less capable of Bergsonian comic "anesthesia" and more prone to feel,

16. Wolfgang Kayser, *The Grotesque in Art and Literature* (1957), trans. Ulrich Weisstein (Bloomington: Indiana University Press, 1963), passim.

17. On Dickens and Hugo see Richard Maxwell, "City Life and the Novel," *Comparative Literature* 30 (1978):161–164, 169–170.

18. See W. M. Frohock, "The Edge of Laughter," in *Veins of Humor*, ed. Harry Levin (Cambridge: Harvard University Press, 1972), pp. 243–254.

"It could happen to us." Is it coincidence that Napoleon liberated European Jews from their ghettoes at the same time that in England a new seriousness transformed the stage presentation of Shylock?

Moby-Dick offers a nice example of how perspective determines our attitude toward a given situation. In "The Mast-Head" (35) Ishmael puts into exemplum the problem and dangers of an excessively speculative overview. If he neglects his work, if he fails to focus his vision in search of whales, the watcher drifts into "reverie" and his mental activity dissolves the man-made world of forms into the energies, the "vortices," that underlie it, causing a tragic fall, a plummet from consciousness to chaos, from the mast-head into the sea. Melville seems to fear abandoning an involved narrator, lest the freedom of a disembodied narrator lead to visionary inspiration that carries one so far from ground that one either remains stranded out of touch with the earth or must return with a thud.[19] In *Little Dorrit* the "stare" menaced those seen, but here danger attaches to the position of the seer.

In "The Hyena" (49), however, Ishmael looks at the world not pantheistically but as "a vast practical joke": "As for small difficulties and worryings, prospects of sudden disaster, peril of life and limb; all these, and death itself, seem to him only sly, good-natured hits." For he has just made his will and can view his life with an uncanny dehumanization from the perspective of beyond the grave: "I looked round me tranquilly and contentedly, like a quiet ghost with a clean conscience sitting inside the bars of a snug family vault." The sudden plunge from the mast-head into death is now calmly anticipated, and what was fate now becomes choice: "Here goes for a cool, collected dive at death and destruction, and the devil fetch the hindmost." No longer the victim of vertigo, Ishmael becomes like Baudelaire's "laughing spectator," the "philosopher," who by quickly splitting himself off into an observing part can laugh at his own fall.[20] This ghostly afterlife achieved by Ishmael makes possible in the later portions of the book his evanescence into a narrator, freed from the limits of personal identity, who has

19. See Paul de Man, "Ludwig Binswanger and the Sublimation of the Self," in *Blindness and Insight* (New York: Oxford University Press, 1971), especially pp. 46–47.

20. "De l'essence du rire," in *Oeuvres complètes de Baudelaire,* ed. Y. G. Le Dantec (Paris: Gallimard, 1954), pp. 717, 727–728.

powers like Dickens's. The first published edition of *Moby-Dick* lacked the "Epilogue" of Ishmael's rescue and thus did not ground the book's narrative in a particular life.

Such matters of perspective figure crucially in Freud's writings on art. If in his early study of jokes he demonstrated the childlike aggressiveness of wit and its origin in that part of the unconscious that he later termed the "id," his late essay on "Humor" sees the superego benignly comforting the ego like a philosophical parent, urging the insignificance of worldly events. Freud comes closest to our present interest, however, in his essay on "The Uncanny," which takes its place with the other two in showing the derivation of specific aesthetic feelings from a structure of relations among the parts of the psyche. Freud's uncanny overlaps very largely with the grotesque. Both derive primarily from the feeling that "automatic, mechanical processes are at work concealed behind ordinary appearances" (Freud), or that "an unknown power is acting within characters" (Kayser), and they bear many further likenesses.

For Freud our feeling of "the uncanny" grows from anxiety at the recurrence of what we have once repressed, regardless of the affect that the repressed thing originally aroused, for although once familiar to us, it has been estranged by repression. ("Estrangement" is also a key category of the grotesque.) Thus in early mental life "the double" was a friendly assurance of immortality, but it later returns, once we have repressed this original belief, as "a vision of terror, just as after the fall of their religion the [pagan] gods took on demonic shapes." Similarly such experiences as déjà vu, or continued "return to one and the same spot," or the observation of other forms of "involuntary repetition" become "uncanny." Freud discusses the "*repetition-compulsion* in the unconscious mind . . . powerful enough to overrule the pleasure-principle, lending to certain aspects of the mind their demonic character" and concludes that "whatever reminds us of the inner *repetition-compulsion* is perceived as uncanny."[21] The insistence of the sun's stare in *Little Dorrit* and the persistence of the ghost's holding his place in the vault (in "The Hyena") suggest the uncanniness in the technical premises of nineteenth-century fiction.

21. Sigmund Freud, "The Uncanny" (1919), trans. Alix Strachey, in *Studies in Parapsychology*, ed. Philip Rieff (New York: Crowell-Collier, 1963), pp. 41–47.

Freud's suggestions offer remarkable insight into the impression that Ahab makes on us. Clearly he who "lacks the low enjoying power" but who is driving ceaselessly onward once again to encounter the whale, he who is "demoniac," is in the grip of the repetition-compulsion. Furthermore, in his fuller exposition of this drive to repeat (*Beyond the Pleasure Principle*), in an analysis of the young child's game of throwing away and then recovering an object whose loss he fears, Freud notes the substitution of an active role in repetition for what had been passive in the initial reality or fear. So a child will play doctor himself after being examined by a doctor. So Ahab: "I will dismember my dismemberer" (37).

A similar "identification with the aggressor" is important to Dickens's art.[22] In the children so frequently his central characters, Dickens show the truth of Lady Macbeth's dictum, "'Tis the eye of childhood, / That fears a painted devil."[23] But if we shift our perspective from character to author, is it not also true in Dickens and Melville that "the eye of childhood" itself paints the devil, using all available colors of rhetoric, in order *not* to have to fear it, in order to "do" it before it "does" you? Anna Freud cites the case of a girl who "was afraid to cross the hall in the dark, because she had a dread of seeing ghosts. Suddenly, however, she hit on a device which enabled her to do it: she would run across the hall, making all sorts of peculiar gestures as she went. Before long, she triumphantly told her little brother the secret of how she had got over her anxiety. 'There's no need to be afraid in the hall,' she said, 'you just have to pretend that you're the ghost who might meet you.'"[24] As well as such a use of introjection, however, one might also employ the mechanism of projection. Dickens was a remarkably energetic, hard-driving man, as largely a self-made success as anyone we may think of, but in his works his own character type is most often exaggerated disapprovingly. The dull if admirable Doyce in *Little Dorrit* is perhaps the most positive instance of this type, while his heroes are rather weak willed. Bounderby in *Hard Times,* who denies his origins in a way that surpasses even Dickens's

22. On identification with the aggressor, see Anna Freud, *The Ego and the Mechanisms of Defense,* trans. Cecil Baines (New York: International Universities Press, 1946), pp. 117ff.

23. See Harry Levin, "Dickens after a Century," in *Grounds for Comparison* (Cambridge: Harvard University Press, 1972), p. 345.

24. Freud, *The Ego,* pp. 118–119.

silence about the blacking factory, most clearly illustrates Dickens's antagonism to the "self-made" go-getter.

Dickens was not only a driving man, but also a driven man, yet his works hold up to laughter the examples of the grotesque, driven people with whom he peoples his world. How does this laughter balance against the anger with which he condemns the society that imposes such mechanical action on people, making them less than what whole human beings should be? Dickens told Forster that he always tended to lose sight of a man, diverted by the mechanical play of some portion of the man's face, which "would acquire a sudden ludicrous life of its own."[25] In a defensive projection, Dickens preemptively does to others what he fears "society" may be doing to him. In a society increasingly given to organized scrutiny of its members' characteristics, he makes himself scrutinizer.

Perhaps Dickens dehumanized people in order to make a fearsome example, to make his readers recognize their own possible fate in his grotesques and act to ameliorate their common situation. But will one recognize in a grotesque either oneself or the results of one's actions or inaction? In *The French Revolution* Carlyle took pains to show that the demonic in people is still part of their essential humanity, but Dickens in *Bleak House* could paint Jo and his kind as "goaded beasts." Some readers no doubt would understand that such a situation called for humane improvements, to help such "beasts" become full human beings, but others, including Carlyle by this time and Dickens himself at many moments, saw only the urgency of more and better police and social control. Even while deploring the abuses of such antiquated and ineffective methods of control as the court system, mocking the newly growing bureaucracy as "Circumlocution," and attacking the humanly destructive control exercised in factories and Benthamite schools, Dickens's narrator is not detached from the system of observation and regulation but repeats anew its action. The narrator's knowledge of his characters is his power over them.[26]

25. Cited in Dorothy Van Ghent, "The Dickens World" (1950), rpt. in *The Dickens Critics*, ed. George Ford and Lauriat Lane, Jr. (Ithaca: Cornell University Press, 1961), p. 215.

26. For a contrary view of Dickens as a detached observer, see the brilliant work of Everett Knight, *A Theory of the Classical Novel* (London: Routledge and Kegan Paul, 1970), chap. 5.

THE FAMILY AND THE CITY: SELVES IN MOTION

NOT ONLY THE OFFICIAL PUBLIC DEVELOPMENT of inspection and centralization, but also the less consciously controlled growth of the city in the nineteenth century bore crucially on how writers imagined a self in relation to others, whether in the household, on the streets, or in some intermediate institution. To contemporary observers the city appeared to further individualism by freeing people from the old bonds that had fixed them, particularly by destroying the stable family existence that was believed to have marked the previous rural condition. These new individuals were often judged negatively, as social problems, as the "deviants and dependents" for whom the "asylum" was developed as a means of social control. Whether looking to crime, poverty, or insanity, early nineteenth-century Americans believed that "almost always a failure of upbringing" and "the collapse of family control" caused deviant behavior.[27] Their fear of this new urban individualism led them to develop institutions—prisons, workhouses, juvenile homes, mental asylums—to restore the deviant individual to a communal environment. The same pattern of analysis, leading to some similar institutional developments, marks the English response to the urban problems of industrialism. Peter Gaskell, whose work looms large historically because Engels incorporated so much of it into his *Condition of the English Working Class,* saw the primary problem of Manchester not as poverty, nor factory labor, nor lack of education, but as "the separation of families, the breaking-up of households, the disruption of all those ties which link man's heart to the better portions of his nature."[28] His chapter on "Education—Religion—Crime—Pauperism" emphasizes the need for moral education to take place in the home. For Gaskell, no less than for his American contemporaries, the public crisis had a private remedy: the well-ordered family.

A related nineteenth-century viewpoint did not question the isolating effect of urban life but questioned whether this urban personality really is more individual than its rural counterpart. This

27. David J. Rothman, *The Discovery of the Asylum* (Boston: Little, Brown, 1971), p. 65.

28. *The Manufacturing Population of England* (London, 1833), p. 7.

view emphasized not the social but the psychological problems of the city, especially the deadening effect of city bustle and hubbub. The intellect hypertrophies, the feelings decay, one become blasé and responsive only to "gross and violent stimulants." This view has a culturally distinguished history, ranging from Wordsworth's preface to *Lyrical Ballads* (1800) and countless midcentury examples to Simmel's study of "The Metropolis and Mental Life" (1902) and the recent critical debates over mass culture. In his study of Baudelaire through the lenses of Bergson, Freud, and Proust, Walter Benjamin elaborately adapts this view, arguing that consciousness grows at the expense of feeling in order to ward off the "shock" characteristic of urban life. To extrapolate from Benjamin's argument, the romantic character convention of the traumatic break with the past represents the central fear of urban experience (brilliantly diagnosed by Henry James in "The Beast in the Jungle"): the fear of sudden engulfment by circumstances, the fear of a shock so great that it overwhelms all defenses. If this is so, then despite the fact that Wordsworth's Oswald, Coleridge's Mariner, Melville's Ahab, and Conrad's Jim suffer their critical moments in isolation at sea, their authors' experiences of urban life are the underlying condition of their creation, fully as much as in the case of Dickens's obviously urban grotesques.[29]

In contrast to these two nineteenth-century views, a more recent, neo-Weberian approach to the relations of city, family, and individual concludes that the growth of the city and the growth of the "nuclear" family are together an integral part of the development of bourgeois, "Protestant Ethic" individualism.[30] The "nuclear" bourgeois family has preserved the residential structure of the traditional poor, rural family, while adding to it the intense intrafamilial relations and emphasis on education that first developed in aristocratic "households."[31] The family, therefore, was not sud-

29. On the relations of sea, city, and crowd, see W. H. Auden, *The Enchafèd Flood* (New York: Random House, 1950), especially pp. 68–71; and Elias Canetti, *Crowds and Power* (1960), trans. Carol Stewart (New York: Viking, 1963), pp. 80–81.

30. Talcott Parsons and Robert Bales, *The Family* (Glencoe, Ill.: Free Press, 1955).

31. Since the seminal but divergent works of Philippe Ariès (*Centuries of Childhood*, trans. Robert Baldick [New York: Random House, 1962]) and Peter Laslett (*The World We Have Lost* [New York: Charles Scribner's Sons, 1965]), research and controversy on the family have

denly threatened by the city but had long been growing together with it, as an adaptive and defensive response to urban life. It was not the failure of the family that created the need for new institutions, but the desire of the family that had finally grown strong enough to try to make the streets safe for its children. The social disparities and anonymity of the city made it all too easy to think that the boy on the street you saw in clothing you would never let your children wear must have no family to look out for him and therefore must be institutionalized. The urban history of England and America in the nineteenth century reveals then not the disruptive triumph of the streets over the family, but the strengthening of "families against the city," clustered around their hearth.[32] And it is against this enclosure that novelists lift rooftops and spring their characters loose into mobility.

Such families did not, however, feel their strength positively but only as a threatened loss, as if each family were under siege: "Households, frail and huddled together, faced the sturdy and wide doors of the tavern, the gaudy opening into a house of prostitution or theater filled with dissipated customers; all the while, thieves and drunkards roamed the streets, introducing the unwary youngster to vice and corruption."[33] Such a mentality produces "intense" families, small, nuclear families that believe family life embodies all significant social experience. This family structure encourages in children a search for a "purified identity," a desire to fix the self as the bearer of good attributes and to impute evil attributes to outsiders, combined with an unwillingness to question the truth of these attributions in the light of experience and action. This is the mentality that we associate with police riots and "over-

---

proliferated. The attempt by Edward Shorter at a synthesis (*The Making of the Modern Family* [New York: Basic Books, 1975]) has yielded to a new onslaught. See Philip J. Greven, *The Protestant Temperament* (New York: Alfred A. Knopf, 1977); Lawrence Stone, *The Family, Sex and Marriage in England: 1500–1800* (New York: Harper and Row, 1977); Christopher Lasch, *Haven in a Heartless World* (New York: Basic Books, 1977); and Mark Poster, *Critical Theory of the Family* (New York: Seabury, 1978).

32. See Alexander Welsh, *The City of Dickens* (Oxford: Clarendon, 1971), especially chap. 9; and Richard Sennett, *Families Against the City* (Cambridge: Harvard University Press, 1970).

33. Rothman, *Discovery of the Asylum*, pp. 70–71.

zealous" political lawbreaking, but it also appears in the tendency of the nineteenth-century novel to present the individual as a pure, essential, given identity, independent of social action. This derivative of Calvinist election installs in the novel a supernatural "beyond," the effect of which may be to justify the existing order.[34] Thus we may judge that for Dickens's heroes and heroines, "who they are and what becomes of them are more important than what they do."[35]

Although this is not the whole truth about these novels (and I present a counterview, especially in Chapter VI), it is significant, and historically the family played a specific mediating role in instilling such beliefs: "The felt hostility of the city intensifies the need for both love and discipline in the home, and the inevitable contradiction of the two parental roles thus exaggerated . . . prevents the nineteenth-century child from growing to adulthood."[36] Paradoxically, then, by infusing youthful fears into modern city life, the "intense" family may actually *not* have succeeded in producing active, exploratory bourgeois individuals. Research has suggested instead that abnormally large or extended families produced proportionally more children marked by exceptional geographic or economic mobility than did the small, nuclear, intense family.[37]

Dickens and Melville, growing up in London or New York, each knew at firsthand urban family life, but in late childhood the catastrophe of the father's failure threw each child from that nest and exposed him to the new and varied experiences that were to become such important material for their fiction. The partial recovery of Dickens's father was propitious for his later literary theme of the "Prodigal Father," an instance of what so often underlies comedy, the displacement to the father of the child's guilt.[38] In *Moby-Dick*

34. On purified identity see Richard Sennett, *The Uses of Disorder* (New York: Alfred A. Knopf, 1970), chap. 1; on the beyond see Knight, *Theory of the Classical Novel,* p. 38.

35. Welsh, *The City of Dickens,* p. 73.

36. Mark Spilka, *Dickens and Kafka* (London: Dobson, 1963), p. 14.

37. Richard Sennett, "Middle-Class Families and Urban Violence," in *Nineteenth-Century Cities* ed. Stephan Thernstrom and Richard Sennett (New Haven: Yale University Press, 1969), pp. 402–408.

38. Van Ghent, "The Dickens World," p. 229. See also Ernst Kris, *Psychoanalytic Explorations in Art* (New York: International Universities Press, 1952), chap. 8.

and especially in *Pierre*, Melville's more shattering experience is written in darker characters.[39] Both Dickens and Melville dread the individual's direct confrontation with the dangers and constraints of society, but neither turns back to the family as the ideal intermediate group. Melville seeks a fraternal anarchism,[40] while Dickens attempts to constitute a "household" in the odd ménages that seem much closer to his ideal than do the perfunctory married families of the happy ending.

The form of social motion least congenial to the writers I am studying, least likely to excite their imaginations or to provide a principle by which to understand their works, is the coming together in marriage and the transmission of property from parents to children. For these writers a happy marriage ends motion; their stories start from displacement—orphanage, usurpation, a failure of succession.[41] The characteristic movements of the books spring from this jarring: the series of journeys to London in *Martin Chuzzlewit*, the bouncing from one to another social meeting in *Our Mutual Friend*, the rush of the railroad in *The House of the Seven Gables* and *Dombey and Son*, the baffled scrambling in the midst of falling houses and rising spirits in *Bleak House* and *The French Revolution*, the thrust of penetration that both the writer and the major characters enact in *Moby-Dick* and Carlyle's lives of heroes. The highly figurative language of these works equally suggests displacement; the properties of things are deflected as the writer transmits

39. David Brion Davis contrasts England and America in the nineteenth century by arguing that the absence of strong paternal authority focused American treatments of murder on fraternal conflict. See *Homicide in American Fiction, 1798–1860* (Ithaca: Cornell University Press, 1957), p. xv. If *Pierre* exemplifies this pattern, however, *Our Mutual Friend* does no less (cf. the chapter title "Better to Be Abel than Cain": IV, 7).

40. Cf. Wilson Carey McWilliams, *The Idea of Fraternity in America* (Berkeley and Los Angeles: University of California Press, 1973), especially pp. 354–357.

41. To elaborate this position, see Edward W. Said, *Beginnings* (New York: Basic Books, 1975), chap. 3. For other nineteenth-century challenges to the "genealogical imperative," see Patricia Drechsel Tobin, *Time and the Novel* (Princeton: Princeton University Press, 1978), pp. 29–46.

them to us. Gaps open up to disrupt any smooth succession from referent to sign just as they do in the attempted succession from generation to generation.

Such fractures obviously determine language and story in Carlyle and Melville, but the marriage stories of Dickens and Hawthorne are no less formally fractured. A failure fully to integrate the growing apprehension of London marks *Martin Chuzzlewit,* and similar impasses affect other works: the failure fully to capitalize on Rokesmith-Harmon's unusual perspective on life in *Our Mutual Friend,* the failure fully to distinguish between good and bad inheritance in *The House of the Seven Gables,* and the failure fully to work out the relation between the railroad and Dombey in *Dombey and Son.* Thus, these relatively simpler works, fully as much as the more obviously experimental works (among which I include *Bleak House* and *Little Dorrit*), are unsettled and leave room for interpretive play that makes it impossible to fix the work into a single, coherent, structured image. The state and the work of art are no longer a Burkean tree but an atmosphere of closely interrelated yet somewhat independent particles, clustering more and less thickly from point to point and from moment to moment, and liable at any moment to part and reveal volcanic fires below or to condense into a thunderous discharge from above. The following chapters are devoted to the history of this new literary form: the tentative process by which it came into being, its characteristic achievements, and its transmutation into yet other ways of writing. In this history the work of Carlyle, Hawthorne, and Melville is all crucial, but the beginning and end emerge most clearly in the career of Dickens.

III

Patterns in Dickens's Career: From *Martin Chuzzlewit* to *Our Mutual Friend*

A COMPARISON OF *Martin Chuzzlewit* (1843–1844) and *Our Mutual Friend* (1864–1865) offers a useful economy by which to abridge and articulate Dickens's career as a novelist. The two works, although separated by over twenty years, resemble each other extraordinarily in basic story material, and each comes at a point of crisis in Dickens's career. The differences between them then allow us some gauge of the directions Dickens was taking at the start and the finish of his career. My comparative studies of Dickens draw on the major social novels between these two end points.

At the time he began *Martin Chuzzlewit,* Dickens faced the danger of self-repetitiveness. He had already written five novels and was world famous, yet it would be hard to discern the coherent shape of a career in what he had done thus far. His extraordinary capacity to capitalize on accidents suggests the wealth of inner resources from which he worked, but he had not yet succeeded in defining his own directions. The first novel that he planned to write, *Barnaby Rudge,*[1] was deferred by the amazing sudden success of *Pickwick* (1836–1837), as he found a way of making a novel out of this series of sketches, and the opportunities of that success projected him into *Oliver Twist* (1837–1838) and *Nicholas Nickleby* (1838–1839) with scarcely a moment's reflective interruption. Dickens intended *Master Humphrey's Clock* (1840–

1. See John Butt and Kathleen Tillotson, "*Barnaby Rudge:* The First Projected Novel," in *Dickens at Work* (London: Methuen, 1957), pp. 76–89.

1841) to relieve the pressure for constant novelistic production by offering a mold to contain whatever miscellaneous writing might come up, but the declining popularity of *Master Humphrey* drove him to work *The Old Curiosity Shop* into a full novel, and he finally wrote *Barnaby Rudge* as well in that weekly format. He had then used up the one project that had been fully his own. Where was he to go? To America, and his tour there moved him significantly toward new self-awareness. In reading Dickens's posthumously published correspondence from this trip, George Eliot remarked upon his "rapid development."[2]

The trip to America effected a physical separation between Dickens and his audience and marked a pause in his relation with them, and in this space Dickens could begin a series of self-definitions. Furthermore, just as the "surprise and distance" achieved by foreign travel often allow a historian newly to conceive of his own native culture,[3] so too for Dickens the experience of surveying a new culture and thinking back comprehensively upon his own changed his view of England. His subsequent work becomes increasingly panoramic, striving toward coherent overview and a sense of totality.

Upon his return, Dickens's relation to his public first reasserted itself in his dealings with his publishers. Chapman and Hall demanded contractually of him that "the new work shall be, in form size and price, precisely similar to the *Pickwick Papers* and *Nicholas Nickleby*." That is, Dickens was to turn away from the experiment with *Master Humphrey* and return to the monthly part serialization that he had made his own in his first great success and repeated in *Nickleby*. Chapman and Hall also claimed in the advance publicity that the new work would offer "matter in the true Pickwickian style."[4] But here began Dickens's first real conflict, both with his public and with his publisher. For *Chuzzlewit* is not very Pickwickian at all, and its low sales chilled his pleasure in returning to his native country after the difficulties that had marked his

2. *The George Eliot Letters,* ed. Gordon S. Haight (New Haven: Yale University Press, 1955), 5:226.

3. Fernand Braudel, "History and the Social Sciences" (1958), in *Economy and Society in Early Modern Europe,* ed. Peter Burke (New York: Harper and Row, 1972), p. 24.

4. J. A. Sutherland, *Victorian Novelists and Publishers* (Chicago: University of Chicago Press, 1976), p. 77.

relations with America. He even decided to change publishers, when Chapman and Hall seemed not supportive enough in his difficulties, but it was less easy to change his public.

In defiance of the lagging sales, however, Dickens in a letter to Forster defended the work's artistic merits:

> You know, as well as I, that I think *Chuzzlewit* in a hundred points immeasurably the best of my stories. That I feel my power now, more than I ever did. . . . That I know, if I have health, I could sustain my place in the minds of thinking men, though fifty writers started up to-morrow. But how many readers do *not* think! . . . If I wrote for forty thousand Forsters . . . I should have no need to leave the scene. But this very book warns me that if I *can* leave it for a time, I had better do so, and must do so. Apart from that again, I feel that longer rest after this story would do me good. You say two or three months, because you have been used to see me for eight years never leaving off. . . . It is impossible to go on working the brain to that extent forever.[5]

Further on in this letter the image of "poor Scott," a "driveller" in his "miserable decay," rises to haunt Dickens as the warning against wrong management of a career.

Despite Dickens's self-confidence in this letter, and despite his insistence in his preface to the first edition of *Martin Chuzzlewit* that he had tried "to keep a steadier eye upon the general purpose and design" and to "resist the temptation" of the monthly unit more than in his earlier works, the novel seems to have trouble finding itself. If not in his overall plot—for Dickens had already decided upon Old Martin's overarching ruse by the third number—or in general theme—for the topic of selfishness emerges clearly from the start—then at least in trying to find the sources of energy to move the whole along, Dickens had repeatedly to begin again: moving Martin to America; introducing Mrs. Gamp; bringing Tigg into the Anglo-Bengalee and working out his deadly relation with Jonas Chuzzlewit. The "gap in the main course of his narrative" that Martin's energizing trip to America cost him, and the technical

5. John Forster, *The Life of Charles Dickens* (Philadelphia: J. B. Lippincott, 1873), 2:69–70.

problems in construction following from that, moved Dickens to much greater care in the preparatory planning of his later books, and starting with his next novel, *Dombey and Son,* the famous memorandum sheets constantly accompany his composition.[6]

From *Dombey and Son* (1846–1848) to *Little Dorrit* (1855–1857) we can unquestionably make out a career, marked by four of the full-size "Pickwick"-type novels. The concern with contemporary life that was adumbrated in *Martin Chuzzlewit,* even though it was set in the coaching days, comes fully to the fore in *Dombey and Son,* engaged firmly with the railroad. The theme of self in *Chuzzlewit* is immeasurably deepened in the semiautobiographical *David Copperfield* (1849–1850). Self and society are fully fused in the massive and astonishing integration of *Bleak House* (1852–1853), achieved through a plot that joins the disparate worlds of the split narrative. *Little Dorrit* explores in a new key the possibilities of *Bleak House.* After *Little Dorrit,* a new period of turbulence shakes the career: Dickens's split with his wife and the transformation of *Household Words* into *All the Year Round;* the compensatory turn to reading aloud as another means of relation to his audience; and the writing of *A Tale of Two Cities* (1859) and *Great Expectations* (1860–1861) as weekly serials, to give *All the Year Round* as firmly as possible the stamp of Dickens's personal distinction.

When Dickens returned to the "Pickwick" form in *Our Mutual Friend,* he was wholly in control of his publisher,[7] but he was also beginning again. More than five years had elapsed since he last wrote in that form, and the experience of the return was extremely taxing. It brought fully to the forefront the concerns of technique and self-conservation that he had first articulated while working on *Martin Chuzzlewit.* In *Chuzzlewit* Dickens avoided the dangers of self-repetition. Even after five works, he wrote the novel less out of his own previous writing than out of the whole available literary tradition as it bore on the possibilities for a novelist, and he began in the work to discover the subject and techniques that he would make wholly his own in his later work. In *Our Mutual Friend* (1864–1865) Dickens redefined his own kind of novel. The work demands to be read in close relation especially to *Bleak House* and *Little Dorrit,* as I do in Chapter VIII, but it even reaches back to

6. Ibid., pp. 44–45, 75.
7. Sutherland, *Victorian Novelists,* pp. 79–80.

Martin Chuzzlewit, for the two novels are remarkably similar in story matter.

In crucial respects *Martin Chuzzlewit* and *Our Mutual Friend* are more like each other than are any other pair of Dickens's novels, even *Oliver Twist* and *The Old Curiosity Shop, Barnaby Rudge* and *A Tale of Two Cities,* or *David Copperfield* and *Great Expectations.* For not just a general given of subject or form—the "progress" of a child to a better world, mob violence in history, or the first-person *Bildungsroman*—links these two, but a very peculiar mesh of theme and construction, which makes them as different from Dickens's other work as they are like each other. The latter parts of both books alternate between a murder story and a ruse put on to bring about good from the evil of inherited money. In both cases the moral of the book puts the greater emphasis on purifying the money, but more interest and energy inhere in the murderer and his psychology. Remarkably enough, both Jonas Chuzzlewit and Bradley Headstone first fail to commit a murder that they have intended, are blackmailed for their attempt—by Tigg Montague and Rogue Riderhood—and then kill their blackmailer. In both cases, fishing clothes out of the water provides important evidence, and in both cases the theme of "the double" develops around the murderer.

The two books' common emphasis on the proper use of money, how to know its real rather than apparent value, generates Dickens's two examples of insurance men——Tigg and Podsnap—both masters of showy appearance. Pecksniff and Wegg play parallel roles as humorous blocking characters, each apparently in control of the rich man enacting the ruse—Old Martin and Boffin. No other of Dickens's novels share so many similar functional roles in the main story lines. Further parallels include Old Martin and Old Harmon, each of whom unnaturally drives out the young hero—Young Martin and John Harmon—while establishing in his will the terms of the young man's marriage.

This attention to the will in the two novels has more than an incidental significance. By the last generation of the eighteenth century, the will as a document had taken on a new function. The wishes inspired by "feelings," "piety," or "affection" were no longer included in the will, which became merely "a legal act distributing fortunes."[8] This change arose from a new intimacy within family

8. Philippe Ariès, *Western Attitudes toward Death,* trans. Patricia M. Ranum (Baltimore: Johns Hopkins University Press, 1974), pp. 64–65.

relations which allowed the dying person to trust that oral instructions would be obeyed without requiring the force of testamentary inscription. This confidence marks a step in the process of internalizing ancestors, building up the superego. Against this new norm, the brutal enforcements of Old Chuzzlewit and Old Harmon are to be measured.

If such overall similarity in subject suggests a lack of invention, our failure to perceive that similarity readily testifies to a mastery of disposition, a tremendous technical skill to offset that lack. But beyond sheer technique we hesitate to assimilate the two books for reasons that relate to Dickens's personal and intellectual development from the forties to the sixties. The female interest in *Our Mutual Friend* is much greater. Mary Graham, Ruth Pinch, and the Pecksniff girls cannot compare as characters with Jenny Wren, Lizzie Hexam, and Bella Wilfer, nor are they so important in determining the book's action. Bradley Headstone attempts to murder Eugene Wrayburn for love of Lizzie, while Jonas Chuzzlewit, whose characterization strongly suggests sexual impotence,[9] tries to murder his father for love of money. Boffin's ruse tests Bella; Old Martin's, Pecksniff and Martin. *Our Mutual Friend* shows a much greater concern with intimate psychology. The change from harsh comedy to melodrama in presenting Jonas Chuzzlewit makes him more "serious" while scarcely bringing us close to him. Our initial involvement with Bradley Headstone's state of suppression, however, leaves us frighteningly near his explosive expression, even as we try to draw back. Finally, *Martin Chuzzlewit* is one of Dickens's funniest books; *Our Mutual Friend,* one of his most sober. The grotesque and macabre, by no means absent in *Martin Chuzzlewit,* predominate in *Our Mutual Friend.* Pecksniff and Mrs. Gamp provoke laughter; Wegg and Mr. Venus, an uneasy snort. The brilliantly detachable portions of *Martin Chuzzlewit* feature the performances of individual characters, while the analogous portions of *Our Mutual Friend* engage the narrator alone—or at least the narrator uses the character more as a prop than a voice.

What most separates the two books is the difference between the imaginative sense of society that each expresses. In *Martin Chuzzlewit* Dickens is articulating his concerns into the pattern that will dominate his following works. He seeks a means of asserting a hidden unity that overrides the variety and individualism that

9. Monroe Engel, *The Maturity of Dickens* (Cambridge: Harvard University Press, 1959), p. 104.

so obviously marked the England of the forties, trying to formulate a "moral law" to order "political and social chaos."[10] After he returned from America in 1842, in the period of writing *Martin Chuzzlewit,* Dickens turned in his own life from the diffuse and enthusiastic radicalism of his youth to the deep and continuous involvement in specific projects of social reform that continued to occupy him throughout his life. By the late fifties, however, around the time he and his wife were separated, Dickens in his writing tried to find a way out of a society that all too obviously fit together rather than to show how it fit. *Our Mutual Friend* strives to discover paths to freedom from a coherence that threatens to be suffocatingly all-enveloping.

Martin Chuzzlewit, then, ends in social and familial union, reconciling Old and Young Martin in life, establishing the relation of intimate trust that supplements the force of the will. *Our Mutual Friend,* in contrast, has Old Harmon dead from the start, and there is no reconciliation even in spirit. For all the formal gimmickry about various states of the Harmon will, the final version revealed in the book's end is then disregarded. There is no fanfare about this in the novel—nothing so dramatic as the burning of the codicil of the Clennam will in *Little Dorrit* in order to spare Arthur Clennam the knowledge of his family history—but the break with the past is even more radical. Dickens undoes through repetition a gesture from his past plots, and in so doing he cuts himself off from that past. One of many analogies that might be adduced from Victorian fiction is Dorothea's choice in *Middlemarch* between obeying the will of the dead Casaubon, or choosing her own will and marrying Will Ladislaw. She enacts no less programmatically than Dickens in his fiction the transfer in the nineteenth century from will as inheritance to will as volition,[11] from career as imitation of an existing pattern to career as the discovery of one's own unique course.

In *Martin Chuzzlewit* Dickens discovers London as a means of organizing his fiction. As the novel moves from the country to the city, Dickens comes upon, invents, his fundamental subject and technique. By *Our Mutual Friend* the motion is more purely spiritual. It begins within London, and its resolving tactic is an internal

10. Everett Knight, *A Theory of the Classical Novel* (London: Routledge and Kegan Paul, 1970), p. 113.

11. Edward W. Said, *Beginnings* (New York: Basic Books, 1975), p. 144.

emigration. Both novels then are innovative, experimental, within his career and in the history of fiction, but in different ways. *Martin Chuzzlewit* first defines Dickens in relation to the whole of previous literature, and our approach to it must be generic; but in *Our Mutual Friend* Dickens defines his current needs against the achievement he himself had brought about to that date and a genetic perspective will be more appropriate. In treating Melville and Hawthorne, I also shift between the generic—emphasized for *The House of the Seven Gables*—and the genetic—predominant for *Moby-Dick.* The two complement each other in providing a full historical context.

At the same time, I should signal another issue of method that follows from the differences I have noted. As a novel of discovery, *Martin Chuzzlewit* needs to be studied sequentially, and I go through it in order, caring less for the themes and overall plan that give it its spatial unity than for the lively work of creative intervention, whether as rejection or invention, with which Dickens redirects the novel. *Our Mutual Friend,* although not totally static, is much more immobilized than *Martin Chuzzlewit.* Dickens's techniques for enforcing analogical coherence are very much stronger and more skilled, and he has thought through the overall shape of the book before composing it. A more synoptic view, therefore, will suit *Our Mutual Friend.*

In dealing with these two novels, as in all my analyses in this study, I am concerned with their realism. By this I intend two things primarily—the author's wish to specify comprehensively the major concerns of his age and the author's critical recognition that there are no literary modes wholly adequate for this task.[12] Old perceptual or organizational techniques and modes, therefore, must be discarded or revised in order to grapple with novelty, yet the new form then made will be no more permanent than was the old form. In realism, the imagination is always at a crisis, passing judgment on the inadequacy of old forms for the urgencies of the

12. This attempt at definition arises from my dissatisfaction with the treatment of the nineteenth century by Robert Alter, *Partial Magic* (Berkeley and Los Angeles: University of California Press, 1975), pp. 84–137. See also George Levine, "Realism Reconsidered," in *The Theory of the Novel,* ed. John Halperin (New York: Oxford University Press, 1974), pp. 233–256. In *Dickens and Reality* (New York: Columbia University Press, 1978) John Romano catches the critical, especially self-critical, dimension of realism but devalues the socially specific.

moment, performing the "capital negation" that destroys "Satan . . . in his tenement," of which Wallace Stevens writes in "Esthétique du Mal":

> The death of Satan was a tragedy
> For the imagination. A capital
> Negation destroyed him in his tenement.
> . . . .
> The tragedy, however, may have begun,
> Again, in the imagination's new beginning,
> In the yes of the realist spoken because he must
> Say yes, spoken because under every no
> Lay a passion for yes that had never been broken.[13]

Within this crisis of rejection, however, there is also "the imagination's new beginning," in which the realist must in his turn say yes, it is good, to the new ordering that has given its shape, its possibility of closure, of fixity, to the work offered to that demanding moment. In that wish to halt the Faustian quest, the devil once more takes his due. The spirit of overview arises.

13. *The Collected Poems of Wallace Stevens* (New York: Alfred A. Knopf, 1954), pp. 319–320.

IV

Problems of Realism in *Martin Chuzzlewit*

Aspects of the Novel: Story, Morality, Society

In exploring the process of realism in *Martin Chuzzlewit,* we may discern three relatively discontinuous aspects of the book. First, there is the story of Martin, the broadly new comic plot of boy gets girl and money. Yet "the hero of the story," as the list of characters calls Young Martin, is totally absent from nine of the monthly parts and is by no means at the center of our interest even when present. The energy of the book lies less in its repetition of this old narrative type than in a second aspect—its debunking observation of contemporary life, its effort to see truth through the obfuscations of form and custom. The work thus holds up to satiric scrutiny a wide range of fresh fictional materials, including not only many individuals from different classes but also certain fundamental institutions of English life. For the first part of the book Pecksniff holds our attention most strongly, and in the later parts the London complex of Mrs. Gamp, Jonas Chuzzlewit, and the Anglo-Bengalee insurance scheme of Tigg Montague. Martin's trip to America does not bring him more fully into focus but makes him less interesting to us than what he encounters, like Gulliver in Lilliput, as American society is anatomized in caricature.

The moral theme of self links this second, satiric aspect of the book to the story of Martin. The perspective of selfishness holds in check the possibly endless heterogeneity of what might be presented. Its technique of meaningfulness emerges most baldly in the American episodes. Dickens uses Bunyan's allegorical analysis of the self to connect Martin's experience in America with the English world juxtaposed to it every few chapters. Whatever novelty America may pretend to, this literary frame still holds it to its British past. The name of "Eden," the pestiferous swamp where Martin has been tricked into buying land, opens up the general possibility of allegory, in a situation that appropriately links two sides of the Protestant Ethic in America: millenarian utopianism and sharp business practice. This Biblical possibility becomes a specific echo of *Pilgrim's Progress*: "As they proceeded further on their track and came more and more to their journey's end, the monotonous desolation of the scene increased to that degree, that for any redeeming feature it presented to the eye, they might have entered, in the body, on the grim domains of Giant Despair" (23).

In this context the literal narrative detail of "journey's end" moves toward the allegorical spiritual pilgrimage of Bunyan. "Eden" threatens to become the final, ironic end of Martin's journey as he sickens and approaches death. The "redeeming" features shift meaning from the financial sense of real estate assessment to the absence in Martin of the spiritually efficacious. "In the body" still differentiates this analogy from the literal level of the action: "Giant Despair" might be found on the page of Bunyan, or in the spirit, but is not yet asserted to be actually present.

Within a few pages, however, the running head announces, "Martin Despairs," and finally a running head summarizes the meaning of the whole Eden episode for Martin as "Discovery of Self": "In the hideous solitude of that most hideous place, with Hope so far removed, Ambition quenched, and Death beside him rattling at the very door, reflection came, as in a plague-beleaguered town." Martin then sees clearly what "an ugly spot" his life has been (33). This traditional allegorical technique of signification enabled Dickens to bring together thematically the instances of selfishness that embody the false principles he sees as guiding life in the England (and America) of his time.[1]

Beyond such moral criticism, a third aspect of the novel emerges from Dickens's wish to systematize his analysis of English society more concretely and circumstantially. The "plague-beleaguered town" of man's soul is "unmetaphored" as Dickens begins to discover in *Chuzzlewit* a principle of organization through the coherent

1. This subject still needs satisfactory treatment, despite the recent work of Jane Vogel, *Allegory in Dickens* (University, Ala.: University of Alabama Press, 1977).

interdependence of individuals in the new urban mass of London.[2] The satiric thrust of Dickens's attacks on the follies and knavery, the fraud and humbug, of his time resonates with the Benthamite attempts to rationalize the antiquated institutional procedures of English society, and Dickens attacked many of the same objects as the Benthamites.[3] Yet in Dickens's organization of his novels through a web of hidden connections and obligations spun out of and around London, one may recognize also an attack on the excessively individualistic emphases of Benthamism, the severing of individuals from each other and the present from the past. Dickens was creating a vision of people's specific interdependence, a sociology to replace the atomism and laissez-faire of Utilitarian psychology and political economy.

In this new myth of London, Dickens speaks "the yes of the realist" and marks the "new beginning" of his imagination after he has discarded all he could bear of what had made sense and shape of life. His new view closely resembles in principle another branch of Utilitarianism. For some Utilitarians emphasized the need for governmental action to create harmonies among people, rather than relying on any invisible hand to achieve such harmony automatically.[4] Inspection and centralization were, as we have noted, the two basic principles of this group, the need to find out all there was to know and to make it all fully available at one spot as a basis for action from that spot—to consolidate knowledge into power. The increasingly spatializing overview that Dickens assumes as the narrative perspective from which to reveal the coherence of his London depends upon, and embodies fully as much as any of the midcentury Utilitarian pioneers of the welfare state, the power of observation.

Indeed, the nineteenth century realized in the social sciences, long

2. On "unmetaphoring" see Rosalie L. Colie, *Shakespeare's Living Art* (Princeton: Princeton University Press, 1974), p. 11.

3. On Dickens's "destructive Benthamism" see Humphry House, *The Dickens World* (2nd ed.; London: Oxford University Press, 1942), p. 91.

4. The classic analysis of this split in Utilitarianism is Elie Halévy, *The Growth of Philosophic Radicalism* (1906), trans. Mary Morris (Boston: Beacon, 1955), e.g., pp. 489–490; on the complexity of Dickens's relation to Utilitarianism, see Raymond Williams, "Dickens and Social Ideas," in *Dickens, 1970,* ed. Michael Slater (London: Chapman and Hall, 1970), pp. 88ff.

before modern physicists did, that no observation is wholly innocent and detached, that observation is already intervention. Etymologically a "detective" is an active "uncoverer," a "lifter-off of roofs"—like Milton's Satan or Lesage's Asmodeus—and the detective is the character within Dickens's fictions who does work like that of the narrator in making the fiction. Just as the detective's revelations bring an individual to judgment, so is there a secular and muted social apocalypse in the narrator's revelations (Greek *apokalypto*, like Latin *detego*, means to reveal, to uncover). From this perspective, I shall now return to the opening of *Martin Chuzzlewit* to examine in detail the textual process by which the three aspects I have defined constitute the book.

THE FIRST NUMBER: TECHNIQUES OF DISLOCATION

Martin Chuzzlewit BEGINS WITH A CHAPTER detailing the "pedigree of the Chuzzlewit family," ostensibly to certify their good "breeding" to a genteel audience of comparable genealogy. As the "origin . . . foundation and increase" of the family is established, it becomes clear that this praise of the greatness of the Chuzzlewits is a mock encomium. Just as the narrator in his role of genealogical "commentator" must perform the "ingenious labor" of "interpretation" to demonstrate the positive values of the family, so must we as readers perform an equal and opposite labor to understand the negative that this ironic construction intends to convey. The chapter is in content a throwaway, for it shows that family history is irrelevant: we all reach back to Adam and to Cain. In undermining the whole claim of the grandeur and authority of the past by reductively defining the activity of its old nobles as "violence and vagabondism," Dickens also warrants the new literary type of the novel, as opposed to the epic and romantic literature of the past. The epigraph he had intended for the work, "Your homes the scene. Yourselves, the actors, here!"[5] defined the world of the novel as the drama of the here and now, in traditional expectations a comedy, in contrast to the more serious forms that attended to the far-off, long-gone, and highborn.

As readers we may feel at home with the stable irony that has so

5. John Forster, *The Life of Charles Dickens* (Philadelphia: J. B. Lippincott, 1873), 2:81.

far defined the strategy of the first chapter, but our situation becomes more complex when we consider the ironies in Dickens's relation to the tradition of the novel. If the whole past is being declared irrelevant to the concerns and techniques of this novel, then the picaresque fiction of the eighteenth century—that earlier fiction that already had eschewed high life for the direct representation of "violence and vagabondism"—is also out of bounds. Yet in turning away from this model, giving us in Martin a hero too bourgeois for the old hit-and-run, Dickens uses one of Fielding's own techniques. This chapter closely echoes Fielding's attack on "greatness" in the genealogical satire of the second chapter of *Jonathan Wild* (1743). The novel, as the form that turns from dead literary models to attempt direct confrontation with life, is caught in the paradox of carrying on an antitraditional tradition, in Harold Rosenberg's phrase, a tradition of the new. At its opening, then, *Martin Chuzzlewit* locates itself in a sequence of apparently spontaneously generated parasitic fictions, works that make themselves up out of material that in using they reject, ranging from *Don Quixote* to Thackeray's explorations of violence and vagabondism in *Catherine* (1839) and *Barry Lyndon* (1844).[6]

Our view of the Chuzzlewit family thus puts aside the issues of direct descent. There remain, however, "patronage and influence," displaced forms of relationship. The "uncle" is the main figure in this relation, and Dickens relies upon our interpretative skills to recognize that he is punning upon a slang term for the pawnbroker. To "dine . . . with Duke Humphrey" is not to eat at all; to attend at the "Golden Balls" of the uncle is to move in lowlife; to acknowledge the magnitude of the uncle's "interest" is to say what you owe him, not what he can do for you. As in *Hamlet,* or in Hawthorne's play with the debilitation that comes from the counterfeit nurture of "Uncle Sam" in the Custom House, this relation with the uncle peculiarly unsettles the relation of words and things and creates a world of hypocrisy. The departed father may have lived in a heroic world, but in the uncle's world money measures all value, although it will not say its own name. Material needs show mutely through as the real bases of human relationships. Dickens at the chapter's

6. This paradox is involved in "The Quixotic Principle," investigated by Harry Levin in *Grounds for Comparison* (Cambridge: Harvard University Press, 1972), pp. 224–243; on parasitism see J. Hillis Miller, "The Critic as Host," *Critical Inquiry* 3 (1977):439–447.

end alludes to Monboddo and Blumenbach, approaching the natural history and biological speculation so important to his French contemporaries and to his own later work. At this point, however, Dickens does not want scientific history, and he rests with a moralist's truth, that people are selfish and eccentric.

Having established, then, through his ironic techniques a satiric perspective on a comic world, Dickens is ready to begin. The opening of the second chapter suggests more "the way of the world" than "the way we live now," for it emphasizes timelessness. The comedy of the Pecksniff household has very little of the particular in it, and we find out neither a name for the town nor a date for the action. There is nonetheless a striking inaugural violence after two pages of fantasia on the wind, as the narrative shifts into the human realm by dropping into farce: the wind slams shut the door and knocks Pecksniff down the stairs.

The thrust of the book from this point is to find as many ways as possible to repeat that ironic plummet from the airy elevation of "sounds and forms" to some humbler ground.[7] Thus Tom Pinch is impressed by Pecksniff's claim "that he could have shed his blood" for Tom, but John Westlock reduces the claim by taking it literally, "Do you *want* any blood shed for you? . . . Does he shed anything for you that you *do* want? . . . Does he shed even legs of mutton for you in decent proportion to potatoes?" So strongly established from the outset is this principle of opening the gap between real wants and empty forms, that it will be extremely difficult for Dickens to make any overall form for the book, beyond a sequence of contradictions, pointing downward. Thus, later in the book, the same kind of coy rhetoric will be used to describe Ruth Pinch as is used in this chapter to characterize the Pecksniff girls. It remains a vexing question for the analyst of the relation between discourse and rhetoric, for the investigator of communication, to define how we know later that Dickens wants us to read the language straight, after so much initial effort to teach us to read with a "bend sinister" (1). Perhaps we do not read the later passages straight but as pure linguistic fiction, the negation of the negation of irony.

The novel, then, has banished the past in the first chapter and established in the second a timeless present, cut off from "the world"

7. For irony as fall, see Paul de Man, "The Rhetoric of Temporality," in *Interpretation,* ed. Charles S. Singleton (Baltimore: Johns Hopkins University Press, 1969), pp. 196–197.

which the coach occasionally bears people off into. The third chapter—the last of the first number—introduces a nostalgia for a past from which things have declined, in its mock elegy on the Dragon, the sign of the local inn, which has grown "faded and ancient . . . of monstrous imbecility." The dragon has become a mere sign rather than a thing, and even as a sign has outworn its use. Unlike what happens in the world of romance, here the dragon will "no longer demand a beautiful virgin for breakfast every morning." The narrator already contaminates that past dragon proleptically with the fate of the present by comparing its appetite for virgins with the wish of "any tame single gentleman" for "his hot roll." This dragon must "rest content with the society of bachelors and roving married men."

Yet just as the novel seems definitively to have removed itself so far from romance as to include only odd traveling salesmen, in another of its abrupt shifts and reversals on come "an old gentleman and a young lady, travelling, unattended, in a rusty old chariot with post-horses, coming nobody knew whence, and going nobody knew whither"(3). Suddenly mystery and romance are present, as the old man, although obviously very sick, refuses any aid except the medicine that his young companion furnishes from a chest she carries. This couple is unlike Dickens's earlier pair of Little Nell and her grandfather, for the old man is not at all broken. Rather, he is "strong and vigorous . . . with a will of iron, and a voice of brass," and with mechanical inflexibility he threatens to leave the house and die on the doorstep if he is not given his way. This threatened curse, the medicine chest, and his evidently "troubled mind" evoke a darkness that suggests sexual irregularity to the landlady: "'Oh!' thought the hostess, 'Then we are in the habit of travelling, and of travelling together.'" When Pecksniff encourages her in this vein, however, our training in how to read his pieties assures us that no January and May relation actually exists, even though the two are unrelated by blood or marriage.

Old Martin is pictured in sharp verbal chiaroscuro, announces that there is a curse upon him, and addresses the landlady in tones of economic worldliness: "'You do your errand, and you earn your fee. Now who may be *your* client?'" When Pecksniff greets the old man as "Martin Chuzzlewit," it seems that we have the central character and that the novel has now really begun, but we learn at the chapter's end that there is a different Martin, a grandson, and the anticipated beginning is again deferred. In response to Pecksniff's claim of cousinship, Old Martin denounces the idea of family, echoing the narrator's perspective in the first chapter. Yet there is only a topical connection of Old Martin's views with those of the first chapter, for the mode of presentation has changed. The narrator tacitly admits the change from satire to a more romantic mode by suggesting that Pecksniff found out that Old Martin wanted to speak to him "on some such principle as prevails in melodramas, and in virtue of which the elderly farmer with the comic son always knows what the dumb girl means when she takes refuge in his garden, and relates her personal memoirs in incomprehensible pantomime." This characterization would allow us a laugh at Pecksniff's expense, except that Martin really does want to talk to him. Even while mocking them, Dickens uses the conventional forms of the popular culture of his age, exempting them from the savage criticism leveled against officially valued forms.

Old Martin suggests that rich men should test the true virtue of others not by pretending to be poor but by making "the search in their own characters" and showing themselves "fit objects to be robbed and preyed upon and plotted against and adulated by any knaves." He thereby adumbrates his ruse to test Pecksniff that will form the overarching frame story to young Martin's reconciliation. Martin continues to emphasize the magical and supernatural qualities of money: "'It is a spectre walking before me through the world. . . . To what man or woman . . . shall I confide such a talisman, either now or when I die? . . . Can you tell me of any . . . living creature who will bear the test of contact with myself?'" Through magical contagion Martin himself has taken on the destructive powers of his money: "'I have been such a lighted torch in peaceful homes, kindling up all the inflammable gases and vapours in their moral atmosphere, which, but for me, might have proved harmless to the end'" (3).

This Timon-like execration of wealth serves an important purpose in the narrative structure of the book, for now that a character within the book has taken on the railer's voice, the narrator is freer to hold up to examination the views which in the first chapter had been his, but now are Martin's.[8] And in the subsequent course of the book the narrator does often take more benign positions than he had in the first part. At this moment which frees the narrator

8. For elaboration of this principle, see Robert C. Elliott, *The Power of Satire* (Princeton: Princeton University Press, 1960), chap. 4.

for constructive work, the metaphors of Martin's speech contain the complex of the ghostly ("spectre") and the pathological (the danger of "contact"), united in an atmosphere. Dickens's later fiction "unmetaphors" this complex, releasing it into the overall world of the novels, which are stories of haunting and sickness. Such language, as we have already seen in *Little Dorrit,* becomes more the narrator's than any character's, and it points toward the biological and social, rather than economic, realms. Old Martin's metaphoric "moral atmosphere" becomes the air people breathe in *Dombey and Son* and *Bleak House,* just as the metaphoric "plague-beleaguered town" (33) of Young Martin's soul becomes the city where they dwell.

Modern Heroism

In the second installment of *Martin Chuzzlewit,* Montague Tigg's appearance abruptly brings the novel up to contemporaneity. Dickens presents him as a type of the present day, "which is currently termed shabby genteel." In examining "Shabby-genteel People" in *Sketches by Boz,* Dickens had suggested that the type occurred only in London. Tigg strikes a triply alien note in this previously isolated and timeless provincial village, for not only is he modern and urban; he is also romantic, a last weed of Byronism. His friend Chevy Slyme is "the highest-minded, the most independent-spirited, most original, spiritual . . . thoroughly Shakespearian, if not Miltonic, and at the same time the most disgustingly unappreciated dog I know" (4). By the reversal with which we read it, Tigg's praise of Slyme casts into disrepute the attempt of the nineteenth century to add depth and glamor to its imaginative life by recourse to the great geniuses of the Renaissance. Dickens thus ironically repeats the *Blackwood's* attacks on the aims of the "Cockney School." Yet Dickens himself will draw on Renaissance sources in *Martin Chuzzlewit,* especially through the interplay of Miltonic, Edenic pastoralism with echoes from Shakespearean tragedy to enrich and integrate his treatment of Jonas's sordid murder of Tigg.

Tigg is "proud as Lucifer" himself, and his mustache is "the regular Satanic sort of thing." The "capital negation" that destroyed Satan "in his tenement" for Stevens has not quite yet happened for Dickens. The narrator, however, is the figure in Dickens's later books who goes far beyond any character in taking on the power that was once the devil's—in Milton's epics or Lesage's satire—of presenting a soaring, comprehensive overview of the kingdoms of the earth and the life of a city. Even so vital a devilish character as Fagin had failed to integrate the world of *Oliver Twist,* and Dickens's growing concern for such integration tempts him into aggrandizing his role as knowing and plotting consciousness.

As much in attitude as in physical appearance, Tigg strikingly prefigures a type that interested Dostoevsky: "He was very dirty and very jaunty; very bold and very mean; very swaggering and very slinking; very much like a man who might have been something better and unspeakably like a man who deserved to be something worse." Like the Underground Man he represents the last gasp of romanticism in confrontation with the materialism that was to dominate increasingly the nineteenth century's thought and actions. Tigg, however, does not go down in a vortex of ideological speculation but swims with the current. As he explains later when he has achieved his position as head of the fraudulent Anglo-Bengalee insurance company, "I rise with circumstances" (27), and *Martin Chuzzlewit* grows increasingly circumstantial as it follows Tigg into contemporary London financial speculation.

Tigg does not float passively. He has a keen grasp on the "circumstances" of his rise. It may seem romantic exaggeration for Tigg to liken Slyme evading debt to "Bonaparte . . . addressing the French army" or to describe Slyme's detention at the Blue Dragon for nonpayment as "a situation as tremendous, perhaps, as the social intercourse of the nineteenth century will readily admit of." Yet together with the irony that reduces Tigg's pretentiousness here, there is also a recognition that we must take his view if we want heroism in the nineteenth century. Thackeray portrays a similar case in "How to Live Well on Nothing a Year" in *Vanity Fair.* Rawdon making money at billiards is "like a great general" and a little later is elaborately compared to "the Duke of Wellington, who never suffered a defeat," but who the French think "cheated at Waterloo" (Thackeray like Pope conflates cards and warfare).[9] The Napoleonic campaigns had spread gambling democratically over Europe,[10] and it comprised for Baudelaire—as in a poem like "Le

9. William Makepeace Thackeray, *Vanity Fair* (1847–1848), ed. Geoffrey and Kathleen Tillotson (Boston: Houghton Mifflin, 1963), chap. 36.

10. Walter Benjamin, "On some Motifs in Baudelaire" (1939), in

Jeu"—a part of modern heroism. Thus Tigg's heroism: in a world in which almost everyone is out for money, he has by far the most practical sense of how to get it. He succeeds in gulling both Pecksniff and Jonas by admitting his corruption and low motives, inviting them to join him as a trickster, and duping them instead. Just as for Raskolnikov it was Napoleonic to butcher an old moneylender or for Julien Sorel to determine to grasp the hand of Mme. de Rênal, so swindling is Tigg's modern heroism.

Napoleon had seemed to offer the last great public opportunities for violence and vagabondism. Resuming a trend from the later eighteenth century, post-Napoleonic crime became more skillful and fraudulent. *Fraser's Magazine* remarked in 1832 that since the exemplary courage of highwaymen, "all this kind of heroism has subsided" into calculation.[11] The new heroism was in a different key. Thus, from 1814 to 1824, Henry Fauntleroy, son of a pious and highly respected dissenting family, carried on huge bank frauds by forgery, until he was discovered, convicted in a sensational trial, and executed. Playing on a slight physical resemblance, Fauntleroy had "dramatized himself as a Napoleon of commerce."[12]

Emerson recognized in Napoleon the synecdochic representative of the materialistic and practical middle class. He was the predominant spirit of the age because "the people whom he sways are little Napoleons."[13] In this heroic age of the bourgeoisie, economics was war carried on by other means. In a society where the desire for social advancement far exceeded the available avenues for such mobility, forgery or destroying wills was a "natural form of economic enterprise,"[14] all the more so since the massive new demands

---

Illuminations, trans. Harry Zohn (1968; rpt. New York: Schocken, 1969), p. 178.

11. Cited in J. J. Tobias, *Crime and Industrial Society in the Nineteenth Century* (London: Batsford, 1967), p. 123.

12. Keith Hollingsworth, *The Newgate Novel* (Detroit: Wayne State University Press, 1963), pp. 41–44. By 1828 Bulwer had incorporated this story into *The Disowned*.

13. "Napoleon; or, The Man of the World," in *Emerson's Complete Works*, Riverside Edition (Cambridge, Mass., 1883), 4:213.

14. Lionel Trilling, *Sincerity and Authenticity* (Cambridge: Harvard University Press, 1972), pp. 14–16; see also Douglas Hay, "Property, Authority, and The Criminal Law," in Douglas Hay et al., *Albion's Fatal Tree* (New York: Pantheon, 1975), pp. 19, 21, 33, 59–60; and Michel Foucault, *Surveiller et punir* (Paris: Gallimard, 1975), pp. 89–91.

for capitalizing industry brought a vast increase in negotiable paper of all kinds. The presses were busy as never before printing shares and books alike.

Tigg then begins as the shabby-genteel character so typical of London and ends as the financial mushroom that is also a London product. Through Tigg, Dickens begins seriously to create his integrated view of London. Dickens's first five novels are more remarkable for their diversity than for their development, but from *Martin Chuzzlewit* on one can see the shape of a career in Dickens's writing. The defining feature of this career is the imaginative apprehension of the city of London as a center of coherence for English life. This coherence is surrounded by mystery as is the city itself, and the means that Dickens uses to expose the coherence of life in *Dombey and Son, Bleak House, Little Dorrit,* and *Great Expectations* is the solution of a mystery in the plot, a mystery which involves the linking, the connection in important ways, of people from seemingly disparate and disjunct ways of life. In *Our Mutual Friend* the emphasis on plot gives way to a looser connection through organized analogy of image and action and yields the novel of Dickens's maturity that can with most accuracy be called symbolical.

ACTIVATING LONDON

THE INCREASING PREDOMINANCE of London and its mysteries emerges in *Martin Chuzzlewit*'s construction. The first seven chapters are set in the country, the last seven chapters in London. As early as the second chapter John Westlock leaves Pecksniff for London and "the world," and after the first London chapters, we only return to the countryside to bring a new character from there to London: Martin, Merry Pecksniff, Cherry Pecksniff, Tom Pinch. Even the establishment of Old Martin with Pecksniff, the one reversal of this direction, is worked in with the departures of other characters. Yet more important than this aspect of the action is the growing sense that the city is the center of meaning for everyone, whether they live in country or city. The last half of the book is dominated by the London figures of Jonas and Tigg, who go out together to the country and work Pecksniff's financial ruin. When Jonas murders Tigg, he makes a double of himself, the disguise as a countryman in which he commits the crime, while his "real self" is supposedly sleeping in London. Yet thinking of that room in

London, Jonas is afraid "not for himself, but of himself." And simply by watching the room in London Nadgett unravels the mystery of Jonas's actions. Finally, Old Martin comes to London in order to pass his final judgment on Pecksniff.

There are three important stages in the developing view of London in *Martin Chuzzlewit,* marked by the first arrivals in London of Pecksniff, Martin, and Tom Pinch.[15] Pecksniff's London shows that the atmosphere of strangeness, of fairy tale or grotesquerie, is present from the first in Dickens's portrayal of London. The description of Todgers's neighborhood is full of high-spirited inventiveness, evoking an atmosphere of romance and mystery that contrasts with the provincial setting of the book's opening. The fruit brokers' stands call up far-off places and impress the reader with London's position as a trading port and the laborious human activity that its needs require.

> One of the first impressions wrought upon the stranger's senses was of oranges—of damaged oranges, with blue and green bruises on them, festering in boxes, or mouldering away in cellars. All day long, a stream of porters from the wharves beside the river, each bearing on his back a bursting chest of oranges, poured slowly through the narrow passages; while underneath the archway by the public house, the knots of those who rested and regaled within, were piled from morning until night.
>
> [9]

The scene is observed from the hypothetical perspective of a "stranger," the reader's surrogate, and is registered in terms of

15. E. B. Benjamin also divides the novel into three stages, finding as I do key points in Chapters 13 and 36. He is not concerned with London, however, but with "selfish hypocrisy." See "The Structure of *Martin Chuzzlewit*," *Philological Quarterly* 34 (1955):39–47; see also Alan R. Burke, "The House of Chuzzlewit and the Architectural City," *Dickens Studies Annual* 3 (1974):14–40; on London in Dickens's work generally, see Donald Fanger, *Dostoevsky and Romantic Realism* (Cambridge: Harvard University Press, 1965), chap. 3; for general context see U. C. Knoepflmacher, "The Novel between City and Country," in *The Victorian City,* ed. H. J. Dyos and Michael Wolff (Boston: Routledge and Kegan Paul, 1973), 2:517–536.

overall "first impressions," a bombardment of the "senses," rather than as an object of knowledge. The oranges are so many bruising impacts upon the retina, just as they themselves have been mysteriously battered and are being slowly transformed. As they fester and molder, are they garbage or is someone purposefully saving them in those boxes and cellars? The second sentence is impressively organized by the close assonance of "porters," "wharves," and "poured" and the many approximations to these sounds in "oranges," "rivers," "bearing," and "bursting"; by the alliterations on *b* and *p;* and by the metaphor that joins the pouring stream of porters to the river that it leads from. But human action has reversed the course of nature. A stream of water could only flow into the river, but the stream of men flows up away from it. In contrast to the orderly oppositions of working outdoors or relaxing indoors, either by resting or by regaling, the "piled . . . knots" present an enigmatic emblem.[16] They bear the traces of all the men indoors, but what do they tell of the men? And how can one untangle these knots?

From this market area we look at churches and cemeteries, thoroughfares and byways, and taverns, until finally we arrive at "the grand mystery of Todgers's . . . the cellarage, approachable only by a little back door and a rusty grating: which cellarage within the memory of man had had no connexion with the house, but had always been the freehold property of somebody else, and was reported to be full of wealth: though in what shape—whether in silver, brass, or gold, or butts of wine, or casks of gun powder—was matter of profound uncertainty and supreme indifference to Todgers's, and all its inmates" (9). This description again opposes the world of human meaning to the physical world. The cellarage is physically part of the house; it is only property rights and the anonymity of urban life that have separated it so that it has "no connexion." The presence of "somebody else," however, that alien presence endemic to the city, arouses gossip, rumor, and speculation that fill the cellar with innumerable phantasmatic shapes and substances, which it seems nonetheless can be safely ignored, for none of these details is more than suggestive, and they play no further role in the action of the book. The cellarage remains forever closed to us. Until Dickens can harness this view of London to a coherent

16. Porter's knot: "A kind of double shoulder-pad, with a loop passing around the forehead, the whole roughly resembling a horse-collar, used by London market-porters for carrying their burdens" (*OED*, s.v. "knot").

plot, the vision will remain much more fanciful than imaginative. When in *Bleak House* the narrator asks, "What connexion can there be?" the answer makes up the rest of the book.

This distinction emerges more clearly in Pecksniff's visit to Ruth Pinch at the brass and copper founder's home. The house is as imposing as "a giant's castle," and indeed the giant inside makes mincemeat of Pecksniff. The sole purpose of the visit is to display Pecksniff's routine of presumption, put down, and recovery and to prepare a contrast with Tom's rescue of Ruth and slaying of the giant. To compare the implications of this visit with the repercussions of Arthur Clennam's observation of Amy Dorrit working for his mother, or of Mr. Dombey's choice of a nurse for Paul, illustrates the difference in organization between *Martin Chuzzlewit* and the later books. Pecksniff's London differs little from that of *The Pickwick Papers* or *Nicholas Nickleby.* Jonas's dinner for Pecksniff's girls evokes the same social milieu as that of Ralph Nickleby or Quilp, and like them Jonas seems a standard old-fashioned villainous type, though we do not yet know just what he will do. Despite the brilliant inventiveness of the writing for Pecksniff's London, the energy that for many readers makes the novel really begin, Dickens also runs the risk of self-repetition.

Martin is the next character to arrive in London (13). He arrives at night and stands "in the dark street with a pretty strong sense of being shut out, alone, upon the dreary world, without the key of it." Disinherited, as he thinks, and without friends, to his knowledge, Martin nonetheless has "great expectations" and his love for Mary to keep him a gentleman. His "dress and manner" prevent him from getting a job as a sailor to America, and there is apparently no work for him in London. His stay in London is treated summarily, as in five weeks the difficulties of his environment reduce him to shameless "listless idleness," "the lowest round" of a tall ladder. When he encounters Tigg in a pawnshop, Tigg's shabby gentility and voluble ease with the pawnbroker cast a worrying shadow, for Martin may be headed permanently toward that level. Both of them, however, are instead on the way up, from the moment of, and because of, that meeting, hailed by Tigg as "one of the most tremendous meetings in ancient or modern history" (13). The encounter will yield from Old Martin the money that Tigg uses to start the Anglo-Bengalee and the money that Martin uses to go to America. Martin, nonetheless, is too concerned with himself to be aware of any mystery or meaning in these coincidences, and he sees Tigg as an embarrassing annoyance, not an omen. Indeed, Dickens probably wrote meaning into the incident only retrospectively, for the passage is handled with no narrative portentousness.

Only with the arrival in London of the last man from the provinces, Tom Pinch, does Dickens begin to create an integrally meaningful overview of London. The five chapters (36–40) from Tom's arrival to his encounter with Nadgett, Tigg, and Jonas at the steamer docks establish the London of hidden connections that will predominate in Dickens's work for nearly twenty years. Yet Tom, surprisingly, is the least romantic or mysterious character in the book. He is rather a mild-mannered voice of common sense in contrast to the overbearingness that so characterizes most of the book's figures.

In the period starting from his disillusion with Pecksniff and continuing through his early stay in London, Tom serves Dickens as an explicit measuring stick of reality, as opposed to fairy tale or romance. First his good sense is contrasted with the Byronic or Timon-like postures that fill the book: "Tom was far from being sage enough to know that, having been disappointed in one man, it would have been a strictly rational and eminently wise proceeding to have revenged himself upon mankind in general, by mistrusting them one and all" (36). Although the "authority of divers poets" supports this fantasy of revenge, Dickens dismisses it as pernicious, like the action of "that good Vizier in the Thousand-and-one Nights, who issues orders for the destruction of all the Porters in Bagdad because one . . . misconducted himself." Tom's quiet irony pricks an extravagant fancy of John's: "'You are on a visit to me. I wish I had an organ for you, Tom!' 'So do the gentlemen down-stairs, and the gentlemen overhead, I have no doubt,' was Tom's reply." Already implicit in Tom's remark is a sense of the city as full of other people that one must care about. This sensitivity to his surroundings, along with his willingness to minimize himself, makes Tom perfect for Dickens's purpose of creating mystery out of everyday life.

As Tom goes out into the streets, his sense of London is colored by a view like that of *Oliver Twist,* and he "was quite disappointed to find, after half-an-hour's walking, that he hadn't had his pocket picked." The narrative marks as a ridiculous fiction such a view of London. Tom is only gratified by John's "inventing a pickpocket . . . and pointing out a highly respectable stranger as one of that fraternity." The general world of London roguery, both from popular legend and picaresque literature, is also present to Tom, but in imagination only, for he actually meets no "preparers of cannibalic pastry . . . ring-droppers, pea and thimble-riggers, duffers, touters. . . . He fell into conversation with no gentleman who swore he had more money than any gentleman, and very soon proved he had more money than one gentleman by taking his away from him" (37). As Tigg shows, crime has moved off the streets into offices; no longer is it the work of isolated individuals or a segregable knot of criminal subculture; rather it has become pervasive and systematic.

Such expectations as Tom's of a glamorous, strange, and visible criminal world are as ridiculous as John's surmises about a possible birth mystery for Tom: " 'Tom,' he said, as they were walking along, 'I begin to think you must be somebody's son.' 'Bless your heart,' replied Tom, 'My poor father was of no consequence, nor my mother either. . . . There's nothing romantic in our history, John' " (39). Now in the city rather than in the country and in a matter-of-fact rather than satiric mode, the consequentiality of the past and of genealogy is again denied, along with the relevance of the fictional models they authorize.

THE YES OF THE REALIST

DICKENS THEN HAS CLEARED the stage of old myths, including some that he earlier shared in, but only in order to establish a space for his own "new beginning," for by the time he explains his background to John, Tom is already involved in mystery. There is a "strange charm" in the "ghostly air" of the "uninhabited chambers in the Temple" where he works: "Every morning when he shut his door at Islington, he turned his face towards an atmosphere of unaccountable fascination, as surely as he turned it to the London smoke; and from that moment it thickened round and round him all day long, until the time arrived for going home again, and leaving it, like a motionless cloud, behind" (40). This is no mere effect of "atmosphere," literal or literary, for here, as in *Bleak House*, where Dickens dwells on "the romantic side of familiar things," there is meaning beneath the atmosphere of foreboding. Yet this mystery will be clarified simply by the arrival of Old Martin.

Within this atmosphere, however, Tom will be first juxtaposed with and then connected to the new London of Montague Tigg. In explaining the Anglo-Bengalee's success to Jonas, Tigg called up the mysteries of the vast city:

"There are printed calculations . . . which will tell you pretty nearly how many people will pass up and down that thoroughfare in the course of a day. *I* can tell you how many of 'em will come in here, merely because they find this office here; knowing no more about it than they do of the Pyramids. . . .

"I can tell you," said Tigg in his ear, "how many of 'em will buy annuities, effect insurances, bring us their money in a hundred shapes and ways, force it upon us, trust us as if we were the Mint; yet know no more about us than you do of that crossing-sweeper at the corner. Not so much. Ha, ha!"

[27]

The laugh and insinuating whisper relate Tigg's temptation to his satanic prototypes, but he has now gone beyond the shabby-genteel world of gambling to apply the same statistical principles of chance and discontinuity to the public sphere. Although any individual—"the crossing-sweeper at the corner"—is as unknowable as the pyramids, a calculus of aggregates allows one to predict crucial facts about such individuals integrated en masse.[17] Yet Tigg also wants to know individual secrets, and to find them out, he hires Nadgett. Nadgett is himself a London type; he belongs "to a class; a race peculiar to the City; who are secrets as profound to one another, as they are to the rest of mankind" (27).[18]

The chapter "Secret Service" (38), in which Nadgett investigates Jonas and comes up with a secret that allows Tigg to blackmail Jonas, opens with a characteristic experience of London life, the passing of two strangers: "In walking from the City . . . Tom Pinch had looked into the face, and brushed against the threadbare sleeve, of Mr. Nadgett, man of mystery to the Anglo-Bengalee Disinterested Loan and Life Assurance Company. Mr. Nadgett naturally passed away from Tom's remembrance as he passed out of his

17. On statistics in the growth of nineteenth-century consciousness of the city, see Louis Chevalier, *Laboring Classes and Dangerous Classes in Paris during the First Half of the Nineteenth Century* (1958), trans. Frank Jellinek (New York: Fertig, 1973), especially pp. 45ff.; and Asa Briggs, "The Human Aggregate," in Dyos and Wolff, *The Victorian City,* 1: especially p. 85.

18. On Nadgett see Ian Ousby, *Bloodhounds of Heaven* (Cambridge: Harvard University Press, 1976), pp. 82–85.

view; for he didn't know him, and had never heard his name." Such urban moments were recognized throughout the nineteenth century as posing a challenge to the artist. Poe met the challenge in his prose fantasia on "The Man of the Crowd," and Baudelaire in such poems as "A une Passante" and "Les Sept Vieillards":

> Fourmillante cité, cité pleine de rêves,
> Où le spectre en plein jour raccroche le passant!
> Les mystères partout coulent comme des sèves.
>
> O swarming city, city full of dreams, where the
> ghost accosts the passer-by in broad daylight!
> Mysteries flow everywhere like sap.

Wordsworth recalls how in London his sense that, "The face of every one/ That passes by me is a mystery," brought on a visionary "second-sight procession" of "shapes" like those that glide over mountains, just as the impact of Baudelaire's experience leaves him at sea "Sans mâts, sur une mer monstrueuse et sans bords!" (mastless . . . on a monstrous, shoreless sea). In contrast to the process by which Dickens moved from urban metaphors toward a direct confrontation with the city, the metaphorizing of these poets' experience led them away from the city. Wordsworth nonetheless recognized the possibility of seeing the city with an "under-sense" that gave a "feeling of the whole."[19]

To contextualize the novelists' perceptions of the city, we must look not only to poets, but also, as we have noted, to the journalists and publicists. They joined in writing of the city in a way that points to the developing social sciences and that strives toward a "feeling of the whole." This complex of relations emerges in a French work contemporaneous with *Martin Chuzzlewit* that takes its title and premise from the overviewing figure of Asmodeus, on which we have already remarked and to which we shall again return. The collaborative devil's-eye view of Paris in the 1840s, *Le Diable à Paris,* curiously condenses a whole history of city writing. It begins as if it were a series of satirical vignettes, including contributions by Balzac, George Sand, Nerval, and Gavarni, but it

19. William Wordsworth, *The Prelude,* ed. Ernest de Selincourt (2nd ed., revised by Helen Darbishire; Oxford: Clarendon, 1959), 1850 text, bk. VII, ll. 628–634, 735–736. *Baudelaire,* trans. and ed. Francis Scarfe (Harmondsworth: Penguin, 1961), pp. 193, 195.

ends with a series of statistical tables, allowing the devil, or reader, the same kind of view Tigg achieved. The chapter on "Un Passant" presents the problem of street-life we have been exploring. A passer-by is "someone who is alone and who remains alone in the midst of everybody; who doesn't concern himself about you and is a matter of indifference to you—wrongly perhaps, for every passerby is a secret." A bypasser is a relative being who only acquires particular value in context: "To an observer, an observation; to a philosopher, a portion of his system." Although to see "all these contrasts passing . . . without so much as noticing each other . . . you might think egoism had triumphed and that in Paris there was no society, only individuals," the piece ends with an organic metaphor that totalizes *les passants* into the warmest blood in the veins of a great city, hailing them as the "formidable People of Paris."[20]

Unwilling to rest with such a sentimental escape, and more insistent on judging the cost of the process by which the city assimilated its inhabitants, was Engels in his social analysis of the condition of the working class. He sees in the "great towns" the ultimate reduction of "human society" into its "component atoms." And in the "restless and noisy activity of the crowded streets" where people "rush past each other as if they had nothing in common," he finds "the isolation of the individual," which has "been pushed to its furthest limits in London."[21] As Dickens develops his scene of strangers passing, he too relates the social disorder of the city, the lack of care of people for each other, to the selfishness of ignorance that refuses to ameliorate the situation of mutual unknowability: "As there are a vast number of people in the huge metropolis of England who rise up every morning not knowing where their heads will rest at night, so there are a multitude who, shooting arrows over houses as their daily business, never know on whom they fall" (38).

Dickens draws tight the irony inherent in such a situation by using his omniscient, novelistic privilege to create a plot linking these two passing strangers. Here the connection that the cellarage failed to establish between "somebody else" and Todgers's materializes.

20. *Le Diable à Paris: Paris et les Parisiens* (Paris: J. Hetzel, 1845–1846), 1:225–228. Translations are my own.

21. Friedrich Engels, *The Condition of the Working Class in England* (1845), trans. and ed. W. O. Henderson and W. H. Chaloner (1958; rpt. Stanford: Stanford University Press, 1968), pp. 30–31.

> Mr. Nadgett might have passed Tom Pinch ten thousand times; might even have been quite familiar with his face, his name, pursuits, and character; yet never once have dreamed that Tom had any interest in any act or mystery of his. Tom might have done the like by him, of course. But the same private man out of all the men alive, was in the mind of each at the same moment; was prominently connected, though in a different manner, with the day's adventure of both; and formed, when they passed each other in the street, the one absorbing topic of their thoughts.
>
> [38]

Two chapters later, however, in the superbly orchestrated scene at the steamer docks, Dickens contradicts himself. Suddenly Nadgett is Tom's landlord, and they in fact do know each other, by face and name. Dickens is now taking up the second possibility in the encounter, the one that initially seemed only a contrary-to-fact hypothesis, the situation of people whose casual acquaintance with each other masks even more surprisingly their deep interconnection.

We have only a few of Dickens's working materials for *Martin Chuzzlewit,* nothing like the increasingly copious "mems" that mark his planning for *Dombey and Son* and the later novels. There is, therefore, no evidence available to inform us with certainty, but it seems likely that in his writing between number XIV (the crossing of Nadgett and Tom connected only by the narrator) and number XV (the steamer scene in which Nadgett activates his connection with Tom) Dickens discovered the sense of London, and correlative technique, that was to inform his subsequent works. The intrigue earlier in *Martin Chuzzlewit* of Jonas's supposed murder of his father creates a simple irony (Jonas thinks he's done it) and makes a moral point (he's as good as done it) but does not create a moral sociology. It is only the grim side of new-comedy and romance birth secrets, like that in *Nicholas Nickleby* that reveals Ralph Nickleby as Smike's father. One may apply this individual retribution as a warning for collective activities, but the collectivity is not directly implicated in the action itself.

Jonas's involvement with Tigg, however, and the further complications of blackmail, fraud, and murder—in which Tom suddenly appears as a short circuit—point in a new direction, involving the whole shared life of the city. But it is too late in the novel to bring Tom into full relation with Jonas and Tigg. After delivering the note to Jonas on the docks for Nadgett, Tom tries to apologize to Jonas the next day and is driven out before he can speak. Jonas therefore does not learn "what unsuspected spy there was upon him" and is not "saved from the commission of a Guilty Deed." The situation is still within the realm of retribution for individual morality: "The fatality was of his own working; the pit was of his own digging; the gloom that gathered round him was the shadow of his own life" (46). The result of the connection is still only a melodramatic irony.

Dickens has not succeeded wholly in reorienting the book from the new beginning of London interconnection and the new social realities of England. The illustration of Pecksniff's last fall (52) shows two book titles, *Paradise Lost* and *Le Tartuffe par Molière.* These seventeenth-century explorations of the self were still available to Dickens for guiding the overall interpretation of the book, just as Bunyan had been for Martin's American sojourn in "Eden." An even clearer instance of this relapse from innovation to convention emerges in Tom Pinch's last and most explicit denunciation of fallacious "poetical justice" such as he might experience were he a "character in a book." He warns of the human dangers for those who imitate literary models and try "to make heroes of themselves out of books," but he can offer in place of such wrong paths only a "much higher justice" (50) that has scarcely been demonstrated in the book, except at such melodramatic moments as Jonas's blindness. In pointing us beyond, that "higher justice" sets us up again for an ironic fall.[22]

In Dickens's following social novels, however, in *Dombey and Son, Bleak House, Little Dorrit,* and *Great Expectations,* the mysteries and connections will lead inevitably to the results of these books that uncover hidden relations of great moral and social import. In *Bleak House,* for example, the "crossing sweeper at the corner" (27), to whom Tigg alluded, will not only appear in the novel in person, but will be a primary link between the various elements of the book. Jo is Captain Hawdon's friend, Lady Dedlock's guide to the cemetery, a witness to Hortense's activities, the object of Mrs. Snagsby's suspicions, and carrier of smallpox to Esther. From the polarity of Tom Pinch and Tigg—the simple touchstone of reality from the country and the exemplar of the mysteries of the

22. On this pattern of relapse in Victorian fiction generally, see Barbara Hardy, *Tellers and Listeners* (London: Athlone, 1975), p. 25.

modern city, the labyrinth of finance and crime—and from their mediation by Nadgett, the man who is nothing in himself but knows everything, Dickens has made a first great step toward articulating a new fiction of how the city works.

OVERVIEW AND UNDERSTANDING: *Chuzzlewit* AND AFTER

THE CHANGE IN THE FUNCTION of London from the early parts to the end of *Martin Chuzzlewit* stands out if we compare two overviews from elevated posts of observation. The famous "view from Todgers's" shows the observer helpless before the energy of random surfaces turbulent with the energy of obscured meaning. The first experience of one who has "climbed to this observatory" is vertiginously disorienting; he is "stunned from having knocked his head against the little door in coming out" and "choked from having looked, perforce, straight down the kitchen chimney." Only after these initiatory "stages" do the "things to gaze at . . . well worth your seeing" emerge. Yet it is not clear what the worth is. If the vista offers "smoke and noise enough for all the world at once," the question remains why we should be assumed to have an appetite for smoke and noise. The Monument, "close beside you" is personified as a fellow observer, "every hair erect upon his golden head, as if the doings of the city frightened him." And well they might in their random multiplicity: "There were steeples, towers, belfries, shining vanes, and masts of ships; a very forest. Gables, housetops, garret-windows, wilderness upon wilderness." The experience is as uncontrollable as the constant bump and jostle of people on the crowded sidewalk. There is no syntax beyond mere contiguity; no clarity emerges from the elevation. Instead "slight features in the midst of this crowd of objects . . . spr[i]ng out from the mass without any reason, as it were, and [take] hold of the attention, whether the spectator would or no." As this incomprehensible assault causes anger in the onlooker, "the tumult swell[s] into a roar; the hosts of objects . . . thicken and expand," and the viewer rushes in fright downstairs lest he be driven "into the street . . . head-foremost" (9).

Contrast the perspective of that specialized city creature Nadgett, explaining his detection of Jonas's crime: "From that garrett-window opposite . . . I have watched this house and him for days and nights." When he sees the strange figure of the countryman

(Jonas in disguise), he says, "I could not comprehend what this meant . . . but, having seen so much, I resolved to see it out, and through. And I did. . . . I kept at that window all day. . . . I think I never closed my eyes. At night, I saw him come out with a bundle. I followed him" (51). Nadgett's watching is purposive and focused; the "worth" of what's being seen quickly emerges from the action that the seeing permits, the "revelation" of the mystery, the uncovering of the meaning of the mysterious surfaces that had seemed to conspire against Todgers's, threatening to "shut the prospect out."

Even Nadgett's view, however, is limited in its comprehension, and in his later fiction Dickens makes of his narrator an even more rarefied and specialized creature of observation. In *Dombey and Son* the narrator broods upon the terrible "revelation" that would follow if we could see the "moral pestilence" that is inseparable from the physically "noxious particles" of "vitiated Air." Not just one murderer would then be found out but a whole world of crimes: "Then should we see depravity, impiety, drunkenness, theft, murder, and a long train of nameless sins against the natural affections and repulsions of mankind, overhanging the devoted spots, and creeping on, to blight the innocent and spread contagion among the pure" (*DS* 47). Such a view can put into proper perspective the question of family history that was so problematic in *Martin Chuzzlewit:* "Where we generate disease to strike our children down and entail itself upon unborn generations, there also we breed, by the same certain process, infancy that knows no innocence" (*DS* 47) and all the other perversions of the ages of man. Dickens calls for a "good spirit," a reformed Asmodeus, to "take the house-tops off" and present the interrelated lives of London in so compelling a vision as to produce social reform.

The abstract analysis of this passage from *Dombey and Son* speaks of the issues that are central to the action of the book: the slums, the warped family relation, the abuses of love, the crime and transportations that figure so largely in the lives of the Browns and associate them with "the thunderbolt" that is about to strike the equally loveless and warped Dombey household. The plot connections, if improbable, are clear and strong. Good Mrs. Brown "borrows" Florence Dombey and thereby causes her nurse to be fired and her relation with Walter to begin. Carker, who has seduced Alice Brown, elopes with Mrs. Dombey. Therefore, Mr. Dombey must humble himself before the Browns to receive information that they have from Biler, who is the son of the dismissed nurse and whose life has been corrupted by Dombey's thoughtless charity. The result is that Carker's secret sin, committed before the book's narrative begins, brings about his own downfall and Dombey's humbling and salvation.

Similarly in *Bleak House* a buried mystery creates the connections, an "infamous alliance" in the past that not even Sir Leicester Dedlock can deny in the present. From Jo at Tom-all-Alone's the path leads to Hawdon at Krook's and thence to Lady Dedlock and Esther. The Jarndyce and Jarndyce suit provides a frame enclosing all the actions arising from the mystery, but it is Lady Dedlock's secret that drives the actions onward. Finally the plague from Tom-all-Alone's spreads through all classes in an analogue of revolution, ending social distinctions. All these elements of the book are caught in the observation of the narrator, who from the first has had the power of aerial perspective, scrutinizing the foggy world of the first chapter as a microscopist would a drop of dirty water, then moving "as the crow flies" (*BH* 2) to Chesney Wold.

Late in the book, the moon has looked down on Tom-all-Alone's and "passed on," but the narrator looks hard and sees that Tom-all-Alone's exacts revenge for society's neglect: "Even the winds are his messengers, and they serve him in these hours of darkness. There is not a drop of Tom's corrupted blood but propagates infection and contagion somewhere. It shall pollute, this very night, the choice stream (in which chemists on analysis would find the genuine nobility) of a Norman house, and his Grace shall not be able to say Nay to the infamous alliance" (*BH* 46).

In *Little Dorrit*, too, the principle is similar. In a passage we have already noted, the narrator presents a panorama centered on Arthur Clennam, returned after long absence to London on a Sunday: "Ten thousand responsible houses surrounded him, frowning . . . on the streets they composed. . . . Fifty thousand lairs surrounded him where people lived so unwholesomely, that fair water put into their crowded rooms on Saturday night, would be corrupt on Sunday morning. . . . Miles of close wells and pits of houses, where the inhabitants gasped for air, stretched far away towards every point of the compass" (*LD* I, 3). Again the scene includes high and low, "houses" and "lairs," and links physical and moral corruption through their common noxious atmosphere. Later in the same book, as Merdle's stocks attract unwary buyers from all levels of society, the narrator observes "That it is at least as difficult to stay a moral infection as a physical one; that such a disease will spread with the malignity and rapidity of the plague; that the contagion, when it has once made head, will spare no pursuit or condition, but will lay hold on people in the soundest health, and become developed in the most unlikely constitutions; is a fact as firmly established by experience as that we human creatures breathe an atmosphere" (*LD* II, 13). The warnings of such a passage find vindication in the catastrophe of Arthur's financial ruin.

Although the plot of *Little Dorrit* is not so well organized as that of *Bleak House,* Dickens still felt the need for a retributive mystery to explain the moral malaise of the book. Dickens drew up two sets of "mems" for the concluding number of *Little Dorrit,* one to summarize what was already known to the reader; the other, to figure out—with some struggle—the initial question about the Clennams: "How connected with the Dorrits?"[23] The will that Mrs. Clennam suppresses is the actual link, although it is not the cause of Dorrit's imprisonment. The gloomy religion that is so caught in its own self-abasement as not to notice the pall it casts over London taints Arthur Clennam's mind before he involves himself in the actual taint of the Merdle speculations; but self-righteous irresponsibility meets its nemesis when the Clennam house collapses. This collapse fulfills the narrator's prophetic, synoptic exclamation as Amy Dorrit thinks of Covent Garden's rats and ratlike children, "Look to the rats, young and old, all ye Barnacles; for before God they are eating away our foundations, and will bring the roofs on our heads!" (*LD* I, 14).

Already in *Little Dorrit,* however, there is considerable discomfort with the organization of which *Bleak House* is exemplary. At the level of plot, Amy's burning of the hidden codicil suggests that the present can free itself healthfully as well as dangerously from the past, that there are some forms of neglect that do not bring about a ghostly return. Furthermore, at the level of reading experience, despite the pleasure in seeing all the loose ends worked in and the portents worked out, despite the reassurance in learning that Arthur was right to suspect *something* wrong, nonetheless, there is no real snapping into place when the hurried explanation finally comes. Indeed, one can hardly remember the details: "It is too obscure and intricate a story to . . . summarize. Towards the

23. Paul D. Herring, "Dickens' Monthly Number Plans for *Little Dorrit,*" *Modern Philology* 64 (1966):58.

end . . . the reader is told the facts, hitherto concealed from him, from which the action springs; with the result, not that he is at last enlightened, but that he falls into a state of complete bewilderment."[24]

In my final chapter on *Our Mutual Friend* I return to the issue raised here. In the next two chapters, however, I look in more detail at the accomplishments of *Dombey and Son* and *Bleak House* that so far I have been able only schematically to sketch. In doing this, I move out again from considering Dickens alone, within the dynamics of his own career, to relate his writing to the problems and achievements of Hawthorne and Carlyle, thereby suggesting a fuller history of mid-nineteenth-century imaginative writing about society. I then focus on Melville's masterpiece in relation to Carlyle's exemplary demands upon the modern writer, to emphasize a different playing out of possibilities similar to those of Dickens. *Moby-Dick* achieves extraordinary poise in its task of getting the whole fluid world of motion fixed within a book. Recognizing the powers, as well as the limitations, of his activity as a writer, Melville holds a balance that soon falls over to the emphasis in "Bartleby" on "dead letters." Reading *Our Mutual Friend* in this context reveals Dickens's similar awareness of his books as fictional and written, though I leave open for investigation elsewhere the reasons (whether psychological, social, or yet other) that Melville's writing was so much more crippled by this self-consciousness.

24. Sigmund Freud, "The Uncanny," trans. Alix Strachey, in *Studies in Parapsychology*, ed. Philip Rieff (New York: Crowell-Collier, 1963), pp. 38–39 (referring to E. T. A. Hoffmann, *The Devil's Elixirs*).

V

The House and the Railroad: *Dombey and Son* and *The House of the Seven Gables*

By juxtaposing Dickens's *Dombey and Son* (1848) to Hawthorne's *House of the Seven Gables* (1851), we can further elucidate the literary history that England and America share in the nineteenth century.[1] Both of these works build up novelistic wholes from the materials typical of the periodical literature of the 1830s, in particular from the forms of the Gothic tale and the sketch of contemporary life. The attempts of Dickens and Hawthorne to integrate these partial, short forms into a comprehensive totality mark their efforts to comprehend in literature a society that seemed increasingly blurred and fragmentary. Considered as social fables, the two novels extraordinarily resemble each other in their organization of material. Both confront a proud, established family, the Dombeys and the Pyncheons, with a society in the turmoil of transition, and both show that the family's fate is to change with society. In both novels the terms of Family and Society are symbolized by an ancestral house and the new railroad. Each ends with the last female of the old family making a mismatch, giving up her proud name to marry a man of lower social origin who has had adventures in the wide world, one who has participated in that new mobility associated with the railroad. Acknowledging this common technical and ideological context allows us to examine English and American

1. I shall not go into problems of influence. Randall Stewart does record Hawthorne's reading of *David Copperfield* while working on *The House of the Seven Gables,* but only in 1856 does evidence appear for his reading *Dombey and Son.* See *Nathaniel Hawthorne* (New Haven: Yale University Press, 1948), pp. 105, 168.

literature, in this case Dickens and Hawthorne, in closer and finer comparison than is possible through nationalist approaches, whether through the American "romance" or the English "Great Tradition."[2]

As I observed in the Introduction, the early nineteenth century saw the establishment of the great quarterly reviews and the proliferation in their wake of many other kinds of magazines. New kinds of literary careers became possible, as old forms gained new popularity and new forms came to prominence. Thus in 1820 *London Magazine* began to publish Charles Lamb's city sketches of "Elia." Magazines also offered new outlets for short fiction, notably the "Germanic" Gothic tales of *Blackwood's* (started 1817) and their American cognates by Poe. Each of these two forms has a typical affectivity, the sketch sentimental, the tale sensational, but each builds its overall effect out of contrasts. The tale mixes comedy and terror, the sketch humor and pathos. Generally the sketch seeks delicate, piquant, and picturesque effects; the tale tends to sublimity, chiaroscuro rather than gradual shading. Both forms prominently displayed the narrator, whose genial presence and politely refined language made acceptable the frequently "low" matter he was presenting. The roots of both these forms reach back into the eighteenth century, the sketch to the *Spectator* and the tale to the fountainhead of English Gothicism, Horace Walpole's *Castle of Otranto* (1765), but the specific institutional opportunities were new to the age.

In this world of periodical literature, Dickens and Hawthorne began their literary careers, each publishing as his first book a collection of reprinted periodical pieces. Washington Irving's *Sketchbook of Geoffrey Crayon* (1820) may serve us, as it did contemporary reviewers, for the model of both *Sketches by Boz* (1836, divided into three sections: "Scenes," "Characters," "Tales") and *Twice-Told Tales* (1837, containing also a number of sketches). The first novel of each writer shows baldly the transition from periodical writing. Hawthorne juxtaposes the long sketch of "The Custom House" to the long tale of *The Scarlet Letter,* while Dickens's comic sketches of cockneys bump against the interpolated dark tales of *The Pickwick Papers.*

This historical context suggests immediate discriminations and

2. For the fullest argument against this nationalistic dichotomy, see Nicolaus Mills, *American and English Fiction in the Nineteenth Century* (Bloomington: Indiana University Press, 1973), chap. 2.

recognitions, both of particular ways of writing and of some problems of construction that may arise in a novel built up from such smaller forms. In *The House of the Seven Gables* the treatment of Hepzibah and her shop clearly derives from the sketch mode, the narrator presenting her with self-conscious apologies for low material in a condescendingly polite mock-heroic voice and then circling round to draw moral lessons from her condition and finally to sympathize with her. Similarly in *Dombey and Son* the quaint shop of the Wooden Midshipman is sketch material and especially resembles Hawthorne in the handling of Captain Cuttle, who from a stock grotesque is rounded and built up toward full moral being. With his severely limited cast of characters, Hawthorne treats one body of material from several different perspectives. Dickens, however, must struggle to integrate the varied materials and treatments across his widely spread plot lines and settings.[3]

GOTHIC RECESSES: THE PAST AND THE SELF

THE CONTINUING LITERARY IMPACT of the Gothic on the writing of Dickens and Hawthorne shows most emphatically in the texture of language that surrounds the house of Pyncheon and the house of Dombey. The conjunction of Gothic methods with a fable of historical change occurs in England in response to the French Revolution. After the fall of that great claustral edifice the Bastille, the Gothic took on new life. The Marquis de Sade saw in such Gothic fiction as *The Monk* (1796) the result of the "shocks of revolution that were felt by all of Europe,"[4] and Hazlitt judged that Mrs. Radcliffe's "mouldering castles" had awakened interest because of the "supposed tottering state of all old structures at the time."[5] For the English the Gothic was popular as a thought experiment for the

3. Cf. Richard H. Brodhead, *Hawthorne, Melville, and the Novel* (Chicago: University of Chicago Press, 1976), pp. 14–20.

4. "Reflections on the Novel," in *The 120 Days of Sodom and Other Writings* (New York: Grove, 1967), p. 109. On the imaginative place of the Bastille see Victor Brombert, *La Prison romantique* (Paris: Corti, 1975), pp. 35–50.

5. "The English Novelists," in *The Complete Works of William Hazlitt*, ed. P. P. Howe (London: J. M. Dent and Sons, 1931), 6:123.

experience of revolution that they hoped to be spared.[6] As the century wore on, however, the Gothic was democratized. Not only the aristocrats of an earlier age, but middle-class families like the Dombeys and Pyncheons could have their ghosts, and writers could find their homes "the scene of events more full of human interest . . . than those of a gray, feudal castle" (*NH* 2:10).[7]

The consistent link in Gothic fiction between character and architecture—leading to such historical climaxes as the collapse of the doomed edifice killing the last member of its doomed family—could by the 1830s blend with scientific concepts. For at this time biology gave both to sociology and to fiction the concept of "milieu," and Carlyle introduced into English the related notion of "environment."[8] The relationship between man and milieu or environment was reciprocal and thereby allowed for a renewal of holistic thought under the aegis of science rather than superstition. Microcosmic relations of part and whole were once again intellectually respectable in theories of "atmospheric influence."

The place of *The House of the Seven Gables* in this tradition emerges clearly from the comment of a contemporary reviewer: "The queer mansion is haunted," for centuries of Pyncheons "have infected the very timbers and walls with the spiritual essence of their lives, and each seems ready to pass from a memory into a presence." These past Pyncheons have made the house into what it now is, and their past actions may wholly define a modern dweller: "To inhabit the house is to breathe the Pyncheon soul and assimilate

6. Cf. Maurice Lévy, *Le Roman "gothique" anglais, 1764–1824* (Toulouse: Association des publications de la Faculté des lettres et sciences humaines, 1968), p. 615.

7. This is part of the process that Alastair Fowler has described as the diffusion of the Gothic "genre" of the late eighteenth and early nineteenth centuries into the Gothic "mode" available for a wide variety of uses from midcentury on. See "The Life and Death of Literary Forms," *New Literary History* 2 (1971):214.

8. See Leo Spitzer, "*Milieu* and *Ambiance*," *Philosophy and Phenomenological Research* 3 (1942):1–42, 169–218; and his application of this research to a text in the tradition of Dickens and Hawthorne, "A Reinterpretation of 'The Fall of the House of Usher,'" in his *Essays on English and American Literature* (Princeton: Princeton University Press, 1962), pp. 51–66. Hawthorne uses the word "environment" earlier than any *OED* citation except those from Carlyle.

the Pyncheon individuality."[9] The atmosphere one breathes, the influences in the air, assimilate the new inhabitant to the old, the present to the past. "Bad air" and "evil spirit[s]" (9) prove to be one. Gothic writing thus encourages a rich sense of the presence of the past, the historical depth that underlies and helps to determine both the shape and the significance of our present.[10] The enduring physical establishment of the house forms an interface between the family and history, just as the established institution of the family joins the individual and society.

In linking dweller and house, Hawthorne exploits the master trope of synecdoche, the reversible relation of representation between part and whole.[11] A brief observation about Hepzibah epitomizes the determining effect of house on inhabitant: "Her very brain was impregnated with the dry-rot" of the timbers of the house (59). On the other hand, the new inhabitant Phoebe can exercise her power to modify her environment. After she sleeps in it once, her room is "purified of all former evil and sorrow by her sweet breath and happy thoughts." Her presence "exorcised the gloom, and now haunted the chamber in its stead" (72). Not even for Phoebe, however, is the Gothic language put aside, and these terms warn that what is fresh now may in its turn become an oppressive burden.

In setting the scene for the third movement of the book, the fateful day of Jaffrey's death, Hawthorne establishes an especially complex and ambiguous set of relations within the "atmosphere" that not only contains the surroundings of the house, but contains also the house itself, the interior of the house, and Hepzibah: "As for Hepzibah, she seemed not merely possessed with the east-wind, but to be, in her very person, only another phase of this gray and sullen spell of weather: the East-wind itself, grim and disconsolate, in a rusty black silk gown, and with a turban of cloud-wreaths on its head! . . . The wet pear-tree branches, sweeping across the small

9. [E. P. Whipple], "Nathaniel Hawthorne," *Atlantic Monthly* 5 (1860):619.

10. Cf. Harry B. Henderson, III, *Versions of the Past* (New York: Oxford University Press, 1974), pp. 60, 207.

11. Kenneth Burke, "The Four Master Tropes," in *A Grammar of Motives* (New York: Prentice-Hall, 1945), pp. 507–509.

windows, created a noonday dusk, which Hepzibah unconsciously darkened with her wo-begone aspect" (223–224).

This passage begins by engaging the complexities of "possession," a term and concept central to this book,[12] which traces the outcome of a history that began with violent physical dispossession and continued through a revenge taken by spiritual possession. The ambiguity by which one may be possessed of something as its master or possessed by it as its bondsman collapses this historical alternation into a moment of the present and relates it directly to the problems of environmental interaction. The description first evokes the metaphorical usage of "east-wind" as the bad humor that Hepzibah seems to possess and then moves to the physical environment, the "atmosphere" of storm, of which she becomes only a "phase," as it possesses her, unsexing her, making her head "its" head and turning her turban into its clouds. She becomes the passive medium through which the weather takes over the air of the house. "Unconsciously" she furthers the work of the weather in darkening the house. This notation suggests the premise so common in the nineteenth-century novel, later to be adopted by Freud and his followers, that by observation of externals one can understand the depths of unconsciousness that are not directly available to the person being observed.[13]

This intimate reversibility between the physical and the moral, the human and the house, develops further in Hawthorne's use of the "heart." From the beginning he links the writer's fidelity to the inner "truth of the human heart" with his management of the external "atmospherical medium" (1). Both physically and psychologically the heart is a privileged center, a crucially representative part, which may determine the condition of the whole, or from which the condition of the whole may be inferred. Thus, we may interpret the outside to understand the state of the heart within, or we may work outward from our knowledge of the heart to interpret the true meaning of external appearances.

With all these complex possibilities of the heart, Hawthorne

12. See Nina Baym, *The Shape of Hawthorne's Career* (Ithaca: Cornell University Press, 1976), p. 155.

13. On such observation as a new principle of life in the nineteenth century, see Richard Sennett, *The Fall of Public Man* (New York: Alfred A. Knopf, 1977), chap. 8.

identifies the house: "The very timbers were oozy, as with the moisture of a heart" (27). Not only physically but spiritually the house is "like a great human heart," for it is "full of rich and sombre reminiscences" (27). Thus the house visibly represents inward meanings, just as the language of "houses" figures the psychological state of the characters. Clifford's "spiritual part" is only a fitful "inhabitant" of the "dark and ruinous mansion" of his body, within which it tries to "kindle the heart's household-fire" (105).

In the second half of the book, building from the complex possibilities for interrelations that he has established, Hawthorne plays further among heart, house, and inhabitant. The scene in which Jaffrey lies dead inside the house while the unwitting organ-grinder tries to stir up some gaiety on the front walk makes the "desolate old house, deserted of life, and with awful Death sitting sternly" within, into an "emblem of many a human heart," forced to confront a discordant world. This climactic moment of the book repeats in action what had already occurred figuratively in the same idiom, when the narrator imaged Jaffrey's creation of his public self, the "character" that he wants to represent his true self, as the building of a "tall and stately edifice," "splendid" and "costly," shiny and "transparent" (229).

In contrast, however, to this "fair" and "noble" "emblem" of character is "the true emblem of the man's character," the hidden evidence of "the deed that gives whatever reality it possesses, to his life": "Beneath the marble pavement, in a stagnant water-puddle . . . may lie a corpse half-decayed and still decaying, and diffusing its death-scent all through the palace! The inhabitant will not be conscious of it; for it has long been his daily breath!" (229–230).

As in Hepzibah's unconscious relation to the atmosphere of the storm, here too the air one breathes, the circumambient influences, are truly part of one. From this buried truth, the corpse that in a mystic's paradox is forever "half-decayed and still decaying," spreads not illumination but miasma, a moral atmosphere that both typifies Jaffrey and determines him. Together the contaminating diffusion of death-scent and the pollution of stagnant water evoke the beginning of the book and of the family history in Colonel Pyncheon's decision to build his house right where the dispossessed Maule had established his, so that the digging of Pyncheon's cellar coincides with the mysterious contamination of Maule's well. In the book's language the order of history and the order of the psyche repeat each other.

In language that echoes an early moment in the narration, Clifford most cogently summarizes this version of repetitive original sin:

> Real estate—the solid ground to build a house on—is the broad foundation on which nearly all the guilt of this world rests. A man will commit almost any wrong—he will heap up an immense pile of wickedness, as hard as granite . . . only to build himself a great, gloomy, dark-chambered mansion. . . . He lays his own dead corpse beneath the underpinning . . . and hangs his frowning picture on the wall, and after thus converting himself into an Evil Destiny, expects his remotest great-grandchildren to be happy there!
>
> [263]

Clifford's analysis is firmly grounded in Gothic tradition. Since Walpole, the model of usurpation in *Hamlet* had been central to Gothic structures and in response to revolutionary challenges had helped to make the Gothic suitable for inquiry into the wrongs of the past. But just as the Romantics turned their attention inward to psychological redemption after the failure of revolution to bring an apocalyptic political renewal, just as the interpretation of *Hamlet* in the nineteenth century grew increasingly introspective and psychological, so Gothic writing too became a means for psychological representation as well as political. Clifford's language begins close to that in which Marx reveals "The Secret of Primitive Accumulation," that original "heaping-up," as the worker's forcible expropriation from the soil. Yet then the language veers from the concretely historical, the material, to the spiritual, from the "solid ground" of real estate to the "pile of wickedness." Finally, his imagery approximates that of a later nineteenth-century writer of psychological Gothic like Freud, for whom the dead ancestor beneath the floor would represent the repressed oedipal wish to kill one's father and the picture on the wall would represent the positive side of our ambivalence toward the dead father, enshrined in the superego. The artistic permanence of the picture all the more effectively hides the truth of underlying corruption, what the narrator called the "evil influence" (21) and Clifford the "Evil Destiny" that the progenitor exerts over his family.

Gothic language of underground foundations for the psyche was as congenial to Freud as it was to Hawthorne. Freud cherished Pompeii for vividly preserving the traces of antique life under the ashes of history, just as the repressed exists timelessly in the unconscious, just as for Hawthorne the corpse remains magically fresh beneath the marble. As Hawthorne has done in the history of the Pyncheons, Freud in *Totem and Taboo* creates an historical narrative to prefigure the individual's psychic structure and development: for both writers murder is the primal crime and hiding it the future task.

Freud's essay "Das Unheimliche" ("The Uncanny") especially prolongs the Gothic tradition in exploring the discomfort provoked by home thoughts. The German term *unheimlich* ("uncanny," "spooky") takes its meaning in opposition to a key word for the home environment, *heimlich* ("homey"), but Freud discovered that *heimlich* had antithetical meanings. The homey itself could be spooky. He cites a text in which people inform a newcomer that a certain family is *heimlich*, "like a buried spring or a dried-up pond. One cannot walk over it without having the feeling that water might come up there again." The newcomer responds to this, "Oh, we call it unheimlich, you call it heimlich."[14] This sense of something underground that makes itself felt even in its absence, and that may return overwhelmingly, links the Freudian uncanny, the return in adult life of perceptions and feelings that were repressed in childhood and from which one has thus grown estranged, to the family history, the cellar and spring, that emblematizes both individual and historical experience for Hawthorne.

Like Hawthorne with the house of Pyncheon, Dickens in treating the house of Dombey develops Gothic motifs with which to explore psychology in the social context and historical depth of the family and thereby also joins in adumbrating what Freud later formalized.[15] In *Dombey and Son* the house contains the book's opening and

14. Sigmund Freud, "The Uncanny," trans. Alix Strachey, in *Studies in Parapsychology*, ed. Philip Rieff (New York: Crowell-Collier, 1963), p. 25.

15. For another underground current that leads to Freud, see Fred Kaplan, *Dickens and Mesmerism* (Princeton: Princeton University Press, 1975) and Taylor Stoehr, "Hawthorne and Mesmerism," *Huntington Library Quarterly* 33 (1969):33–60.

then is orchestrated through the book in a complex rhythm. Fourteen of the nineteen installments present important action in the house, focusing on a series of crucial ceremonial events: Paul's birth, christening, and death; Florence's mourning; redecoration for Edith, her wedding, and housewarming; the anniversary dinner; the final auction. From the beginning we learn that "the house had been inhabited for years by [Mr. Dombey's] father" and was "old-fashioned and grim" (3). Paul's nurse, therefore, sees Mr. Dombey in the house "as if he were a lone prisoner in a cell, or a strange apparition" (3). The Gothic note is thus struck early and connected to the generational ties of birth and death, preparing for the end of the book, when Dombey, near suicide, "wandered through the despoiled house like a ghost" (59).

The early description of Dombey's relation to the house and the weather outside it at the time of Paul's christening party shows Dickens exploiting synecdochic representation as Hawthorne has in describing Hepzibah and the storm. Once again the day is "iron-grey" and there is a "shrewd east wind blowing" outside, while inside, "Mr. Dombey represented in himself the wind, the shade, and autumn of the christening." When he glances out at the trees, "Yellow leaves came . . . down, as if he blighted them." The weather is "in keeping with the proceedings," and the rooms of the house correspond as well, for they are "black" and "cold" and "seemed to be in mourning, like the inmates of the house." Mr. Dombey catches the essence of the weather and in turn his essence is captured by one part of the house: "The stiff and stark fire-irons appeared to claim a nearer relationship than anything else there to Mr. Dombey, with his buttoned coat, his white cravat, his heavy gold watch-chain, and his creaking boots." Growing "colder and colder," this "atmosphere" is ominous of "desolation and decay," portending as ill for Paul as Hepzibah's storm does for Jaffrey (5).

Dickens capitalizes on the psychological possibilities offered by the Gothic sense of the house as abode of spirits most especially in the sequence of Florence's solitude in the house. After Paul's death, while her father is off courting Edith in Leamington, "Florence lived alone in the great dreary house, and day succeeded day, and still she lived alone." The repetitive rhythms of this narrative prose initiate a process of "uncannying," as the house that has been Florence's dwelling becomes estranged from her: "No magic dwelling-place in magic story, shut up in the heart of a thick wood, was ever more solitary and deserted to the fancy, than was her father's mansion in its grim reality, as it stood lowering on the street." In the regressive, fairy tale mode of "fancy," the life that should be part of her "youth and beauty" passes into the "walls," which become malevolent, "Gorgon-like," threatening to make her "into stone" in their place (all 23). The question the "un-heimlich" asks is when is a home not a home, and the answer here is, when no one is living there, when the life is all in the things, only latent in the people, like springs under stone.

Florence herself reaches a mental state of "fancy" that echoes the narrator's animistic and uncanny view of her situation. In her solitude day after day she performs rituals of propitiation toward her absent father and dwells on the thought of her dead mother and dead brother meeting in heaven and caring for her, neglected as she is on earth.[16] Suddenly she fears that in "weeping for [her father's] alienated heart, she might stir the spirits of the dead against him," and at this "half-formed thought" her "loving nature" begins to "tremble." She recognizes the accusation against her father implicit in her wishful appeal to the spirits, and, "from that hour Florence strove against the cruel wound in her breast, and tried to think of him whose hand had made it, only with hope." Instead of thinking any longer of her father's "alienated heart," she alienates her own heart. It must be all her fault: "Her father did not know—she held to it from that time—how much she loved him." Her own weaknesses and deprivations become an accusation against herself: "She was very young, and had no mother, and had never learned . . . how to express to him that she loved him" (all 23). It is as if she has been transformed into stone, and whatever is inside her is trapped there, invisible and unknowable, though still uncannily radiant, as her father's later sense of her testifies.

Freud's *Totem and Taboo* is as relevant here as it was for Hawthorne. Like the obsessional neurotics Freud describes, Florence has developed a primitive religion, complete with ceremonials and a cult of the spirits of the dead. The ambivalent coexistence of desire and prohibition that for Freud underlies such primitive ritual is equally present in the wishes and fears of Florence's mental processes. Like Florence, primitives and obsessives "tremble at the

16. For quite a different view of Florence's relation to death, see Alexander Welsh, *The City of Dickens* (Oxford: Clarendon, 1971), pp. 185–191.

half-formed thought," the hostile wishes that must be feared for their magical powers and continually warded off, lest they destroy loved ones.

Although Florence's inhibitions come repeatedly to our attention in the course of the book, Dickens is too committed to an ideal of woman as child-angel to question the rightness of Florence's course in any direct way or to focus for long on the complex activity of her embattled consciousness. Nonetheless, the book shows the heavy price of living up to such an ideal and reveals enough of the dynamics that generate it to allow a judgment that Dickens might contradict if it were stated explicitly. Certainly a sentimentally conventional scene like Florence's fantasy of a tearful reconciliation with her father on her deathbed, for example, takes on new significance if we keep in mind that Florence believes in the power of the spirits of the dead—whom she then would be about to join—to take vengeance on the still living. Gothic models give Dickens the means to suggest an acute psychology of resentment, the revenge of those powerless in their love.

SKETCHED SURFACES: VIEWS OF MODERNITY

IN ORGANIZING THEIR BOOKS around houses and the relations between houses and their inhabitants, and in using this system of relations as an idiom for historical and psychological speculation and analysis, Dickens and Hawthorne continue and augment earlier Gothic writing. In portraying the impingement of the railroad and its mobile energy upon the worlds of the houses, both writers develop the tradition of sketch writing in its appropriation of new, contemporary subject matter for literature.[17] In his sketch of "The Old Apple Dealer," for instance, Hawthorne had introduced the "steam fiend" of the railway to bring out by contrast the evasive "moral picturesque" in his human subject (10:445,439). In these novels, however, Dickens and Hawthorne treat the railroad not

17. I differ here from Patrick Parrinder, who relates the Victorian novel to the romantic sketch only through the "cultivation of private experience . . . insulated . . . from the pressures of social reality." See *Authors and Authority* (London: Routledge and Kegan Paul, 1977), pp. 61–62.

directly as an object of the narrators' perceptions but as it is seen and felt by the characters in the texture of their lives.

Thus for Clifford in *The House of the Seven Gables,* after thirty years of imprisonment, the "steam-devil" appears as an instance of the modernity that he cannot cope with. Nonetheless, its "terrible energy" evidently fascinates him, for he leans "a little way from the arched window to catch a glimpse of the trains" (160–161). Clifford combines the childish innocence of a man who has never lived in the world with the physical and mental decay of one who has been long imprisoned. Thus at age fifty he can still cry, "I want my happiness" (157). He is like a Wordsworthian child with a few clouds of glory still trailing about him despite nature's stepmotherly treatment: "All his life long he had been learning how to be wretched as one learns a foreign tongue" (149). Clifford's long and unmerited suffering has isolated him from his fellow men and their common life, first in prison and then in the house, and made him the "most inveterate of conservatives" (161). He continues to live only in his own past until Jaffrey's death exhilarates him and liberates him to leave the "defunct nightmare" (252) and go off with Hepzibah on the railway.

The railroad proves a microcosm of society: "They had been drawn into the great current of human life." The varied group of people whom they encounter as passengers seems "life itself." This society, furthermore, is in transition.[18] The "world racing past them" en route offers a view of history like that of time-lapse photography: "At one moment they were rattling through a solitude;—the next, a village had grown up around them;—a few breaths more, and it had vanished, as if swallowed by an earthquake." Clifford's sense of time is reintegrated, as everything is "unfixed from its age-long rest" (256–257). Although constantly recurring to the old house as a point of contrast, Clifford moves into speculations about the future, leading to his condemnation of the human desire for the "solid ground to build a house on." He wishes to unhouse mankind, for "the soul needs air" (261), and he insists that we can and must free ourselves from the terror of memory, that we abolish the past, not just bury it.

As their fellow passengers grow increasingly suspicious and incredulous, the two old children jump off at a little stop and find themselves in a disenchanted world, with nowhere to go but back

18. See Frank Kermode, *The Classic* (New York: Viking, 1975), pp. 91–105.

to the house. It has not been a demonic experience, as in Hawthorne's earlier allegory of "The Celestial Railroad," yet there is something eerily disturbing in this galvanic return of vitality to Clifford after his persecutor's death. This ecstatic, triumphant escapade marks the only release that these characters experience from the house and its precincts until the end of the book.

The house so predominates in the reality of the book that we are tempted to discount the radical exhortations of Clifford on the train or of Holgrave in the garden as overcompensatory reactions to being out of the house, which seems so totally unescapable when one is inside. That Holgrave and Clifford at these moments express such similar social views allows these views great weight as the universal wish of the dispossessed, but it also defines them as suspiciously unsettled, merely the result of dispossession. Thus Holgrave like Clifford has inveighed against ancestral houses, urging the need of each generation to build its own, but he finally settles down with Phoebe and gives up his characteristic mobility. Although the novel is premised on the uncanny paradox of Hawthorne's notebook entry, "To inherit a great fortune. To inherit a great misfortune" (8:293), it ends happily with a great inheritance. Yet as the inhabitants of the House of the Seven Gables leave it to settle in their new possession, what ghosts must await them at Jaffrey's house?

As Hawthorne had done, Dickens also explicitly links the railroad in its first appearance to the process of social and economic change. In the set piece that describes the clearing of Staggs's Gardens to make way for the London-Birmingham railway, the terror that we might feel at the great forces working is calmed by the association of the railroad with the strength and love of the Toodle household. The railroad provides Toodle (husband of Paul Dombey's nurse) with a new job that allows him to support eight children in decency and with a new house that is far superior to the squalid dwellings that the railroad swept away. By the second appearance of the railroad, order seems fully imposed upon its energy, the trains are running, and life is better for all concerned.

Even this relatively straightforward presentation poses some problems. When Dickens introduces Toodle, before he works for the railroad, the following exchange occurs:

> "You were going to have the goodness to inform me, when we arrived at the door that you were by trade a—"
>
> "Stoker," said the man.

> "A choker!" said Miss Tox, quite aghast.
> "Stoker," said the man. "Steam Ingine." . . .
> "And how do you like it sir?"
> "Which, Mum?" said the man.
> "That," replied Miss Tox. "Your trade."
> "Oh! Pretty well, Mum. The ashes sometimes gets in here," touching his chest, "and makes a man speak gruff as at the present time. But it *is* ashes, Mum, not crustiness."
>
> [2]

Toodle is a choker passive, not active. The upper classes need fear no criminal activity from him but must recognize that his job subjects him to discomfort that endangers his health and encrusts his good nature. Yet once Toodle has gone to work for the railroad, we never again hear of his chest problem. Nor does anything come of the menacing comment by a neighbor: " 'He knowed Toodle,' he said, 'well. Belonged to the railroad didn't he?' " (15). This eager acquiescence in paternalism is not the Dickens we usually admire; yet as I have tried earlier to suggest, it may be related to his own narrative power to present us with a world of his own, to which every part belongs.

The two subsequent appearances of the railroad, however, present it in a different light; we see it through the lenses of the different characters' disturbed emotional states. After his son Paul has died, Dombey en route to Leamington experiences the train on which he rides as "a type of the triumphant monster, Death" (20), although Dickens's narrator carefully distances himself from this view, remarking that if Dombey had been less self-involved in his misery he would have seen things differently. Nonetheless, Carker, Dombey's treacherous assistant, in a mood of hysteria rather than melancholy, also sees the railroad as death, and in fact the "fiery Devil" kills him (55). Despite the admirable social progress that Dickens saw represented in the railroad, his imagination responded strongly to its terrible aspects as well.

This problematic ambivalence in Dickens's sense of the railroad emerges particularly in the relation that the book establishes, but never quite avows, between the railroad and Dombey. Just as the railroad uproots the old way of life at Staggs's Gardens and replaces it with a bustling chaos of construction, so Dombey abolishes Florence's old, solitary life by sending teams of workers into his house for "alterations." The "Babel towers of chimneys . . . piles of scaffolding, and wildernesses of bricks" created by the railroad echo the "labyrinth of scaffolding . . . heaps of mortar, and piles of wood" that Dombey brings about (6, 28).

Furthermore, for Dombey the train had been a type of Death because the relentless "speed" by which it was "whirled along" echoed mockingly the "swift course" on which Paul had been "borne away so steadily" to his "foredoomed end" (20). Yet Dombey himself had wished to hasten Paul "to the great end of the journey," when he would be old enough for business. Dombey had been impatient for that "time to come . . . impatient to advance into the future" (8). Death and the railroad, then, whirl along with the force that Dombey had wished for, although the "end" is not the one he had set. Dombey and the railroad both represent a society, like that which Dickens had discovered in his *American Notes,* that cares more for the future, for getting ahead, than for the present or the past. Here, in contrast to the experience of Dickens's brother-in-law Austin noted in Chapter I, the railroad lays bare the previously hidden slums, but it rushes by them without doing anything about them or helping one to understand why they are there.

The danger for life of such new powers emerges from Carlyle's anatomy of the "mechanical" in "Signs of the Times" (1829), and Melville brings it explicitly into his fiction through Ahab's soliloquy on the quarterdeck after he has nailed up the doubloon and sworn his men to Moby-Dick's death: "Swerve me? Ye cannot swerve me. . . . The path to my fixed purpose is laid with iron rails, whereon my soul is grooved to run. . . . Naught's an obstacle, naught's an angle to the iron way! (37).[19] We have seen that Melville supplements this fixed perspective with Ishmael's views and then dissolves Ishmael into a ghostly overview. Likewise Dickens is driven to strangely disruptive shifts of view to bring the "iron way" to general human use.

Not Dickens's narrator, not Dombey himself, but only Carker in the book identifies Dombey with the railroad, as Carker transfers to the railroad his fear of Dombey in his final delirium, and the intuition of this unscrupulous but artistically sensitive character seems sound. For the railroad carries out Dombey's murderous wish against Carker, running him down as Dombey looks on. Does not Dombey

19. See Leo Marx, *The Machine in the Garden* (New York: Oxford University Press, 1964), pp. 294–295.

and Son bear down all before it? Yet for the narrator directly to assimilate Dombey and the railroad would have been to suggest too strongly Dombey's total unconvertibility, his being unswervable like the fixed course of rails, all iron without a drop of human warmth.[20] And by the same token, to liken the railroad to Dombey would seriously question the positive value of its larger effects.

Thus Dickens votes for the future with the railroad, while simultaneously showing in Dombey that his society's orientation toward the future may be terribly and dangerously inhumane. The positive countervalues that the Wooden Midshipman group provides against Dombey in the book's economy are guaranteed by the shop's being "old-fashioned" and never selling anything, not a commercial milieu but one of maritime legendry and archaic Dick Whittington success stories. In the closing pages, however, Dickens attempts to align this configuration with modernity by suggesting that Mr. Gills was providentially ahead of his time, as his "old investments" come to fruition in "the fulness of the time" (62), as if the rhythm of the growth of capital were like that of the growth of nature.

The thematic incoherence that thus marks *Dombey and Son* and *The House of the Seven Gables,* the twists of plot that seem to subvert the books' established structures of social values in order to bring about the happy endings, points to the ways in which Dickens and Hawthorne share the confused and compromised political views that we call Victorian. Both are finally more moralists than social critics in their exposure of the self-enclosed egoism of the Gothic house, the prison of self from which sympathetic human intercourse provides the only escape, discordantly echoed in the railroad's bustle and change and movement. In contrast to what Hawthorne calls the "big, heavy, solid unrealities" (229) of property and place, both books value warm human relations as truer and more enduring. Yet committed as they are to shared rather than solitary human values and virtues, in order to show the success of their characters' integration into society, such unreal yet public tokens are all they find at their disposal. Here again, as in *Martin Chuzzlewit,* endings pose a special difficulty.

20. Cf. Julian Moynahan, "*Dealings with the Firm of Dombey and Son:* Firmness *versus* Wetness," in *Dickens and the Twentieth Century,* ed. John Gross and Gabriel Pearson (Toronto: University of Toronto Press, 1962), pp. 121–131; see also Gabriel Pearson, "Towards a Reading of *Dombey and Son,*" in *The Modern English Novel,* ed. Gabriel Josipovici (London: Open Books, 1976), pp. 54–76.

OVERVIEWS: PAUL PRY VERSUS THE GOOD SPIRIT

WITHIN THIS GENERAL SIMILARITY in the interaction of their social views with the workings of their novels, Dickens and Hawthorne nonetheless project differing images of their tasks as writers. Faced with a world in which people build up deceitful structures to present their characters, the "tall and stately" edifices that hide a corpse beneath their floors, Hawthorne locates the possibility for truth in a "seer." Beneath his "sadly gifted eye," the "whole structure" of such a house of character "melts into thin air, leaving only the hidden nook, the bolted closet . . . or the deadly hole under the pavement, and the decaying corpse within" (230). Such a seer penetrates the sham of appearance to reach the underlying reality, the psychological depths beneath social surfaces. The artist's insight yields disillusioning knowledge that tends to set him apart.

Dickens, however, hopes that the artist's work will have wider and more integrative social consequences, that the representation of social reality carries a moral power that moves people to action. In a passage we have already noted, the resonance of which extends through his whole later oeuvre, Dickens calls "for a good spirit who would take the house-tops off" to reveal the pestilence, both physical and moral, that London breeds at night: "the pale phantoms rising . . . from the thick and sullen air where Vice and Fever propagate together." After such a "view," a "blest" morning would rise, "for men, delayed no more by stumbling-blocks of their own making . . . would then apply themselves . . . to make the world a better place!" (47).[21] In his role as "good spirit," looking down from above, removing the stumbling blocks that impede vision at the ground level, and trying to show to everyone the detailed reality of everyone else's life, Dickens differs most drastically from Hawthorne. Both men work within the Gothic tradition of spirits and seers and the secrets of houses, and both share the holistic view, the moral sociology of public health, that joins "Vice and Fever," the "evil spirit" and the "bad air" (9), but for Dickens's "good spirit" to lift off the roofs is not the same as for Hawthorne's "seer" to lift off the whole house, dispelling everything but the buried

21. For further discussion of this passage, see Raymond Williams, *The English Novel from Dickens to Lawrence* (New York: Oxford University Press, 1970), pp. 32ff.

body. Dickens recognizes the existence of society without needing to reduce it to its psychological substrata.

Hawthorne had toyed in one of his earliest sketches with a mode of perception similar to the one which Dickens here deploys. In "Sights from a Steeple" Hawthorne speculates on a "mode of existence" like that of a "spiritualized Paul Pry," and he wishes that "the Limping Devil of Le Sage would perch beside me here, extend his wand over this contiguity of roofs, uncover every chamber, and make me familiar with their inhabitants!" (9:192). This limping devil, the Asmodeus of Lesage's *Diable boiteux* (1707, 1726) whom we have earlier remarked, had from a steeple in Madrid uncovered the roofs and revealed the hidden lives to young Cleophas. His view, however, had been truly a devil's-eye view, that of a destructive satirist with neither sympathy nor a wish to reveal a complex system of social interrelation, preferring the cynical exposure of individuals. Hawthorne understandably abjures this fantasy of detached, sadistic omniscience.[22]

Dickens also knew this prototype of the nineteenth-century omniscient narrator, and in *American Notes* he links it to the vilest qualities of irresponsible journalism, "dealing in round abuse and blackguard names; pulling off the roofs of private houses, as the Halting Devil did in Spain; pimping and pandering for all degrees of vicious taste."[23] Popular periodicals of the 1830s and 1840s, bearing such titles as *Asmodeus in London*, had placed the city in overview "at [the reader's] feet" and lifted "away . . . the roofs of the houses" out of no moral purpose, but only for "curiosity," a love of "scandal" that led even to "blackmail."[24] Thus in *Dombey and Son*, as in the passage from *Household Words* cited in Chapter I, we must recognize the emphasis on the *good* spirit called upon, who must work, Dickens insists, with "a more potent and benignant hand than the lame demon in the tale" (47). This narrative perspective will transform the satirist's view into one that combines the insight

22. On the continuing fascination for Hawthorne of invisible spectatorship, see Edgar A. Dryden, *Nathaniel Hawthorne* (Ithaca: Cornell University Press, 1977), pp. 26–30.

23. Charles Dickens, *American Notes* (Leipzig: Tauchnitz, 1842), chap. 6.

24. Louis James, *Fiction for the Working Man* (1963; rpt. with extensive corrections Harmondsworth: Penguin, 1974), pp. 20–21.

of sympathy and the breadth of statistics in order to work as a tool of both individual and social improvement.[25]

Only in *Bleak House* (1853) does Dickens begin fully to realize the program of the good spirit. In *Bleak House* physical and moral pestilence are firmly locked together in the plot as well as verbally associated, and the sketch and the Gothic tale are brought into full harmony. The picturesque City haunts of Elia prove to be as haunted as Chesney Wold. Not just the ancestral countryside, not just London, but England as a whole becomes a haunted house. As if in obedience to Hawthorne's injunction to "connect a by-gone time with the very Present that is flitting away from us" (2), Dickens endows his characters with powerful relations to the past, links the personal history of the Rouncewells and Dedlocks to the sweeping changes in English history, and juxtaposes chapters of present-tense narrative to the retrospective narration of Esther Summerson.

In *The Blithedale Romance* (1852) Hawthorne at the same time was revealing through the narrative of Miles Coverdale the impotence of a utopian fresh start, dragged down by the weight of all the old human weaknesses; and the self-exposure of Coverdale that emerges from his unreliable narration reveals as well the impotence of a ground-level "Paul Pry." In this divergence we can begin to chart a differential history of English and American fiction in the nineteenth century, but any such attempt would be premature if it failed to reckon with the profound institutional similarities in the literary backgrounds and early careers of Dickens and Hawthorne that continue to mark their methods, techniques, and concerns.

25. The complexity of literary technique allows Dickens to escape the "indifference to the specifically human" that accompanied the "distance" taken by nineteenth-century painters who sought "totality" through "the panoramic." See Linda Nochlin, *Realism* (Harmondsworth: Penguin, 1971), pp. 175–176.

VI

Narrative Form and Social Sense in *Bleak House* and *The French Revolution*

We have gained a fuller sense of nineteenth-century fiction by correlating English and American novels, and we may further deepen our understanding by relating fiction to forms of writing that we consider nonfictional. Just as the short periodical forms of tale and sketch contributed to novelistic wholes, so did the short periodical form of the review-essay. This form was the training ground for historians, who learned as well from a novelist like Scott (himself a major review writer). Thus they combined intellectual clarity with vividness in a way equally available to novelists. In French and German the terms for "story" and "history"—*histoire, Geschichte*—overlap, and a smooth spectrum thus joins *Dichtung* to *Wahrheit*, poetry to truth.[1] Although English does not offer the same semantic ambiguity, the two overlapped in practice,[2] and

1. For discussion of this topic, see H. R. Jauss, ed., *Nachahmung und Illusion* (Munich: Eidos, 1964), pp. 190–195, 233–236.

2. On the relations of history and literature, see Roland Barthes, "Historical Discourse," in *Introduction to Structuralism*, ed. Michael Lane (New York: Basic Books, 1970), pp. 145–155; Leo Braudy, *Narrative Form in History and Fiction* (Princeton: Princeton University Press, 1970); David Levin, *History as Romantic Art* (Stanford: Stanford University Press, 1959); George Levine, *The Boundaries of Fiction* (Princeton: Princeton University Press, 1968); James C. Simmons, "The Novelist as Historian: An Unexplored Tract of Victorian Historiography," *Victorian Studies* 14 (1971):293–305. Closely linked to problems of truth and fiction, history and literature, are those of philosophy and rhetoric, treated by John Holloway, *The Victorian Sage* (London: Macmillan, 1953).

English and American readers of the mid-nineteenth century turned both to overtly fictional and declaredly nonfictional writing to satisfy their quests for reality.

A symbolic beginning for this interplay of fiction and history is the meeting of Herder and Goethe in Strasbourg in 1771. Herder introduced the youthful Goethe to Shakespeare and thereby "in a special sense to the world of history."[3] This introduction provoked not only Goethe's essay on Shakespeare but also his neo-Shakespearian history play *Goetz von Berlichingen*. This play was translated by Walter Scott as his first signed work (1799). Lockhart judged that Percy's *Reliques* had awakened Scott to editing as a means of historical re-creation, but only *Goetz* revealed to him history's availability for "high art."[4] Scott's model in turn was decisive for the great generation of historians born with the century, whether for Thierry's emulation or Ranke's revulsion.[5] The French novelists Stendhal and Balzac were enabled by their personal experience of radical political and social transformations to profit directly from Scott and to integrate a sense of historical process with existing methods of realistic representation of contemporary life.[6] In England, however, Scott's fiction needed an historian's mediation before Dickens's great novels of contemporary history became possible. France had the Revolution, England Carlyle.

In depicting the "Condition of England" in *Chartism* (1839) and *Past and Present* (1843), Carlyle's revision of Scott gave English novelists a method of approaching the problems of industrial development and political unrest, for it brought home to them that just as flesh-and-blood, everyday people had made and lived history

3. Friederich Meinecke, *Historism* (1936), trans. J. E. Anderson (London: Routledge and Kegan Paul, 1972), p. 380.

4. J. G. Lockhart, *Memoirs of Sir Walter Scott* (1837–1838; rpt. London: Macmillan, 1900), 1:257–258.

5. For Scott and the historians see Emery Neff, *The Poetry of History* (New York: Columbia University Press, 1947); and H. R. Trevor-Roper, *The Romantic Movement and the Study of History* (London: Athlone, 1969).

6. See Georg Lukács, *The Historical Novel* (1937), trans. Hannah and Stanley Mitchell (London: Merlin, 1962), pp. 81–85; Erich Auerbach, *Mimesis* (1946), trans. Willard Trask (Princeton: Princeton University Press, 1953), pp. 474–482; Harry Levin, "Society as Its Own Historian," in *Contexts of Criticism* (Cambridge: Harvard University Press, 1957), pp. 171–189.

in the past, so were people now living in and making history. Thus the English "social novel" of the 1840s represented new social groups, new social issues, and new forms of speech, as if obeying Carlyle's injunction to "understand and record what is *true,*—of which, surely, there is, and will forever be, a whole Infinitude unknown to us, of infinite importance to us!" (28:178).[7] Carlyle hoped to quash novel writing by insisting that "the only genuine Romance (for grown persons) [is] Reality," but the result was that Dickens dwelt "upon the romantic side of familiar things" (*BH* Preface).

DEFINING A VICTORIAN MODE OF WRITING

JUXTAPOSING *The French Revolution* and *Bleak House* allows us to define more clearly the Carlylean feeling of Dickens at his best and to begin describing the literary mode that history and the novel share in Victorian writing. Although Dickens wanted to have "Carlyle above all" present when he read *The Chimes* (1844),[8] dedicated *Hard Times* (1854) to Carlyle, and praised the "philosophy" of Carlyle's "wonderful" *French Revolution* in the preface to *A Tale of Two Cities* (1859), I do not wish to treat Carlyle's influence on Dickens.[9] I will instead consider Carlyle's work in its public role in the institution of literature, as the first book to embody and articulate a mode of writing, a fusion of techniques and attitudes, that became dominant in early-Victorian England.

The reception of *The French Revolution* marks it as the work of Carlyle's that most demands our attention in analyzing a typically Victorian mode, for it defined him for his audience. Its success gained an English publisher for the previously rejected *Sartor Resartus* (1838), spurred the publication of Carlyle's collected

7. See Louis Cazamian, *The Social Novel in England: 1830–1850* (1904), trans. Martin Fido (London: Routledge and Kegan Paul, 1973); and Kathleen Tillotson, *Novels of the Eighteen-Forties* (Oxford: Clarendon, 1954), especially pp. 150–156.

8. Edgar Johnson, *Charles Dickens: His Tragedy and Triumph* (New York: Simon and Schuster, 1952), 1:522.

9. For studies of Carlyle's influence on Dickens, see G. B. Tennyson, "The Carlyles" in *Victorian Prose: A Guide to Research*, ed. David J. DeLaura (New York: Modern Language Association of America, 1973), p. 63. For the most comprehensive recent survey of Carlyle's impact on the Victorian novel, see the untitled review essay by U. C. Knoepflmacher, *Nineteenth-Century Fiction* 32 (1977):73–80.

Essays (1839), and created the lecturing opportunities from which *Heroes and Hero-Worship* (1841) resulted. Praise for *The French Revolution* resounds from the first reviews (1837) by Thackeray and J. S. Mill, who proclaimed it an "epic" and a work of "genius," to obituary notices (1881) by Andrew Lang and R. H. Hutton, who considered it "by far the greatest" of Carlyle's works, "the book of the century."[10] Of Dickens it is said that "he carried a copy of it with him wherever he went" on its first appearance, and at the time of beginning *Bleak House* he mentions reading "that wonderful book *The French Revolution* again, for the 500th time.[11] Even Carlyle's biographer and disciple Froude, one of the coterie of intellectuals who were especially moved by *Sartor Resartus,* called *The French Revolution* "the most powerful of Carlyle's works, and the only one which has the character of a work of art."[12]

The French Revolution achieved its exemplary status as "work of art" in the Victorian mode by breaking with the literary procedures that characterized the visionary mode of romanticism. In response to the historical experience of the French Revolution, writers of the 1790s transformed earlier eighteenth-century views of historical progress into violently apocalyptic plots, organized around a visionary speaker, the "Bard," who presents a "panoramic view of history in a cosmic setting, in which the agents are in part historical and in part allegorical or mythological."[13] By the early nineteenth century, however, both political repression and disillusionment with the course of the Revolution drove writers inward to a

10. I quote from the valuable collection by Jules Paul Seigel, *Thomas Carlyle: The Critical Heritage* (London: Routledge and Kegan Paul, 1971), pp. 52, 73, 509, 503.

11. James Anthony Froude, *Thomas Carlyle: His Life in London* (New York: Harper and Brothers, 1885), 1:53; John Forster, *The Life of Charles Dickens* (Philadelphia: J. B. Lippincott, 1873), 2:440.

12. James Anthony Froude, *Thomas Carlyle: A History of the First Forty Years of His Life* (New York: Harper and Brothers, 1882), 2:243.

13. M. H. Abrams, *Natural Supernaturalism* (New York: W. W. Norton, 1971), p. 332. My whole paragraph draws upon Abrams's analysis. Gerald L. Bruns also uses Abrams as a point of departure for comparing Victorian to romantic in "The Formal Nature of Victorian Thinking," *PMLA* 90 (1975):917; and see Peter Alan Dale, *The Victorian Critic and the Idea of History* (Cambridge: Harvard University Press, 1977), pp. 78–79, who places Carlyle in this tradition but looks for his analogues only in Victorian poetry, not the novel.

personal vision, in which refreshed perception rather than revolution created a "new heaven and new earth." The language of politics and redemption shifted into metaphors for states of consciousness; symbols grew more private and opaque; the "Bard" became a "Solitary."

These changes within romanticism demonstrate that a mode of writing is "an act of historical solidarity," the means through which the human intention to create form connects itself to the great crises of history.[14] In a given historical moment those writers undertaking moral responsibility for their time will share techniques of presentation, patterns of plot, and structures of language that in their interrelationships define a mode of writing. In the new political situation that had emerged in England by the later 1820s, as Catholic Emancipation and Reform agitation marked the unfreezing of counterrevolutionary repression, a new mode was necessary, a renewed relation between the writer and the public. To us a work like *Sartor Resartus* may seem satisfyingly modern in its self-consciousness, hesitancy, and discontinuity, but we have earlier noted the challenge to his age inscribed in Carlyle's prose. His contemporaries were distressed by the obliquities of *Sartor,* and even those who most admired the work considered them a prime defect.[15] Carlyle himself strove in his writing of *The French Revolution* for directness, clarity, and fluency, as emerges from his work on "The Diamond Necklace," a trial piece for the full history.[16]

In addressing a newly defined audience, *The French Revolution,* therefore, transforms the constellation of elements that composed romantic writing. Carlyle rescues the public voices and public concerns of the 1790s while keeping also the personal message that had come to later dominance. In *The French Revolution* a voice like that of the "Bard" ranges over history, attending to all levels of significant action. This voice speaks directly to its age the words

14. Roland Barthes, *Writing Degree Zero* (1953), trans. Annette Lavers and Colin Smith (New York: Hill and Wang, 1968), p. 14.

15. See the letters to Carlyle by John Sterling in Seigel, *Critical Heritage,* pp. 26–33; John Stuart Mill in *Letters,* ed. Hugh S. R. Elliot (London, 1910), p. 64; and Emerson in *The Correspondence of Emerson and Carlyle,* ed. Joseph Slater (New York: Columbia University Press, 1964), pp. 98–99.

16. Carlisle Moore, "Carlyle's 'Diamond Necklace' and Poetic History," *PMLA* 58 (1943):537–557.

that are most important to be heard correctly, but its story tells of no imminently accessible apocalypse. There is no final ending. The irony created by this gap between a disillusioning plot and a visionary means of representation furnishes one of the work's most striking sources of power. Through it Carlyle and his readers can safely reexperience the revolutionary hopes and master the trauma of their disillusionment. His ironic narrative control makes available to his contemporaries both the meaning of a clearly told story and the vividness of immediate presence.

To find some such method of representing human lives in action that would join the "soundness and depth" of "Reason" and the "vividness" of "Imagination," to combine the virtues of "theory" and "fiction," was the task Macaulay had set his age in his essay on "History,"[17] and it was the problem that Carlyle too had perceived as the legacy left by Sir Walter Scott. Scott's fiction had made clear, as the histories of Hume or Gibbon could not, that history had been made by "living men . . . with colour in their cheeks, with passions in their stomach," and before projecting any "philosophy," the modern historian must succeed as well as Scott had in capturing the "idioms, features and vitalities" of concrete human "experience" (29: 77–78). As Macaulay defined it, the "Novel" is one extreme, the "Essay" the other, and to history belongs the disputed but fertile ground in between. This sense of the centrality of history, based for both Macaulay and Carlyle on their belief that history could truly teach while fiction could merely amuse, persists in the practice of Victorian novelists. In their attempt to prove that they too could be true teachers of the age, novelists drew upon the resources of the essay and thereby made their work more like history in ways that will soon be specified.

This focus upon the essay points to one of the major institutional facts of literature in the years around 1830, what, we recall, Bulwer defined as the "revolution that has been effected by Periodical Literature."[18] The reviews and magazines had monopolized the talent and thereby caused a "deterioration" of "standard" book literature. Carlyle and Macaulay, as outsiders whom periodical writing allowed to come to prominence, exemplify the new careers that this revolution in the fourth estate allowed for. The review

17. *Edinburgh Review* 47 (1828):331–332.

18. Edward Lytton Bulwer, *England and the English* (1833), ed. Standish Meacham (Chicago: University of Chicago Press, 1970), p. 262.

journalist was above all a judge, weighing for his readers the work under consideration and defining the meaning of its thought in the broad terms of general human nature. Narrative could exist only as panorama and had constantly to be interrupted for its significance to be unfolded. There was no place for everyday experience.

Dickens also began his literary career as a periodical writer. Not Macaulay, however, but Lamb, not Edinburgh but the *London Magazine* suggest his situation, as we have earlier noted. The collected pieces of *Sketches by Boz* (1836), Dickens's analogue to the "Critical and Miscellaneous" collections of the review writers, are written not by a judge but by an observer close to the level both of his subject and his audience. Specific incidents, not general considerations, formed the basis of these sketches; not the clear outline of a broad panorama, but the nuance of a distinctive atmosphere, not meaning but mood or incident was their goal. Thus, as they turned to book-length writing, Carlyle and Dickens faced opposite problems of continuity and coherence.

Therefore, similar principles of formal organization in *Bleak House* and *The French Revolution* have different meanings in the contexts of their authors' whole careers but are especially significant as a middle ground on which opposed literary practices could meet. *The French Revolution* and *Bleak House* are about the same length, and Carlyle's subdivisions into twenty books parallel the nineteen monthly parts in which *Bleak House* originally appeared. But neither work is the "medley" that often resulted from the agglomeration of periodical writing into longer forms.[19] Despite the constant shifts in actors, *The French Revolution* holds together through the generalizing narrative voice that describes, both analytically and symbolically, the continuity of the process that different people at different times are engaged in carrying on. To engage the reader's activity in synthesizing these parts into a whole, each chapter bears a brief and pointed, often enigmatic, title: not a mere listing of events, but a puzzle whose meaning must be considered in advance and a catchphrase, laden with significance, to carry away after reading. The process of reading is a series of challenges and initiations.

From his first novel *The Pickwick Papers* (1837) Dickens realized that sketches could be built into installments and installments into a

19. Jerome Beaty, "All Victoria's Horses and All Victoria's Men," *New Literary History* 1 (1970):271–292.

book by stringing episodes along the movement of a central character, and in his early novels the chapter titles strive to maintain a clear narrative continuity. They are almost wholly of the "In which . . . " type that describes at some length what will be going on in the chapter to follow. However, the use of an historical episode to interrelate a variety of lives in *Barnaby Rudge* (1841), the growing apprehension of London as a center of coherence that we have observed in *Martin Chuzzlewit* (1844) and *Dombey and Son* (1848), and even the somewhat abortive attempts to organize these latter two novels by the moral themes of selfishness and pride respectively, all indicate a wish to discover methods of bestowing some abstract, intellectual significance on narrative. Just as Carlyle used novelistic "vividness" to go beyond Hume and Gibbon, so Dickens drew on the essay for "theory" to surpass Lesage and Smollett.

We have seen that in *Dombey and Son* the uninterrupted linear rush of the railroad, like a narrative moving just on the level of events, reveals only a senseless sequence of fragments, a vision of death (*DS* 20), and the book's narrator therefore pleads for "a good spirit who would take the house-tops off" and from this synoptic perspective reveal to everyone the reality of everyone else's life. The comprehensive knowledge gained from such vision would lead men, no longer blinded "by stumbling-blocks of their own making," "to make the world a better place" (*DS* 47). In *Bleak House* (1853) Dickens presents a narrator who consistently plays the part of this "good spirit." The titles of the chapters in which this narrator appears—such as "Telescopic Philanthropy," "The Appointed Time," "Enlightened"—are consistently of Carlyle's type (e.g., "Questionable," "As in the Age of Gold," "Sanculottism Accoutred"). Like Carlyle's titles they interrupt the flow of reading, emphasize not *mythos* but *dianoia*, not actions but attitudes, relations that are paradigmatic rather than syntagmatic. No less than Carlyle in *The French Revolution* this narrator by both analogy and analysis draws together the classes of society and the different individual lives that make up the multiple plots of *Bleak House*. The historical irony of Carlyle's abrupt references to Napoleon, present at some action in his youthful obscurity, or of his remarks on the strange destiny that joins Marat and Charlotte Corday, also appears in *Bleak House* as the air of fatality that allows the narrator to pose arch questions and to speak knowingly about strange social interconnections that will be revealed. Through these means *Bleak House* becomes more "spatialized" than Dickens's earlier works.[20] In this mode both Dickens and Carlyle combined the linear aspects of narrative with the solidity of completed significance.

The panoramic unity in these works absorbs a great variety of narrative perspectives that the full worlds of the books combine and comprehend in one whole. Carlyle quotes directly from contemporary sources, vigorously narrates in his own voice actions that he has pieced together from such sources, jumps into the trenches shouting with Achilles by means of a participatory "we," and rises to the visionary heights of summary and interpretation, like Dickens taking the reader on "an Asmodeus' Flight" (3: 291). Dickens divides *Bleak House* between two narrators, a floating visionary eye like Carlyle's "eye of History" (2: 15), and Esther Summerson's retrospective "I." In both books the past tense is used in narration by the actors—Esther or Carlyle's contemporary sources—but the impersonal narrator speaks in the present tense. One's relation to one's own past must be mediated by time, but to the narrator's vision, as to Ranke's God, all is immediate. A letter of Dickens's, written around the time that he was reading *The French Revolution* for the "500th time," shows the potency that he attributed to such narration. He is planning a series of sketches, to recount in the present tense historical moments, under the general title of "Shadow": "I understand each phase of the thing to be *always present before the mind's eye. . . .* Whatever is done, must be *doing.*"[21]

The mode of writing shared by *Bleak House* and *The French Revolution* includes not only techniques of narrative unity and variety, but also a similar plot of social action. As the major action of *The French Revolution* is the Phoenixlike "death-birth" of a society, so *Bleak House* portrays the passing of an old order of society and its replacement by a new. In this work Dickens's impatience is matched only by his respect for realities. Dickens shows

20. See Joseph Frank, "Spatial Form in Modern Literature," in *The Widening Gyre* (New Brunswick: Rutgers University Press, 1963), pp. 3–62; H. M. Leicester, Jr., "The Dialectic of Romantic Historiography: Prospect and Retrospect in 'The French Revolution,'" *Victorian Studies* 15 (1971):7–17; Elliot L. Gilbert, "'A Wondrous Contiguity': Anachronism in Carlyle's Prophecy and Art," *PMLA* 87 (1972):432–442.

21. *The Letters of Charles Dickens*, ed. Walter Dexter (London: Nonesuch, 1938), 2:334.

this change in terms that relate closely to the historical events of England in his lifetime. *Bleak House* charts not a change of heart, no Scrooges or Dombeys, but a change in the structure of social and economic power.

This historical consciousness of old and new shows most clearly in the story of Chesney Wold. In the course of the book the Dedlock family, a distinguished line "as old as the hills, and infinitely more respectable" (2), slips finally toward extinction. To characterize Chesney Wold, Dickens uses the Burkean language of value, terms far from the vitriolic picture of "the good old days" in *Barnaby Rudge* or the ridiculous self-exposure of sentimental medievalists in *The Chimes* or *Dombey and Son.* This house, however, has passed its great days and has now become a seat of deathly immobility. Yet it has brought forth new life. The housekeeper's son Rouncewell has left home and gone north, where he becomes not an anonymous Chartist, as Sir Leicester Dedlock imagines, but an ironmaster and a politically important figure, who has been asked to stand for a seat in Parliament. Sir Leicester finds in this no proof of the flexibility of British institutions, but rather speaks of it "as if there were a general rising in the North of England" (28). He laughably misses the point, for Rouncewell has named his son Watt not after Sir Leicester's bogey Wat Tyler, the medieval insurrectionary, but after the inventor of the steam engine, the source of what the Victorians came to recognize as the Industrial Revolution: the bourgeois Phoenix born from the ashes of aristocratic decay.[22]

SCIENCE AND SUPERSTITION: VICTORIAN CULTURAL CODES

THE VICTORIAN MODE OF WRITING shared by *Bleak House* and *The French Revolution* goes beyond techniques of narration and overarching movements of plot to include the articulation and interweaving of particular "cultural codes."[23] In particular three lexical systems—let us call them Gothic, Scientific, and Apocalyptic—are

22. For a Chartist called "Wat Tyler" see Harvey Peter Sucksmith, "Sir Leicester Dedlock, Wat Tyler, and the Chartists: The Role of the Ironmaster in *Bleak House*," *Dickens Studies Annual* 4 (1975):119.

23. Roland Barthes, *S/Z* (Paris: Editions du Seuil, 1970), pp. 27, 104–105, 210–212.

organized by synecdoche, the rhetorical figure that connects part and whole. Thus by the end of *Bleak House,* Chesney Wold as an outward whole echoes the condition of Sir Leicester, its dominant inward part, and has itself become a "body without life," full only of "ghostly likenesses" (66). But this haunted house repeats the condition of Tom-all-Alone's, the ruinous slum held in Chancery and debated over in Parliament, the representation in small of the whole political system that Sir Leicester supports, and that props him up.

In literary history, as my previous chapter has argued, this play of similarity between dweller and dwelling, between the House of Dedlock and the edifice of state, the decay of institutions and the decay of what is "in" them, derives from the Gothic fiction that was so popular in the years following the fall of the Bastile; and these same years saw political writings filled with images of the tottering house of state.[24] A Gothic code thus links several adjacent practices of discourse. To recall the pervasive power in the nineteenth century of Gothicism as an idiom of historical representation, think of the "spectre" that haunts Europe at the opening of *The Communist Manifesto,* the echo of Hamlet's ghost in the "old mole" of revolution in *The Eighteenth Brumaire,* and the atmosphere of mists, vapor, and insubstantial spirits that marks man's mystification under the "fetishism of commodities" in *Capital.*[25]

24. Cf. Sir Walter Scott: "We have already compared the monarchy of France to an ancient building . . . decayed by the wasting injuries of time . . . standing, from the mere adhesions of its parts. . . . If its materials have become dry and combustible, still they may long wait for the spark which is to awake a general conflagration," in *Life of Napoleon Bonaparte, Miscellaneous Prose Works of Sir Walter Scott* (Edinburgh: Cadell, 1851), 8:73; and William Hazlitt: "When a government, like an old-fashioned building, has become crazy and rotten, stops the way of improvement, and only serves to collect diseases and corruption, the community . . . 'pull down the house, they abate the nuisance,'" in *The Life of Napoleon Buonaparte, The Complete Works of William Hazlitt,* ed. P. P. Howe (London: J. M. Dent and Sons, 1931), 13:38–39. Howe attributes the quotation within the passage to Burke.

25. Cf. Jeffrey Mehlman, "A partir du mot 'unheimlich' chez Marx," *Critique* 31 (1975):232–253; and on how "Gothic conventions . . . become the vehicle of social commentary," Richard C. Maxwell, Jr., "G. M. Reynolds, Dickens, and the Mysteries of London," *Nineteenth-Century*

The use of such language by Marx and Engels suggests its availability for the most serious purposes and its compatibility with scientific intentions, a commitment to the truth, as best one understands it, about the historical depth of a given social situation. The mysterious correspondences that link character and architecture in Gothic fiction could blend with the new, holistic scientific language of the later eighteenth and early nineteenth centuries to create striking descriptions of the coherence of social process. Just as Herder's historism tried to grasp as one whole the unique process of a given culture, so *Naturphilosophie* in Diderot, Goethe, Schelling, and others sought to define the cosmos as a dynamic continuum of becoming, in which physical and human moral significances were unavoidably linked.[26] Thus, when Carlyle considers the "swell of the public mind" before the revolution, he notes that "there are swells that come of subterranean pent wind . . . even of inward decomposition, of decay that has become self-combustion:—as when, according to Neptuno-Plutonic Geology, the World is all decayed down into due attritus of this sort; and shall now be *exploded*, and new-made" (2: 80). Identical organic processes operate to change both the earth and society. These processes express themselves both in people's physical activities and their mental activities: "One reverend thing after another ceases to meet reverence: in visible material combustion, château after château mounts up; in spiritual invisible combustion, one authority after another" (3: 106–107).

This synecdochic sense of shared essence combated a mechanical sense of isolated cause and effect.[27] For many areas of scientific discourse had not yet been Newtonianized, formalized, reduced to comparisons of quantity. Diderot, for instance, understood chemistry as the science of quality and metamorphosis. He argued that even for the physicist not the attraction of discrete particles but phenomena of blending and continuity, such as resonance, fire, electricity, and sulphurous exhalation should be the focus of attention. The concrete historical science of geology replaced the mathematical

---

Fiction 32 (1977):196. Gothic receives only minimal attention in the generally valuable study by S. S. Prawer, *Karl Marx and World Literature* (New York: Oxford University Press, 1976).

26. Charles Coulston Gillispie, *The Edge of Objectivity* (Princeton: Princeton University Press, 1960), pp. 178–201.

27. Cf. Hayden White, *Metahistory* (Baltimore: Johns Hopkins University Press, 1973), pp. 16–17, 35–36.

sciences as the focus of popular interest.[28] In their biological speculations Buffon, Goethe, and Geoffroy St.-Hilaire propounded a similar metamorphic holism.[29] As we saw in Chapter V, the transfer to social theory of language from such scientific writing marks the beginnings of the characteristic nineteenth-century terms of historical perception that describe the relations of part and whole: "milieu," "circumstance(s)," "influence," "air," "element," "atmosphere," "medium," "conjuncture," "mentality," "background," and "environment."[30]

Carlyle, who had first learned German to study Werner's "geognosy,"[31] found in German the whole linguistic complex that we have been charting, and he joined the holistic tradition of sociology, contributing to English the word "environment." As the sense of society in Dickens's novels grows more complex and cohesive, his categories of representation become simultaneously more Gothic and more Scientific.[32] In *Martin Chuzzlewit* we found that he mentions the biological theories of Monboddo and Blumenbach only to dismiss them (*MC* 1), but in *Dombey and Son* the plea for a "good spirit" arises from the wish to make visible the "moral pestilence" that is "in the . . . laws of outraged Nature . . . inseparable" from the "noxious . . . vitiated air" found in the slums by "those who study the physical sciences, and bring them to bear upon the health of Man" (*DS* 47).

The world of *Bleak House* is full of both disease and mysterious spirits. Yet like Marx, Dickens does not allow his pleasure in a thick, portentous rhetoric to override a central aim of clarification. Ghosts arise from human actions and may be dispelled by them. They are not supernatural at all; their explanation is social. As dirt is "matter

28. Charles Coulston Gillispie, *Genesis and Geology* (Cambridge: Harvard University Press, 1951), p. xi.

29. Peter Demetz, "Balzac and the Zoologists: A Concept of the Type," in *The Disciplines of Criticism*, ed. Peter Demetz et al., (New Haven: Yale University Press, 1968), pp. 397–418.

30. Leo Spitzer, "*Milieu* and *Ambiance*," *Philosophy and Phenomenological Research* 3 (1942):1–42, 169–218.

31. G. B. Tennyson, "*Sartor*" *Called* "*Resartus*" (Princeton: Princeton University Press, 1965), pp. 20–21.

32. For Dickens and science see Ann Y. Wilkinson, "*Bleak House*: From Faraday to Judgment Day," *ELH* 34 (1967):225–247.

out of place,"[33] so the ghosts of *Bleak House* arise from displacements in social relations: undervaluing close relationships or overvaluing distant ones. Thus the case in Chancery of Jarndyce and Jarndyce, the opposition of those whose interests should be identical, becomes the "family curse," "the phantom that has haunted us for so many years" (29).

Lady Dedlock is the center around whom most of the book's ghosts congregate. Her "secret"—her premarital liaison with Captain Hawdon, their child whom she abandoned and believed dead, and her continuing love for Hawdon despite her marriage to Sir Leicester—has caused her to distance herself from those to whom she should be close and to give herself distant airs among her present company, while this very distance draws too close to her those who suspect that it hides something. Her love for a man of lower station, despite her marriage to an aristocrat, awakens echoes of the seventeenth-century Lady Dedlock, who chose the revolutionary cause despite her husband's Cavalier sympathies. No less than revolution once did, Hawdon now threatens the upper classes, for dead and buried in a hideous city burial ground he will be "raised in corruption: an avenging ghost" to pollute the air with disease (11). Once Esther learns that Lady Dedlock is her mother, she is obsessively drawn to Chesney Wold, but the sound of her "warning feet" makes her identify herself with the seventeenth-century ghost and feel that she is "haunting" the house (36). Terrified of herself, she runs away. Injustice and secrecy make people incomprehensible even to themselves, while they appear to others as spirits of doom.

To pierce Lady Dedlock's icy façade, the family lawyer Tulkinghorn involves many people in his secret machinations. Thus, the house of Snagsby the stationer "becomes ghostly" (25) and the object of gossip and rumor. The involvement of Guppy the law clerk brings him to Krook's shop for a midnight rendezvous, "haunted by the ghosts of sound" (32). Finally, Tulkinghorn himself is shot and becomes a "ghost" to be "propitiated" (53). Unlike Tulkinghorn,

33. William James, *The Varieties of Religious Experience* (London: Longmans, Green, 1902), p. 133. A close variant reappears in English (in quotation marks without attribution) in the essay on character and anal erotism (1908) by Sigmund Freud, *Gesammelte Werke* (London, Imago Publishing Co., 1941), 7:206; and the phrase is cited familiarly as "the old definition" by Mary Douglas, *Purity and Danger* (New York: Frederick A. Praeger, 1966), p. 35.

who wishes to collect and hoard secrets, Bucket, the detective, makes public both the solutions to the mysteries and the means by which he has solved them. Like the "good spirit" of *Dombey and Son,* he demystifies. Even Lady Dedlock can dispel the ghosts around herself by actively avowing her situation, removing herself from Chesney Wold to seek the grave of her lover Hawdon. As she leaves Chesney Wold at dawn, the whole "spectral company" of shadows vanishes into "the realities of day" (55).

Carlyle's book, too, is what Froude called a "spectral" history.[34] Like Dickens, Carlyle suggests states of alienation through the code of the supernatural. People need to make sense out of their experience, and if they cannot find some comprehensive explanation in themselves, they will seek to interpret every event as part of some mystery. Thus Dickens's Snagsby "always is . . . under the oppressive influence of the secret that is upon him. Impelled by the mystery of which he is a partaker, and yet in which he is not a sharer, Mr. Snagsby haunts what seems to be its fountainhead. . . . It has an irresistible attraction for him" (33). Compare with Snagsby's state of possession the state of Camille Desmoulins in the last days before the Terror. He has got his head "so saturated through every fibre with Preternaturalism of Suspicion" that he sees "Behind, around, before, it is one huge Preternatural Puppet-Play of Plots, Pitt pulling the wires. Almost I conjecture that I, Camille myself, am a Plot and wooden with wires" (4: 156).

Carlyle describes at some length the popular psychology of suspicion. For example, in 1789 a lack of confidence in the state's economy caused people to hold on to their money. Trade slowed, and food grew scarce in the markets. People discovered that "they need not die while food is in the land" and some arose to help themselves to it, the Brigands. But this "actual existing quotity of persons" became the object of rumor and so "long reflected and reverberated through so many millions of heads, as in concave multiplying mirrors, become a whole Brigand World; and, like a kind of Supernatural machinery, wondrously move the Epos of the Revolution. . . . Not otherwise sounded the clang of Phoebus Apollo's silver bow, scattering pestilence and pale terror; for this clang too was of the imagination; preternatural; and it too walked in formless immeasurability, *having made itself like to the Night*" (2: 126).

34. Froude, *Thomas Carlyle: His Life in London,* 1:51.

Thus Carlyle assimilates the "Great Fear" to the plague that opens the *Iliad* and reveals the social genesis and propagation of a moral epidemic. Certainly the social disorder and political unrest that marked the first great European outbreak of cholera (1830–1832) strengthened the links in the cultural code between epidemic disease and revolution. For reasons of nutrition and sanitation, the disease killed mostly poor people, and it thereby set social inequality in high relief. It appeared to the poor as the result of a murderous conspiracy against them by the rich, and it exacerbated the awareness of the rich that the existence of the poor masses posed a great threat. Perhaps the most potentially explosive demonstration in nineteenth-century London was the popular protest against the declaration of a cholera fast day, 21 March 1832.[35] The renewed outbreak of cholera in 1848–1849 engraved these connections all the more deeply. Dickens and Carlyle resemble each other and typify their time in trying to show the particularities of social mediation through which the plague, both physical and moral, spreads. Carlyle finds the source of plague in irresponsibility by those in power, which undermines popular faith in social institutions. If the institutions no longer work, people will turn to what resources remain to them; they will form irregular institutions and thus create the turmoil that suspicion paranoiacally interprets, thereby growing greater.

The opening pages of *The French Revolution* relate physical, moral, and social evil in the code of plague. Louis XV is dying from hideous "confluent small-pox," and since he is himself "France," his condition is also the condition of the nation. As he has lived in an "enchanted . . . Armida-Palace" built by "black-art" and devoted himself to pleasure rather than to administration, the nation too is

35. David Eversley, "L'Angleterre," in *Le Choléra,* ed. Louis Chevalier (La Roche-Sur-Yon: Imprimerie centrale de l'Ouest, 1958), p. 183. I also draw upon Chevalier, "Paris," in *Le Choléra,* pp. 1–45; R. Baehrel, "Epidémie et terreur: histoire et sociologie," *Annales Historiques de la Révolution Française* 23 (1951):113–146; Asa Briggs, "Cholera and Society in the Nineteenth Century," *Past and Present,* no. 19 (1961), pp. 76–96; and Charles E. Rosenberg, *The Cholera Years* (Chicago: University of Chicago Press, 1962). For general orientation see William H. McNeill, *Plagues and Peoples* (Garden City: Anchor Press/Doubleday, 1976), pp. 261–278. McNeill shows the spread of cholera from India to Europe as a consequence of the British industrial revolution.

"smitten (by black-art) with plague after plague" and suffers hunger and misery (2: 3–5). The king's "putrid infection" (2: 16) spreads, sickening and killing courtiers, while "the cardinal symptom of the whole widespread malady" is that "Faith is gone out" (2: 14). In his review John Stuart Mill shows how easy it was to translate from the medical to the sociological code: "The loathsome deathbed of the royal debauchee becomes . . . the central figure in an historical picture, including all France; bringing before us, as it were visibly, all the spiritual and physical elements which there existed, and made up the sum of what might be termed the influences of the age."[36]

To show the same pattern in *Bleak House,* we might analyze the famous opening, in which the anaphora syntactically, the fog visually, and the present participle temporally reduce the condition of England to one hideous atmosphere. But if Chancery is the center of that scene, Tom-all-Alone's, because it is "in Chancery," is equally central. At night it is filled with blackness and is as inhospitable to life as its silvery antithesis the moon. Despite talk in Parliament, Tom-all-Alone's

> only may and can, or shall or will, be reclaimed according to somebody's theory, but nobody's practice. And in the hopeful meantime, Tom goes to perdition head foremost in his determined spirit.
>
> But he has his revenge. Even the winds are his messengers and they serve him in these hours of darkness. There is not a drop of Tom's corrupted blood but propagates infection and contagion somewhere. It shall pollute, this very night, the choice stream (in which chemists on analysis would find the genuine nobility) of a Norman house, and his grace shall not be able to say nay to the infamous alliance. There is not an atom of Tom's slime, not a cubic inch of any pestilential gas in which he lives, not one obscenity or degradation about him, not an ignorance, not a wickedness, not a brutality of his committing, but shall work its retribution, through every order of society, up to the proudest of the proud, and to the highest of the high. Verily, what with tainting, plundering, and spoiling, Tom has his revenge.
>
> [46]

36. Seigel, *Critical Heritage,* p. 58.

Dickens personifies this slum quarter as "Tom" and assimilates the quarter synecdochically with its inhabitants, thereby combining the medical dangers of disease and the political dangers of revolution. The sexuality of "infamous alliance" hints at venereal disease and more directly evokes the liaison of Lady Dedlock and Captain Hawdon and her pilgrimage to the graveyard where he is buried, itself as loathsome as Tom-all-Alone's.[37] Through its inhabitant Jo, Tom-all-Alone's has revealed to Lady Dedlock the spot where she will die and has infected her daughter Esther with smallpox. Sir Leicester neglects his political responsibility, and Tom-all-Alone's falls into ruin; Lady Dedlock neglects her moral responsibility, and her lover falls into ruin. Both poison the air.

Dickens conveys less a specific physical description of the slum ("slime," "gas") than an attitude of scientific precision about it ("chemist," "analysis," "atom," "cubic inch"). Dickens's insistence on "truth" in his preface to *Bleak House,* his wish to be a Carlylean "bringer-back of men to reality" (5: 133), leads him to draw whenever he can on scientific authorities, for he was convinced that there was no conflict between science, rightly understood, and the imagination. The "poetry of fact" was always his aim. But accurate description, the truth, the facts, included such moral qualities as "ignorance," "wickedness," and "brutality." The most effective vocabulary in such a context is simultaneously scientific and moral: "spoil," "taint," "corrupt," "pollute," "contagion," and "infection." "Infection" is the key word and concept of this passage. Etymologically it derives from Latin *inficere,* whose primary meaning is to stain or color; to put or dip into something, especially a dye. It then comes to mean to mix with something else, especially a poison, to taint, spoil, corrupt. *Inficere* had a direct counterpart in Greek *miaino,* whose nominal form, *miasma,* referred to the mysterious elements suspended in air that defiled the air and caused plague. The crucial analogy was between a tincture where a small drop of dyestuff colors the whole fluid, and the way that an evil smell from a single source could diffuse through the air, especially the smell from the decay and putrescence of organic bodies.[38] The concept of

37. On the shift in mentality that made old churchyards objects of loathing and led to modern, individualized cemeteries, see Philippe Ariès, *Western Attitudes toward Death,* trans. Patricia M. Ranum (Baltimore: Johns Hopkins University Press, 1974), pp. 69–72.

38. My philological information comes from Owsei Temkin, "An

infection, then, is itself synecdochic in its emphasis on a whole "atmosphere."

In the "Author's Preface" to *Bleak House,* with reference to the lawyers in the book, Dickens cites "an apt quotation from Shakespeare" (Sonnet 111):

> My nature is subdued
> To what it works in, like the dyer's hand:
> Pity me then, and wish I were renewed!

The poem continues beyond what Dickens quotes:

> Whilst, like a willing patient, I will drink
> Potions of eisell 'gainst my strong infection.

The violation that moral nature suffers from degrading employment is like that which physical nature suffers from plague. Through this allusion Dickens engages the whole etymological complex of *inficio.* The "dyer's hand" typifies the professional deformation that has often been a source of comic amusement. In *Bleak House,* however, the cause of professional deformation, what Carlyle called the "environment," comes under critical scrutiny. Phil Squod's Vulcanic deformity results from a warping occupational environment, Jo's ignorance and disease from a pernicious physical environment, and Esther's diffidence and fearful desire to justify herself from an oppressive moral environment. The book offers countless other examples, for such deformations are like a plague ravaging society.

TRANSFORMATION AS PROCESS: APOCALYPSE DEFERRED

WHAT HOPE FOR RENEWAL do the worlds of *Bleak House* and *The French Revolution* offer? Dickens and Carlyle share the ambivalence appropriate to a plot that brings about change but frustrates the apocalyptic hope for total change. We have noted that a detective's

---

Historical Analysis of the Concept of Infection," in *Studies in Intellectual History,* ed. George Boas et al. (Baltimore: Johns Hopkins Press, 1953), pp. 123–147. See also K. J. Fielding and A. W. Brice, "*Bleak House* and the Graveyard," in *Dickens the Craftsman,* ed. Robert B. Partlow, Jr. (Carbondale: Southern Illinois University Press, 1970), pp. 115–139.

revelation is only a diminished apocalypse. In contrast, the revolutionary French sought to cleanse their whole world with fire. Prevalent versions of *Naturphilosophie* gave scientific cachet to popular millenarian expectations, and the revolutionaries, despite French Catholicism and Enlightenment, shared the apocalyptic hopes of their supporters in Protestant lands.[39] The troubled hope and fear of the early 1830s again aroused apocalyptic tremors. In England the concurrence of Catholic Emancipation, the second French revolution, the cholera epidemic, and the intense agitation for reform led many to look to the "signs of the times." Dr. Thomas Arnold was "half-inclined to believe" that the glossolalia in the congregation of Carlyle's friend Edward Irving was a "sign of the coming of the day of the Lord," at least in the sense that "an epoch of the human race was ending."[40]

A consciousness of possible apocalypse permeates *The French Revolution* from its first episode, the death of Louis XV: "Thou, whose whole existence hitherto was a chimera and scenic show, at length becomest a reality: sumptuous Versailles bursts asunder, like a dream, into void Immensity; Time is done" (2: 20). Since what is true of the king is true of the kingdom, the people rejoice, "Behold a New Era is come" (2: 26). The hope is located within the historical actors themselves. Carlyle traces throughout his work how millenarian psychology fed into revolutionary activities, and he especially emphasizes the constant disappointment. Time and again the actors are deceived in their belief that at last the new era is at hand. The motif of incongruous confrontation, the failure of people to recognize themselves as brothers and sisters when social barriers are torn down, articulates this disappointment. When a crowd of Sansculottes breaks into the king's chateau, the parties "brought face to face after long centuries" can only "stare stupidly at one another" (3: 263). The traditional apocalyptic figure of Holy Marriage ironically describes another failure. The Festival of the Con-

39. Georges Lefebvre, "Foules révolutionnaires," in *Etudes sur la révolution française* (Paris: Presses Universitaires de France, 1954), p. 183; and Robert Darnton, *Mesmerism and the End of the Enlightenment in France* (Cambridge: Harvard University Press, 1968), pp. 107–125.

40. Owen Chadwick, *The Victorian Church,* Part 1 (New York: Oxford University Press, 1966), pp. 36–38. On the apocalyptic temper of the early 1830s, see further Patrick Brantlinger, *The Spirit of Reform* (Cambridge: Harvard University Press, 1977), pp. 11–17.

federation, 14 July 1790, should have been a mystical union of all France (as Michelet asserts that it was).[41] Carlyle, however, considers it an inappropriate bit of mummery: "Think of a . . . Nation of men spending its whole stock of fire in one artificial Firework! . . . Shall we say then that the French nation has led Royalty, or wooed and teased poor Royalty to lead *her*, to the hymeneal Fatherland's Altar . . . and has, most thoughtlessly, to celebrate the nuptials with due shine and demonstration—burnt her bed?" (3: 68).

The constantly frustrated hope for a final judgment, for some great consummation, is equally present in *Bleak House*. The very first chapter ends with the wish that Chancery and all its injustice and misery could be locked up "and the whole burnt away in a great funeral pyre." In Esther's narrative we meet Miss Flite, who "expects a judgment": "'Shortly. On the Day of Judgment. I have discovered that the sixth seal mentioned in the Revelation is the Great Seal. It has been open a long time!'" (3). The death by spontaneous combustion of Krook, the metaphorical "Lord Chancellor," has overtones of the desired apocalypse, but although totally consumed, he takes nothing with him.[42] His firetrap of a shop remains as it was, even as Chancery itself goes on beyond the exhaustion of Jarndyce and Jarndyce. There is no total judgment, no way to begin the world anew beyond the individual. Both books share a mood of hope and apprehension, and both teach the patience needed when there is no end.

A comic outburst, however, without promising a new world may afford a temporary renewal within society. Carlyle describes the procession from Versailles leading the royalty back to Paris after the Insurrection of the Women: "It was one boundless inarticulate HaHa;—*transcendent* World-Laughter; comparable to the Saturnalia of the Ancients. Why not? Here too . . . is Human Nature once more human" (2: 288). This moment is only one of the many false new beginnings, but it exemplifies an important source of the

41. For one of the greatest humanistic apocalypses, see Jules Michelet, *History of the French Revolution*, trans. Charles Cocks (1847), ed. Gordon Wright (Chicago: University of Chicago Press, 1967), pp. 440–453.

42. Northrop Frye notes the overtones but not the frustration in his preface to Gaston Bachelard, *The Psychoanalysis of Fire* (1938), trans. Alan C. M. Ross (Boston: Beacon, 1964), p. viii.

energy that keeps people going. Dickens often builds long stretches of his novels up to comic reversals, in which life and decency triumph over the blocking figures: Micawber denounces the "Heep of infamy" in *David Copperfield,* and in *Martin Chuzzlewit* the plots and counterplots end with masks dropped, roles reversed, and the scoundrels driven out, as Pecksniff receives the last of his many knockings.

Bleak House offers no such comic triumph. Only the reaction to the end of the Jarndyce case resembles it. Amidst "immense masses of papers of all shapes and no shapes," spectators emerge laughing "more like people coming out from a farce or juggler than from a court of justice" (65). Here, however, the blocking figure is an institution, not a person, and this relief, this Bergsonian triumph of humanity asserting itself over the dead things that so often control life, is still not enough to save Richard Carstone. The case is "all up with at last," but so is Richard. The contrast of the romantic Richard consumed by his smoldering combustion and Rouncewell the ironmaster, who husbands his fire in engines rather than wasting it in torchlight demonstrations, echoes the meaning of Carlyle's "Close thy *Byron;* open thy *Goethe*" (1: 153).[43]

For Carlyle to turn from Byron to Goethe was to abandon a posture of titanic alienation and to assert that people can and must form their world, their environment, by productive activity: "Whatsoever thy hand findeth to do, do it with thy whole might" (1: 157). The redemption of Bleak House demonstrates this power over the environment. Old Tom Jarndyce gave the house its name and "left the signs of his misery upon it," for as he wasted himself in the family lawsuit, the wind and rain and weeds ruined the house. But John Jarndyce turned from the lawsuit to work at hand and created a charming home, now ironically misnamed. Dickens's discarded titles show that he closely associated Tom-all-Alone's and Bleak House as alternative images of Chancery-ruined edifices, and the parallel makes clear that Tom-all-Alone's name need not determine its

43. Georg Lukács observes that in the great fiction of the nineteenth century the resolution is "less a heroic explosion than suffocation," *Goethe and his Age* (1947), trans. Robert Anchor (London: Merlin, 1968), p. 47; and Jacques Cabau notes that for Carlyle "le feu volé par Promethée finit dans la machine à vapeur victorienne," *Thomas Carlyle ou le Promethée Enchaîné* (Paris: Presses Universitaires de France, 1968), p. 171.

nature. The pathbreaking reports on public health of the 1830s and 1840s emphasized equally that the atmospheric impurities that caused disease could be removed by action.[44]

In his assertion through narration that Esther, Woodcourt, Rouncewell, and others can do valuable, productive work despite the politicians, Dickens echoes Carlyle's recognition that "the true Constitution" was not "made . . . by Twelve hundred august Senators," but grew "unconsciously, out of the wants and efforts of these Twenty-five millions of men" (3: 244). For Carlyle went beyond Burke or Scott in recognizing that, since France survived the Revolution, there must have been some principles of social cohesion beneath the apparent chaos.[45] Thus, in the idiom of *Naturphilosophie* Carlyle visualizes the Reign of Terror as a vexed and eddying circulation of energy, flowing out to the borders to fight aristocratic invasion and flowing inward to fight domestic subversion. Although his explanations are not scientific by our standards, Carlyle felt that history's task was not to "shriek" (4: 203) but with its "imaginative organ" (4: 207) truly to see, to articulate the realities of the human past.

Carlyle's moral dynamics locate humanity between two realms, the cultural above, the physical below. Symbols, "realized ideals" (2: 5), compose the upper realm. These have been made by man for man, to embody and channel human energies. Energy itself makes up the lower realm. It is unformed, destructive in itself, but the source of all life, all *being* and *doing* and *reality*. These two realms must be in touch with each other. Otherwise the upper realm dies, rots, dissolves, burns, and spreads its infection: "As for Falsehood . . . what should it do but decease, being ripe; decompose itself, gently or even violently . . . too probably in flames of fire?" (2: 213). Furthermore, when the two realms are out of touch, the lower breaks loose as ravaging fire, water, and electricity. Nonetheless, human effort reorganizes this energy into a new realm of

44. Francis Sheppard, *London 1808–1870* (Berkeley and Los Angeles: University of California Press, 1971), pp. 251–252.

45. For Carlyle's radical appropriation of conservative organicism, see Philip Rosenberg, *The Seventh Hero* (Cambridge: Harvard University Press, 1974), pp. 124–127; on Carlyle's place in historiography, see Hedva Ben-Israel, *English Historians on the French Revolution* (Cambridge: Cambridge University Press, 1968).

symbols and institutions. Again and again Carlyle tries to set out his terms for his reader:

> French Revolution means here the open violent Rebellion, and Victory, of disimprisoned Anarchy against corrupt worn-out Authority: how Anarchy breaks prison; bursts-up from the infinite Deep, and rages uncontrollable, immeasurable, enveloping a world; in phasis after phasis of fever-frenzy;—till the frenzy burning itself out, and . . . elements of new Order . . . developing themselves, the Uncontrollable be got, if not reimprisoned, yet harnessed, and its mad forces made to work towards their object as sane regulated ones.
>
> [2: 211–212]

The skeptical loss of faith that precipitated the Revolution prevented the "unconsciously" acting participants from seeing significances as clearly as Carlyle can. Tragically, their failure to comprehend the events that caught them up led to the conflicts that exacerbated the process of dissolution and increased the total suffering. Carlyle, however, does not consider it impossible to understand one's own historical environment: "Had they understood their place, and what to do in it, this French Revolution, which went forth explosively in years and in months, might have spread itself over generations; and not a torture-death but a quiet euthanasia have been provided for many things" (3: 232–233). We may think of Sir Leicester Dedlock, not carried off by apoplexy, but doomed nonetheless. Carlyle and Dickens both are trying to help the English gain the understanding of their physical, moral, and historical environments that will allow them to avoid the horrors of a revolution by avoiding the stagnation of conservatism. Like many others in the 1840s, Dickens and Carlyle turned away from electoral and constitutional politics, but their constant social emphasis ensures that their reality remains larger than merely "personal experience, the private, the domestic."[46]

46. Francis Mulhern, "Comment on 'Ideology and Literary Form,'" *New Left Review*, no. 91 (1975), pp. 86–87. On the theoretical basis for the move from the political to the social, see Sheldon S. Wolin, *Politics and Vision* (Boston: Little, Brown, 1960), pp. 286–294; and for the concrete situation of "Anti-Politics of the 1840s," J. D. Y. Peel, *Herbert Spencer* (New York: Basic Books, 1971), chap. 3.

Both books express the wish for apocalypse, but both ironically expose the hope for total transformation to the reductive laughter of basic humanity. The Gothic language in both expresses the fear that humankind is prey to incomprehensible forces of the past, but Gothic appearances are reduced to social and psychological processes in the present. *Naturphilosophie* provides a synecdochal view of the world by which the works assert that human energies are at one with the forces of nature and thus that people do have the power to change the world. The spatializing power of narrative overview demonstrates the human ability to comprehend the world, while the personal narratives ensure that such "philosophical" comprehension is constantly tested by juxtaposition to "experience." The heterogeneous narrative technique that encompasses such diverse voices constantly draws attention to the writer at work, who at every moment determines by choice the form of the book's world, and thus it suggests the validity of the writers' appeals to their readers to change their world. As Carlyle says, our world is "most fictile" and people the "most fingent plastic of creatures" (2: 6).

VII

Heroism and the Literary Career: Carlyle and Melville

THE *French Revolution* AND *Bleak House* exemplify writing as a means of relation to the world capable of changing the world. The power of retrospect on the past and overview of the present allows a prophetic orientation toward the future. Such a renewal of the public dignity of literature, such a reestablishment of the writer's control over circumstances—to shape and direct what is at hand—made possible, and perhaps necessary, a new relation to the history of literature itself. It inspired in Melville a confident freedom toward the literary past that distinguishes *Moby-Dick*, yet also marks it as of its times.

Not until *The Waste Land* was American literature to see another masterpiece so thoroughly made up of books as *Moby-Dick*. "Imitation is often the first charge brought against real originality" (*MD* 544), as Melville recognized, and contemporary reviewers flocked to name the work's sources or analogues: Thomas Browne, Robert Burton, Defoe, Sterne, Monk Lewis, Maturin, Charles Lamb, Washington Irving, Marryat, Poe, Hawthorne, and Emerson, as well as Carlyle.[1] Yet for Melville, all these were only markers on the course of his own career: "All that has been said, but multiplies the avenues to what remains to be said" (545). Melville includes within *Moby-Dick* an exhilarating avowal of the relation that joins writer, book, and reader to the historical institution of literature. No more than Eliot did Melville passively receive an enriching influx from "sources"; rather, he exemplifies a choice of influence, the transformation, or even deformation, that a young writer imposes upon

1. See the reviews collected in *"Moby-Dick" as Doubloon*, ed. Harrison Hayford and Hershel Parker (New York: W. W. Norton, 1970).

his work to differentiate it from the conventions of his generation.[2] In England, to write like Carlyle was to be of the moment; in America, it was a conscious, decisive choice.

Thus, as Melville grew impatient with his own youthful Byronism and the false impressions of the sea that *Childe Harold* had promulgated, might he not turn to Carlyle, who had said, "Close thy *Byron;* open thy *Goethe*" (*TC* 1: 153)? Yet Carlyle not only offered an escape from romantic excesses; he was also himself a disruptive liberator, shaking the genteel complacency of the New York literary world in which Melville briefly rested.[3] As a model for prose, Carlyle's "run-a-muck style" opposed the "health" of Rabelais, and philosophically he set the profound Kant against the simple clarity of Locke. In many of Melville's steps to break away from the orbit of the *Literary World,* Carlyle was explicitly or implicitly present. If Melville flouted Duyckinck by going to hear Emerson lecture, Emerson was the leading American spokesman for Carlyle. If Melville began to read the subversively antiorthodox Bayle, Carlyle was the period's leading analyst of Enlightenment skepticism. When Melville traveled to England in 1849 as a writer rather than sailor, he sought to meet Carlyle, and, even though he failed, nonetheless his choice of books to buy and read there reflects an imaginary dialogue with Carlyle.[4] Most important for *Moby-Dick,* Carlyle's vision of heroism invigorated Melville's own developing conception

2. See Claudio Guillén, "A Note on Influences and Conventions," in *Literature as System* (Princeton: Princeton University Press, 1971), p. 61.

3. See the portrait of that world by Perry Miller, *The Raven and the Whale* (New York: Harcourt, Brace, 1956).

4. For biography I rely on Leon Howard, *Herman Melville* (Berkeley and Los Angeles: University of California Press, 1951); Jay Leyda, *The Melville Log,* 2 vols. (New York: Harcourt, Brace, 1951); and *The Letters of Herman Melville,* ed. Merrell R. Davis and William H. Gilman (New Haven: Yale University Press, 1960).

An early letter suggests that Melville was familiar with the *Edinburgh Review,* in which he may have first read Carlyle (*Letters,* p. 7). A letter to Lemuel Shaw requests help in getting an introduction "from Mr. Emerson to Mr. Carlyle" for Melville's trip to England (*Letters,* p. 90). This request and the evident acquaintance shown with Carlyle's works in *Mardi* suggest that Melville borrowed Duyckinck's *Sartor Resartus* and *Heroes and Hero-Worship* in 1850 for rereading. See Merton M. Sealts, "Melville's Reading," *Harvard Library Bulletin* 3 (1949):119–120.

of his role as a writer and helped him to the new way of reading that underlies his interpretations of Shakespeare and Hawthorne.

PORTRAIT OF CARLYLE

TO UNDERSTAND MORE FULLY what Carlyle could have meant to Melville in the crucial years from 1848 to 1851, we must further renew our image of Carlyle. In *Sartor Resartus* (1833) Carlyle wished to register the conquest of doubt and despair and the transcendence of an isolating and paralyzing self-consciousness. Yet this triumphant Yea-saying, although the book's moral, is not its entire message. Its form and style still betray self-consciousness, for neither in his life nor in his work did Carlyle fully achieve the goals that he preached and free himself from the tensions and uncertainties that he felt compelled to mask but which kept showing through.

In the first important critical comment on Carlyle, the letter that elicited Carlyle's defense of his revolutionary prose, John Sterling judged that *Sartor Resartus* was a great work which would find only a small audience. Through analyzing Carlyle's stylistic innovations, he discovered a "startling whirl of incongruous juxtaposition" that "coheres with, and springs from, the whole turn and tendency of thought." Despite the theistic "opinions" of Carlyle's protagonist Teufelsdröckh, his true "state of mind" reveals itself to Sterling as godless. The very interpretive method by which Carlyle had exposed natural theology as atheism laid him open to such across-the-grain readings of his own text. Sterling finds in Teufelsdröckh an anguished titanism and an aching nostalgia, expressed in his "strong inward unrest" and "storm-like rushing over land and sea": "He writhes and roars under his consciousness of the difference in himself between the possible and the actual. . . . He holds himself aloof in savage isolation . . . and would even perhaps be willing to exchange the restless immaturity of our self-consciousness . . . for the unawakened undoubting simplicity of the world's childhood."[5] Melville, whose own arc of feeling moves from the idyllic plenitude of *Typee* to the titanic nihilism of *Pierre*, and who embodies in Ahab and Queequeg such contrasting images of modern, overconscious and of primitive, unconscious heroism, may well have also felt and responded to such strains in Carlyle.

5. Jules Paul Seigel, ed., *Thomas Carlyle: The Critical Heritage* (London: Routledge and Kegan Paul, 1971), pp. 31–32.

William Thompson found that Carlyle's *Heroes and Hero-Worship* (1841) pointed to revolution. The common character of these heroes is "*radical pugnacity*," for Carlyle defines the primitive Norse figure of Odin as "*Wuotan*, Movement, i.e. *agitation*, the very watchword of a true radical. . . . His heroes all offend against magistrate, priest, or law."[6] These charges acutely note those qualities in Carlyle that might help the creator of insurgent outcasts like Pierre or John Paul Jones in *Israel Potter*. Even Emerson, friend and promoter of Carlyle, complained of him as if he were an Ahab: "His imagination, finding no nutriment in any creation, avenged itself by celebrating the majestic beauty of the law of decay. . . . Where impatience of the tricks of men makes Nemesis amiable and builds altars to the negative Deity, the inevitable recoil is to heroism or the gallantry of the private heart, which decks its immolations with glory, in the unequal combat of will against fate."[7] Walt Whitman, however, more positively asserted Carlyle's stature in striking terms: "Rugged, mountainous, volcanic, he was himself more a French Revolution than any of his volumes." Even after his death he still "splashes like leviathan in the seas of modern literature."[8]

The style that had so troubled Sterling was praised by Emerson for the "magnificence" of its epic sweep and microscopic comprehension and for its power to "pounce on a fact as a symbol which was never a symbol before." In its overview, like that of an "air-balloon or bird of Jove," Carlyle's prose accomplished "the first domestication of the modern system with its infinity of details. . . . London and Europe tunneled, graded, corn-lawed, with trade-nobility, and East and West Indies for dependencies, and America, with the Rocky Hills in the horizon, have never before been conquered in literature." It took the revolutionary prose of this book "full of treason" to tame the modern world.[9] Melville in his writing also builds a full world through the elaboration of metaphors from a far-flung range of human activity, whether through the sudden unfolding of a fact of whaling into cosmic significance, or through the simile that conquers modernity by suddenly bringing frontier or factory and whaleship together. Yet Emerson criticizes the "lurid

6. Ibid., pp. 185–186.

7. *English Traits,* in *Emerson's Complete Works,* Riverside Edition (Cambridge, Mass., 1883), 5:237.

8. Seigel, *Critical Heritage,* pp. 456–457.

9. Ibid., pp. 224–225, 222.

stormlights" that make Carlyle's world resemble the "Creation or Judgment Day" of the painter John Martin instead of "the common earth and sky." To Emerson's optimism, as often to Wordsworth, the sublime effects of artistic heightening, whether in response to landscape or history, are unworthy of human greatness: "The sun and stars affect us only grandly, because we cannot reach to their smoke and surfaces, and say, Is that all?"[10] Both Carlyle and Melville, like John Martin, needed at least as much black as light in their scenes; neither could ever say, "Is that all?" to any natural fact; and both writers suffered under the sense of frustration which that inability provoked.

During his time at Walden, Thoreau wrote an essay that emphasizes Carlyle's relation to the common, working man. In his approach to idiomatic speech, Carlyle's prose works at "emancipating the language" from conventional literary style.[11] Furthermore, it has initiated Americans into "the privileges of the century" by showing "what philosophy and criticism the nineteenth century had to offer." Carlyle's writings are not part of an elite culture but are "such works of art only as the plough, and corn-mill, and steam-engine": highly useful, more necessities than amusements, not ornamental but productive. Thoreau adopts Carlyle's own concept, and almost his voice, to call him "the hero, as literary man," and he proclaims that "there is no more notable working-man in England" than Carlyle. To make this point, Thoreau "cannot do better than quote [Carlyle's] own estimate of labor from Sartor Resartus," that remarkable paean to "the toil-worn craftsman" and "the artist," as well as the Christ-like union of the two.[12]

Like Emerson, however, Thoreau objects to Carlyle's excessive attention to "the grimmer features of life." *The French Revolution* needs more "sun" in it. Adding chapters on "Work for the Month," "Altitude of the Sun," "State of the Crops and Markets," "Meteorological Observations," "Attractive Industry," or "Day Labor" would "remind the reader that the French peasantry did something beside go without breeches, burn châteaus, get ready knotted cords, and

10. Ibid., pp. 222–223.

11. *Early Essays and Miscellanies,* ed. Joseph J. Moldenhauer and Edwin Moser (Princeton: Princeton University Press, 1975), p. 232.

12. Ibid., pp. 223, 234, 243. For the European resonance of such union between artist and worker, see Jean Seznec, "Michelet in Germany: A Journey in Self-Discovery," *History and Theory* 16 (1977):7–10.

embrace and throttle one another by turns." Although Carlyle "hinted at" such aspects, "they deserve a notice more in proportion to their importance. We want not only a background to the picture, but a ground under the feet also."[13] Even Carlyle's hints at the quality and continuity of daily life during the Revolution were (as I have noted earlier) historiographically innovative, but Thoreau goes far beyond him toward the position of some modern scholars that precisely what does *not* change during a given period is the true object of historical investigation.[14] Through the detailed attention to ordinary conditions of work in *Moby-Dick,* in chapters titled like those Thoreau suggested to Carlyle, Melville gives us not just a background to the tragedy of Ahab and the Whale, but a ship under our feet as well.

His response to Carlyle finally moves Thoreau to declare that modern literature must speak to "The Man of the Age, come to be called Workingman," and to speak "to his condition" the writer must also be "in his condition."[15] Thoreau thus later characterized what he had done at Walden as going "before the mast and on the deck of the world." From the first paragraph of *Typee,* his first book, Melville made clear that such was also his condition. And in his writing years Melville continued to be a whole workingman. After one of the most eloquent descriptions of his problems writing *Moby-Dick,* he continued his letter to Hawthorne, "I'm rather sore, perhaps, in this letter; but see my hand! four blisters on this palm, made by hoes and hammers" (1 June 1851). No less than Thoreau's, Melville's sense of the relation of work and writing bears the mark of his imaginative dialogue with Carlyle.

In its focus on the problem of vocation—the yielding of clerical calling to literary career, what it means to work as a writer, and what relation a writer may achieve with his audience—the correspondence of Emerson and Carlyle helps further to place those elements in Carlyle that might have made him especially useful to

13. Thoreau, *Early Essays,* p. 248.

14. On "that other, submerged history, almost silent and always discreet, virtually unsuspected either by its observers or its participants, which is little touched by the obstinate erosion of time," see Fernand Braudel, *The Mediterranean and the Mediterranean World in the Age of Philip II* (1949), trans. Siân Reynolds (New York: Harper and Row, 1972), 1:16.

15. Thoreau, *Early Essays,* p. 251.

Melville.[16] For all his theoretical individualism, Emerson emerges in these exchanges as a socially settled Yankee, knowledgeable in the ways of power and money, while Carlyle, though a theorist of social cohesion, finds himself isolated, a proud, almost penniless middle-aged Scot struggling in the literary world of London. Thus, from the security of his place in the Concord community and his established position as a popular lecturer, Emerson located the source of Carlyle's stylistic problems in his "despair of finding a contemporary audience," and he urged Carlyle to "defy" the "diabolism" that such despair provokes.[17] Carlyle agrees that he speaks "*alone* under the *Heavens*" but insists that his "diabolism" is fundamental. When writing *The French Revolution*, his "view" had been "such as Satan had from the pavilion of the Anarch old. . . . I also know what it is to drop *plumb:* fluttering my pennons vain."[18] The "air-balloon" may not hold; overview is as precarious for Carlyle as for Satan or for Ishmael on the mast-head.

Emerson hoped to cure Carlyle with a lecture tour in America, where the Lyceum was "the most flexible of all organs of opinion," and its "popularity" and "newness" would free the speaker from "any shackles of prescription." In that "great institution" a living, responsive audience would allow him to join in society and "become that good despot which the virtuous orator is." But Carlyle resisted, for his America was a place where in "daydream" he imagined he might enjoy isolation and be free of the urge to social responsibility, "in the Backwoods, with a rifle in my hand."[19] No less than his American contemporaries Carlyle is building up the heroic figure of "Man in the Open Air."[20] He also expressed this mythic sense of America in his public writings, where it was one of the initial handles by which Melville, while still closely associated with the

16. See Henry Nash Smith, "Emerson's Problem of Vocation—A Note on 'The American Scholar,'" *New England Quarterly* 12 (1939):52–67. See also Quentin Anderson, *The Imperial Self* (New York: Alfred A. Knopf, 1971), pp. 29–32.

17. *The Correspondence of Emerson and Carlyle*, ed. Joseph Slater (New York: Columbia University Press, 1964), pp. 98–99.

18. Ibid., pp. 103, 134.

19. Ibid., pp. 143, 159.

20. For the significance of this phrase from Whitman, see F. O. Matthiessen, *American Renaissance* (New York: Oxford University Press, 1941), chap. 14.

New York literary nationalists, could grasp him. In *Heroes and Hero-Worship* Carlyle judges that in "the American Backwoods" one "catches tones" of the "grim humour" of Norse mythology, "mirth resting on earnestness and sadness, as the rainbow on the black tempest" (5: 39). In *Sartor Resartus* we respond as ambivalently to the heroism of Napoleon as to the "American Backwoodsman, who had to fell unpenetrated forests" even at the cost of "rioting" and "theft" (1: 143). America gripped his imagination, but Carlyle never did come over. The success of his *French Revolution* (1837) gave him the chance to try lecturing in London. Although always acutely ill at ease with his audience, Carlyle finally succeeded in saying what he thought was true and important in his series on "Heroes." Instead of "setting out for America,"[21] however, and repeating the lectures there, he wrote them for publication. He had tried speaking to a live audience, and it was not what he needed; instead he dedicated himself to London and the life of writing.

Carlyle's letters reveal his writing as a solitary agony. It cut him off wholly from outer life; it "girdled" him round "like a panoply"; it was like going "down into primeval night," where he would "live alone and mute with the Manes," uncertain whether he would "ever more see day." Emerson found, however, that Carlyle's style rewarded the reader with the presence of all that the writer had had to sacrifice. Through giving up the city in life, Carlyle gains an organic possession of it in prose: "Your strange genius [is] the instant fruit of your London. It is the aroma of Babylon. Such as the great metropolis, such is this style: so vast, enormous, related to all the world, and so endless in details."[22]

By contrast, Emerson, who appears so socialized in his letters as he describes his lecturing, his various acquaintances, and his work on Carlyle's behalf with publishers, emerged to Carlyle from the pages of his books as "a *soliloquizer* on the eternal mountain-tops. . . . Only the *man* and the stars and the earth are visible." Just as Carlyle's sentences chart an urban labyrinth, so Emerson's reveal not a society but a collection of individuals: "The sentences are very *brief;* and did not . . . always entirely cohere for me. . . . They did not, sometimes, rightly stick to their foregoers and their followers: the paragraph not as a beaten *ingot,* but as a beautiful

21. *Correspondence of Emerson and Carlyle,* p. 275.
22. Ibid., pp. 151, 327, 161.

square *bag of duck-shot* held together by canvas!"[23] In each case the style presents the writer's social vision, rather than representing the society in which he lived.[24]

The same restless dissatisfaction that he felt toward a live audience marked Carlyle's attitude toward nature: as concrete actualities both were lost forever. For Carlyle an untroubled existence in nature is part of mankind's, and each individual's, childhood, a necessary state of passivity that lays the foundation for a later life of activity. Nature is "a mystery" that "will have us rest on her beautiful and awful bosom as if it were our secure home; on the bottomless boundless Deep, whereon all human things fearfully and wonderfully swim, she will have us walk and build. . . . Under all her works . . . lies a basis of Darkness" (28: 3–4).

The "as if" balances between a necessary fiction and a deceitful imposture. To grow into adulthood one must fall into realizing that "our being is made up of Light and Darkness. . . . Everywhere there is Dualism. . . . A perpetual Contradiction dwells in us," just as it does in nature (28: 27). From this perspective Carlyle can define literature as "a quarrel, and internecine duel, with the whole World of Darkness that lies without one and within one" (10: 104). He continually emphasizes the "boundless Deep" and the Calvinistic "blackness" to which Melville was so sensitive. In contrast, Emerson's *Nature* as a whole is a paean to what Freud calls "the omnipotence of thought." Despite moments on "the brink of fear," Emerson's usual sense of himself in *Nature* is as an infant at the breast of a good mother. The "lover of nature" retains "the spirit of infancy." The "transparent eyeball" through whom "the currents of the Universal Being circulate" replicates the situation at the breast, if not *in utero*. There is none of the distrust, the "as if," the insistence on struggle that marks Carlyle. The dualisms of surface and depth, dark and light, are not there.

Even in a moment that, logically considered, opposes man and nature, Emerson's language resonates with uncanny infantile beatitude. When English friends (in a group including Carlyle) asked about his "house" in America, Emerson instead of answering fell into fantasy: "There . . . in America, lies Nature sleeping, overgrowing, almost conscious, too much by half for man in the picture,

23. Ibid., p. 371.

24. My argument here reflects the thesis of Richard Poirier, *A World Elsewhere* (New York: Oxford University Press, 1966).

and so giving a certain *tristesse,* like the rank vegetation of swamps and forests seen at night, steeped in dews and rains, which it loves; and on it man seems not able to make much impression. There, in that great sloven continent, in high Alleghany pastures, in the sea-wide sky-skirted prairie, still sleeps and murmurs and hides the great mother."[25] Such a great maternal "Nature" is the "house" of Emerson the writer, not of the social traveler among his friends. Both Emerson's call to individual enjoyment and Carlyle's summons to social engagement are counterstatements to the oppressive environments they felt around them, but the terms of Carlyle are so much closer to those of the man who wrote "The Whiteness of the Whale" and "The Try-Works," that we can easily see why for Melville to begin with Emerson might have led so quickly to Carlyle.

HEROISM IN THE AGE OF WRITING

IN HIS CONTEMPORARY CONTEXT, then, Carlyle appeared to himself, to some who knew him personally, and through his writings to some of his most perceptive readers, as an ambiguous and satanic figure. Yet he played such a role despite himself. As we have noted, his desire was not to stand titanically alienated from a fallen society, but to reunite all individuals in a redeemed society. *Heroes and Hero-Worship* is Carlyle's most comprehensive survey of the prospect and problems of this attempt, more concretely historical and less metaphysically symbolical than *Sartor Resartus,* broader in range than *Past and Present,* and, crucially, most concerned with defining his own task as a writer. By writing *Heroes and Hero-Worship* he had solved his problem of vocation, abandoned any further plans for lecturing, and committed himself to continuing his writing, an activity the value of which he never again so strongly asserted as in this book, though his personal devotion to it never flagged. Melville's increasingly uncompromising commitment to his own literary career at the time of writing *Moby-Dick* and his creation of the heroic character of Ahab both grow from his response to the book that sealed Carlyle's direction.

Carlyle's heroes are men of action in historically determined roles —divinity, prophet, priest, poet, man of letters, king—for he sees heroic capability as a permanent human potential, though circumstances mold the peculiar form of its expression. This substantial

25. *English Traits,* in *Emerson's Complete Works,* 5:273.

identity allows for a rich play of analogy linking one hero to another. Carlyle considers the process of his heroes' lives closely, comes close to writing biographical sketches of them, as they respond to strong challenges from life, almost all changing their course in middle age or midcareer. They hold an adversary relation to society and lack any easy Emersonian capacity for possessive assimilation of what the world around them offers.[26] Carlyle's heroes are disruptive creators within a progressive framework. Thus he sees Napoleon as carrying into European politics the democratic trend inaugurated by the Reformation.

One vital aspect of Carlyle's work in *Heroes* is obscured by our modern tolerance and only emerges clearly from contemporary reviews. Carlyle's choice of heroes was deeply shocking. His sympathy with the Norse Paganism of Odin, with Mohammed, with Cromwell, and with Napoleon was particularly outrageous. He was trying to socialize demons, to show the historically and humanly positive values and achievements of these men in their own societies and thus introduce them as positive forces into his own. This integrative attempt recalls also Goethe's attempt to screen himself from the fearful principle of the "Demoniac" by writing *Egmont,* so as to bury that principle in historical dialectic. Carlyle's heroes are like the men Goethe describes as predominantly manifesting the demoniac: full of "tremendous energy," exercising "wonderful power," and "to be overcome by nothing but by the universe itself."[27] Certainly Ahab's dominance over the crew and final defeat by the whale fits this paradigm, and even if Melville had read this in Goethe, his specific receptivity to it grows from Carlyle's heroes.

Cromwell is the Carlylean hero who most resembles Ahab, so much so that one feels here a direct appropriation. Ahab's role in its broadest outlines poses a democratic interrogation of Carlyle's authoritarian emphases. Carlyle insists that if you "find . . . the ablest man that exists" in a given situation, "raise *him* to the supreme place, and loyally reverence him, you have a perfect government" (5: 197). Melville shows such a perfect government leading to perfect disaster. He may also be questioning Carlyle's ability to

26. For a valuable comparison of *Heroes and Hero-Worship* with Emerson's *Representative Men,* see Kenneth Marc Harris, *Carlyle and Emerson* (Cambridge: Harvard University Press, 1977), chap. 2.

27. *The Autobiography of Goethe: Truth and Poetry: From My Own Life,* trans. John Oxenford (London: Bell, 1891), 2:159.

deal with individual tragedy. Carlyle draws solace from the progressive course of history to which an individual has contributed, but if, democratically, every man counts in his own right, there can be no consolation. Even though Melville holds a confident view of history, the *Pequod* is a case too small for the overall design to govern.

Despite this ironic qualification of his role, Ahab is very much a Carlylean hero, as in the organic imagery that valorizes his leadership, helping to provide the positive side of what Melville criticizes. Thus, as the second day of chase begins, the ship has achieved such a union of disparities that "the rigging lived. The mast-heads, like the tops of tall palms, were outspreadingly tufted with arms and legs" (134). Ahab's concealment of his real goal, using his captaincy against the owners' purposes, since "the only real owner of anything is its commander" (109), echoes Carlyle's casuistry over Cromwell's supposed "Hypocrisy," "Lies," and "dissimulation." Carlyle insists, in language that echoes his defense of his own devious prose style, "Such a man must have *reticences* in him. If he walk wearing his heart upon his sleeve . . . his journey will not extend far" (5: 220). Even if Melville does not fully accept Carlyle's advocacy, he follows his emphasis, opposing our moralistic tendency to damn our demons too easily.

In language as violent and vivid as Melville's was to be, Carlyle described the epistemological struggle. He found "something of the savage in all great men," a wild "wrestling naked with the truth of things" (5: 192–193), and pictured the "rugged outcast Cromwell" as a "savage *Baresark*," who "grappled like a giant, face to face, heart to heart, with the naked truth of things" (5: 209). Whalemen, Melville tells us, are of all men "the most directly brought into contact with whatever is appallingly astonishing in the sea; face to face they not only eye its greatest marvels, but, hand to jaw, give battle to them." Ahab lost his leg in confronting the whale like a "duellist," showing the will of a giant to pierce through the blubber to the "fathom-deep" heart of things (41).

More specific details of Carlyle's Cromwell link him to Ahab. Cromwell as "Baresark" echoes Melville's comparison of "fighting Quakers" to "Scandinavian sea-king[s]" (16). Melville's jottings in his edition of Shakespeare about the Quaker who sells his soul parallel Carlyle's report of an officer's claim that he saw Cromwell "sell himself before Worcester Fight" to a "black Spectre, or Devil in person" (5: 212). In general, Carlyle's concern to investigate the value of the seventeenth century, the age of Cromwell and of the first Quaker George Fox, made him speak the more directly to America, where the English seventeenth century in many ways still endured, as much of Hawthorne's fiction may remind us.

Carlyle's summary of Cromwell shows a figure so much like our image of Ahab that no citation of Melville is needed to make the resemblance felt. Cromwell showed "an outer hull of chaotic confusion" and suffered from "visions of the Devil, nervous dreams, almost semi-madness," and yet "in the heart" of that turmoil was "a clear determinate man's energy working" that yielded him "insight . . . into the heart of things" and "mastery . . . over things": "The man's misery . . . came of his greatness" (5: 217).

This heroic image of Cromwell helped Melville to create Ahab, and the figure that Carlyle draws of Dante shows that "The Hero as Poet" shares the same qualities as the hero of action. Dante's "lip is curled in . . . godlike disdain of the thing that is eating-out his heart," and his face is that "of one wholly in protest, and lifelong unsurrendering battle, against the world" (5: 86). Yet "congealed into sharp contradiction" on this "ground of eternal black" appear also the "rainbows" of "tenderness," "longing," and "love" (5: 94–95). Carlyle's image of Shakespeare and vision of "The Hero as Man of Letters" carried this line further and offered models that helped Melville to develop as a reader and to achieve the definition of himself as a writer that made *Moby-Dick* possible. In his letter to his publisher on *Mardi,* although he describes his impulse to write "a *real* romance" and longs "to plume [his] powers for a flight," he is still eager to be accepted as a "gentleman" who has "read the Waverly novels" (25 March 1848). Only a year and a half later, despite the commercial successes of *Redburn* and *White-Jacket,* Melville no longer wishes to associate himself with the conventional popularity and respectability of Scott but avows his "earnest desire to write those sort of books which are said to 'fail' " (6 October 1849). Like Dickens a few years earlier, Melville rejects the example of Scott's career. Whether or not Melville's sense of alienation from his audience and dissatisfaction with what he considered hackwork antedate his engagement with Carlyle's work, he found much in Carlyle to support and direct this sense.

In "The Hero as Man of Letters" Carlyle had defined the contradictions of the writer's situation in the current age. "With the art of Writing, with the art of Printing, a total change" has come over that communication "of man to man" which the pulpit had been intended to facilitate in an age of speaking. Echoing his earlier correspondence with Emerson, Carlyle declared, "The Writer of a Book, is not he a Preacher preaching not to this parish or that, on this day or that, but to all men in all times and places?" (5: 159). Thus even before he knew the name of his "Germanick new-light writer," Emerson was awakened by Carlyle's words in the *Edinburgh Review* and therefore blessed the art of printing that "joins me to that stranger by this perfect railroad."[28] The steam press like the steam engine transforms the possibilities of communication.

Paradoxically, as his universal significance increases, the relation of the writer to the communal life of his time diminishes. At best "he is of some importance" only "to a certain shopkeeper, trying to get some money for his books. . . . He is an accident in society. He wanders like a wild Ishmaelite" (5: 159). This of course is Carlyle's sense of his own condition, and it leads him to create an ideal community of departed spirits to fill the place of a real contemporary readership. Rousseau, Johnson, and Burns are his exemplars, because, unlike Goethe, "the conditions of their life . . . resemble what those of ours still are": "These men did not conquer. . . . They fought bravely, and fell. They were not heroic bringers of the light, but heroic seekers of it. They lived under galling conditions. . . . It is rather the *Tombs* of three Literary Heroes that I have to show you . . . the monumental heaps, under which three spiritual giants lie buried" (5: 158).

During his stay in London, when he had hoped to meet Carlyle, Melville bought and began to read Goethe's autobiography, Rousseau's *Confessions,* and Boswell's *Life of Johnson.* The conditions of Rousseau and Johnson were indeed like those of Carlyle and Melville. All four had found intolerable their youthful experiences as schoolmasters, thrust upon them by their status as impoverished young proto-intellectuals, and went on from there to embattled literary careers.[29] All four were, compared to Goethe or Emerson,

28. *The Journals and Miscellaneous Notebooks of Ralph Waldo Emerson,* ed. William H. Gilman et al. (Cambridge: Harvard University Press, 1960—), 4:45.

29. Cf. the reference by Matthew Arnold (apropos of Goldsmith, Hartley Coleridge, and Maurice de Guérin) to "that common but most perfidious refuge of men of letters . . . the profession of teaching," in *The Complete Prose Works of Matthew Arnold,* ed. R. H. Super (Ann Arbor: University of Michigan Press, 1960–1977), 3:28.

outsiders to the sphere of culture and leisure. Thus, Melville felt compelled to reject the serenity of Goethe's "Live in the All," objecting to Hawthorne how impossible this was when one had "a raging toothache" (1 June 1851). The aches of labor and hunger were equally present to him.

In a democratic adaptation of Carlyle's rhetoric of heroism, Melville turns to two examples of persecuted writers from the seventeenth century and to the rough backwoods hero who was the closest American analogue to Cromwell in revolutionary political impact. His subject is "not the dignity of kings and robes" but "that democratic dignity . . . shining in the arm that wields a pick or drives a spike":

> If, then, to meanest mariners, and renegades and castaways, I shall hereafter ascribe high qualities, though dark; weave round them tragic graces; . . . if I shall touch that workman's arm with some ethereal light; if I shall spread a rainbow over his disastrous set of sun. . . . Bear me out in it, thou great democratic God! who didst not refuse to the swart convict, Bunyan, the pale, poetic pearl; Thou who didst clothe with doubly hammered leaves of finest gold, the stumped and paupered arm of old Cervantes; Thou who didst pick up Andrew Jackson from the pebbles; who didst hurl him upon a war horse; who didst thunder him higher than a throne! [26]

This invocation to the democratic Muse as God catches up Carlyle's theme of workmen and colors it with the Carlylean contrast of "dark" qualities overspread by "rainbows": the "mournful" and "the exalted." It is through toil and struggle, not through serene ease, that his characters act and that he writes.

Looking back to Shakespeare, Carlyle admires the victory by which he achieved the laughter of the comedies, but he is more concerned to exclaim, "How much in Shakespeare lies hid":

> his sorrows, his silent struggles known to himself; much, that was not known at all, not speakable at all: like *roots,* like sap and forces working underground! Speech is great; but Silence is greater. . . . All his works seem, comparatively speaking, cursory, imperfect, written under cramping circumstances; giving only here and there a note of the full utterance of the

> man. Passages there are that come upon you like splendour out of Heaven; bursts of radiance, illuminating the very heart of the thing. . . . Such bursts, however, make us feel that the surrounding matter is not radiant; that it is, in part, temporary, conventional. Alas, Shakespeare had to write for the Globe Playhouse; his great soul had to crush itself . . . into that and no other mould. It was with him, then, as it is with us all. No man works save under conditions.
>
> [5: 108–110]

Shakespeare, then, faced modern problems, although he greatly overcame them. Even so, much of him lies buried, if not so much as of Rousseau, Johnson, and Burns. They were "seekers" of light, he, one of the "bringers" of light, even if only in "bursts." Carlyle has transformed the organic critical metaphor of harmonious growth ("roots") into disruptive violence ("forces"). As with Hugo a few years earlier, Shakespeare moves Carlyle to the critical sublime. The implicit image of the titanic volcano links the underground personal spiritual activity, the physical burial mound, and the heavenly cultural expression flashing out against that dark ground. Melville cries out in a moment of creative exaltation, no less serious for its self-mockery, "Give me Vesuvius' crater for an inkstand" (*MD* 104).

Carlyle's Shakespeare is very much Melville's Shakespeare.[30] In his annotations Melville challenged the claim that Shakespeare produced his works "without any throes or labor of mind." He wished that Shakespeare were free from "the muzzle" his Elizabethan circumstances placed on him: "Even Shakespeare . . . was not a frank man to the uttermost. And, indeed, who in this intolerant universe is, or can be? But the Declaration of Independence makes a difference" (3 March 1849). Melville like Carlyle insists that particular circumstances make universal human problems either more or less bearable.

In this letter Carlyle's perspective on Shakespeare has helped Melville declare his own independence from Duyckinck's circle in terms that anticipate his position in "Hawthorne and his Mosses,"

30. To understand how greatly Carlyle's interpretation of Shakespeare differed from that prevalent in the American 1840s, see John Stafford, "Henry Norman Hudson and the Whig Use of Shakespeare," *PMLA* 66 (1951):49–61.

that to "write like a man" is "to write like an American" (546). Carlyle commented to John Sterling that he had written *The French Revolution* "in the character of a man" only, and many found in his work a "character" rather than a "thinker"; more a "man of letters" and a "preacher" than a "philosopher."[31] But Carlyle's great impact came from his power to awaken people and set them an example in concern and commitment without binding them to a system. He gave such different writers as Dickens, Engels, and Melville license to be themselves.

In the essay on Hawthorne, Melville echoes Carlyle's view of Shakespeare not only in his own interpretation of Shakespeare, but also in the method of reading Hawthorne (as Blake read Milton) by which he implicitly warrants his own practice in *Moby-Dick*. Melville grounds his analysis of Hawthorne's "blackness" on its similarity, both technically and thematically, to Shakespeare, and he claims to show that "the world is mistaken" about Hawthorne just as it is about Shakespeare. Shakespeare is great not for "Richard-the-third humps and Macbeth daggers,"

> but it is those deep far-away things in him; those occasional flashings-forth of the intuitive Truth in him; those short, quick probings at the very axis of reality:—these are the things that make Shakespeare, Shakespeare. . . . The immediate products of a great mind are not so great, as that undeveloped, (and sometimes undevelopable) yet dimly-discernible greatness, to which these immediate products are but the infallible indices. In Shakespeare's tomb lies infinitely more than Shakespeare ever wrote. . . . Shakespeare . . . was forced . . . by circumstances [into] the popularizing noise and show of broad farce and blood-besmeared tragedy.
>
> [541–542]

The "circumstances" of Melville's analysis correspond to the "cramping circumstances" that Carlyle's Shakespeare had to face. Consequently, the deepest truth of Melville's Shakespeare emerges only in "flashings-forth" like the "bursts of radiance" in Carlyle, while

31. James Anthony Froude, *Thomas Carlyle: His Life in London* (New York: Harper and Brothers, 1885), 1:50; Octavius Brooks Frothingham, *Transcendentalism in New England* (1876; rpt. Philadelphia: University of Pennsylvania Press, 1972), p. 93.

the most of him lies still in his "tomb," an enigma for interpretation; for as Carlyle had proclaimed, silence is greater than speech.

In the midst of composing *Moby-Dick,* Melville writes, "I am so pulled hither and thither by circumstances. The calm, the coolness, the silent grass-growing mood in which a man *ought* always to compose,—that, I fear, can seldom be mine. Dollars damn me; and the malicious Devil is forever grinning in upon me. . . . What I feel most moved to write, that is banned,—it will not pay. Yet, altogether, write the *other* way I cannot. So the product is a final hash, and all my books are botches" (1 June 1851). The "grass-growing mood," the "All-feeling," is dispelled by market necessities, which, despite the Declaration of Independence, still "muzzle" writers and "ban" their truths. "Man in the open air" and "circumstances" are locked in struggle.[32] Melville's own situation greatly resembles that of the Shakespeare he discovered in Carlyle, "forced by circumstances" toward a way of writing that he felt was unnatural for him, driven toward allegory and silence.

WRITING AND EXPERIENCE IN *Moby-Dick*

IN HIS ROLE AS MAN OF LETTERS, as modern writer, Melville draws constant attention to the "writtenness" of *Moby-Dick.*[33] He opens with the purely bookish array of "Extracts" compiled by the "sub-sub-librarian." Ishmael's narrative, although writers often use the first person to pretend to be speakers, is not set in any speaking context, such, for example, as Conrad always uses. As early as chapter 23 the reference to the "six-inch chapter" as "the stoneless grave of Bulkington" places the book in the tradition of writing as commemorative inscription, reaching across time to strangers. Later Melville uses the classic trope of book as voyage: "Already we are boldly launched upon the deep; but soon we shall be lost in its unshored,

32. These two semimythical entities both derive from the semantic complex of "*milieu* and *ambiance*" and illustrate the abyss that may open to separate meanings one would expect to share common ground. See Leo Spitzer, "*Milieu* and *Ambiance,*" *Philosophy and Phenomenological Research* 3 (1942):1–42, 169–218.

33. Cf. Rodolphe Gasché, "The Scene of Writing: A Deferred Outset," *Glyph,* no. 1 (1977), pp. 150–171.

harborless immensities" (32).[34] In "The Crotch" Melville describes his enterprise in romantic, organic imagery, "Out of the trunk, the branches grow; out of them the twigs. So, in productive subjects, grow the chapters" (63). Shandy-like, Melville relates the state of knowledge about "The Fountain" up to the moment of writing, "fifteen and a quarter minutes past one o'clock P.M. of this sixteenth day of December, A.D. 1850" (85). But he brings us even further into the moment of writing: "In the mere act of penning my thoughts of this Leviathan, they weary me, and make me faint with their outreaching comprehensiveness of sweep, as if to include the whole circle of the sçiences, and all the generations of whales, and men, and mastodons, past, present, and to come, with all the revolving panoramas of empire on earth" (104). The Carlylean theme of writing as heroic labor and the ambition that Emerson saw in him, to be "related to all the world" and "endless in details,"[35] are both raised here to the level of program and fulfilled in the rest of the work.

Ishmael humorously literalizes the ideal of "the whole man" as writer by recording the whale's dimensions on his skin, leaving off the odd inches because he "wished the other parts of [his] body to remain a blank page for a poem [he] was then composing" (102). For Melville as for Carlyle, books and living beings are enigmatic. The whale's skin is hieroglyphically marked (68), and so is Queequeg. His tattooing makes him "in his own proper person . . . a riddle to unfold, a wondrous work in one volume; but whose mysteries not even himself could read, . . . and these mysteries were therefore destined in the end to moulder away with the living parchment whereon they were inscribed" (110). If, however, like Shakespeare, one transfers these mysterious but "infallible indices" from "living parchment" to paper, then one's "greatness" may yet be "dimly discernible" to future readers. So Queequeg copies his body's tattoos onto the coffin that carries Ishmael safe from the *Pequod*'s wreckage.

Melville gives further emphasis and value to the writtenness of *Moby-Dick* by inserting, as subordinate parts of the book's polyphonic whole, examples of the major forms of spoken discourse cur-

34. See Ernst Robert Curtius, *European Literature and the Latin Middle Ages* (1948), trans. Willard R. Trask (New York: Pantheon, 1953), pp. 128–130.

35. *Correspondence of Emerson and Carlyle*, p. 161.

rent in his time. As captain of a small ship, Ahab occupies one of the few positions in which the spoken word stands alone as means of command. At a time when even such political orators as Webster and Calhoun made much of their impact through the printed circulation of their words, the ship was remarkable for having no written adjunct to the leader's speech.[36] Nonetheless, Ahab's word lives for us only as reported in writing by the surviving Ishmael. It has not been able to prolong itself in oral tradition. Although Mapple's sermon is impressive in its ability to bring together the scattered congregation, as Ahab's word welds into one the scattered isolatoes of the *Pequod,* the sermon clearly fails to comprehend the book's whole experienced presentation of the whale. By going from the sermon to sharing in Queequeg's pagan rituals, Ishmael immediately undercuts its authority.

"The Town-Ho's Story" particularly illuminates the book's implicit contrast of speech and writing. The story, told to a specific, actively participating audience, is exactly what *Moby-Dick* is not.[37] It contrasts with *Moby-Dick* by having no nonsense about it. Ishmael presents himself as swearing on a Bible to the veracity of the tale, but we are disappointed in our hope that here at last is "gospel cetology," for the tale is simply and rigorously an account of human beings in action, and the whale appears as part of their story rather than as subject and center in itself. When the Teneriffe man sees the whale and Ishmael announces, "It was Moby Dick," the listener asks, "Do whales have names? whom call you Moby Dick?" Ishmael replies, "a very white, and famous, and most deadly immortal monster, Don;—but that would be too long a story" (54). The effect is momentarily vertiginous, as the whole book that we're reading becomes a delayed digression to one of its own interpolated stories. The larger point, however, is clear. A book allows a fullness of detail and multiplicity of perspective for which spoken discourse has no room: this gospel must be scripture. Melville, like Carlyle,

36. See Alan Heimert, "*Moby-Dick* and American Political Symbolism," *American Quarterly* 15 (1963):498–534; and Ann Douglas, *The Feminization of American Culture* (New York: Alfred A. Knopf, 1977), especially p. 306.

37. For a different view of Ishmael as "raconteur," see Walter L. Reed, *Meditations on the Hero* (New Haven: Yale University Press, 1974), pp. 160–163.

finds the book, rather than direct speech, the most valuable contemporary form of communication.

By its very detail and multiplicity, writing can be simultaneously more critical and more reverential than speech, by showing us all sides of what it presents. Carlyle warns lest nature become ordinary to us, "Hardened round us, encasing wholly every notion we form, is a wrappage of traditions, hearsays, mere *words*. . . . It is a poor science that would hide from us the great deep sacred infinitude . . . whither we can never penetrate, on which all science swims as a mere superficial film" (5: 8).

"To know a thing," says Carlyle, one must be "related to it" (5: 107). The writing of *Moby-Dick* attempts to undermine "mere words" and to replace "hearsays" and "traditions" with the testimony that comes of real relation. The book's action is continually to unpeel "wrappage." We move from the great society of land to the small ship-society, from the sea's surface to what lies beneath, and from the whale's outside to the inside. Melville embodies in action Carlyle's metaphors of floating and penetration. In *Moby-Dick* no less than in *Sartor Resartus* the point lies "much in the Author's individuality, as if it were not Arguments that had taught him, but Experience" (1: 40–41). Melville follows Carlyle in trying to inaugurate a "reign of wonder" in his readers (1: 55).[38]

In attempting this project, Melville follows closely Carlyle's epistemology. For Carlyle, as for Goethe, "Doubt of any sort cannot be removed except by Action," since "All Speculation is by nature endless, formless, a vortex amid vortices: only by a felt indubitable certainty of Experience does it find any centre to revolve around" (1: 156). Thus Ishmael tries to cure his malaise by going to sea as a sailor. However, such embodiment of speculation in action is a "symbol," a blend of "concealment" and "revelation," of "Speech" and of "Silence" (1: 175). Thus, one can never say right out in words the meaning of the action undertaken against uncertainty. In fact, despite the pretense of trying to "order this chaos" (cf. *MD* 32), the writer actually multiplies words in an attempt to have one word, one image, undo the previous, and to replace solidifying formulas with fresh, living wonder.[39] Thus Ishmael's elaboration of

38. See further Tony Tanner, *Reign of Wonder* (Cambridge: Cambridge University Press, 1965).

39. The best treatment of this important aspect of Melville is James

a fish story, his need to write what he told the Don in Lima "would be too long a story."

In *Moby-Dick* "wonder" and "experience" chase each other in a dizzying circle. The whaleman's "habit" may blind him to the "true terror" of living encircled by the whizzing line (60), and "by the continual repetition of impressions" man may lose his "sense of the full awfulness of the sea" (58). But then, if one were always a "beginner" on the mast-head, one would have no chance for the pleasure of speculation (35). In the cetological chapters Melville emphasizes the need of his subject to be "enlarged upon, in order to be adequately understood," and just as *Sartor Resartus* brings us Teufelsdröckh's biography in fragments that mimic experience, so Ishmael wishes not "to perform [his] task methodically," but to "produce the desired impression by separate citation of items . . . known to me as whaleman" (45).[40] If "in a whaler wonders soon wane" (50), it becomes all the more the writer's task to revivify these wonders for his readers.

In the chapters on the heads of the sperm and right whales, through the prolonged address to the reader as "you," Ishmael tries to engage us as closely as possible, by the vicarious experience of reading, with the actual whale. He invites us right onto the "summit" of the right-whale's head to "look at these two *f*-shaped spout-holes":

> You would take the whole head for an enormous bass-viol, and these spiracles, the apertures in its sounding-board. Then, again, if you fix your eye upon this strange, crested, comb-like incrustation on the top of the mass—this green, barnacled thing, which the Greenlanders call the "crown" and the Southern fishers the "bonnet" of the Right Whale; fixing your eyes solely on this, you would take the head for the trunk of some huge oak, with a bird's nest in its crotch. At any rate, when you watch those live crabs that nestle here on this bonnet, such an idea will be almost sure to occur to you; unless, indeed, your fancy has been fixed by the technical term "crown" also

---

Guetti, *The Limits of Metaphor* (Ithaca: Cornell University Press, 1965), chap. 2.

40. For a more straightforward view of Melville's "thrust toward explication," see Warner Berthoff, *The Example of Melville* (Princeton: Princeton University Press, 1962), p. 208.

> bestowed upon it; in which case you will take great interest in thinking how this mighty monster is actually a diademed king of the sea.
>
> [75]

Was there ever a less pictorially composed description? Insistently cajoling us into submission to the narrator, who dictates our responses, the passage reveals the power of perspective and of names to influence our apprehension of a thing. There is a constant struggle with inarticulateness. One cannot rest with the vagueness of "mass" and "thing," yet the words almost fly apart when one tries to speak of "live crabs" in a "bonnet," and even a would-be "technical" term like "crown" may "fix" our response on an inappropriate literary association. This insistence on active involvement in experience as the only way of knowing finally pushes in the direction of silence: "But to learn all about these recondite matters, your best way is at once to descend into the blubber-room" (94). Alas, for us landlubbers!

This failure of explicitness before mute experience, this recourse to the mystic's rhetoric of ineffability, leads to that sea of troubles which critics with all their arms have failed to end. In *Sartor Resartus* Teufelsdröckh's biography turns out to be only "hieroglyphically" authentic, for you cannot know anything by "stringing together beadrolls of what thou namest Facts. The Man is the spirit he worked in; not what he did, but what he became. Facts are engraved Hierograms, for which the fewest have the key" (1: 161).[41] Facts are no longer part of the public realm of preaching and oratory; their meaning belongs only to a dispersed readership. Melville repeatedly forces upon us the inadequacy of facts by showing Ishmael's need to interpret them and urging us to interpret them also. In the very first chapter Ishmael tries to unfold the relation between "meditation and water." He insists, "Surely all this is not without meaning," and offers us "the key to it all," but the key is only "the image of the ungraspable phantom of life," hardly a key that will open many doors. In The Spouter-Inn the strangely chaotic oil painting was "enough to drive a nervous man distracted," but this distraction arose from the urge "to find out what that marvel-

41. For background see John T. Irwin, "The Symbol of the Hieroglyphics in the American Renaissance," *American Quarterly* 26 (1974): 103–126.

lous painting meant" (3). When Mapple draws up the ladder after him, Ishmael feels that it "must symbolize something unseen" (8).

As the book goes on, however, Ahab takes over much of the interpretive activity, and Ishmael begins to be skeptical. He says of Ahab's response to the fish moving from the *Pequod* to the *Albatross*, "to any monomaniac man the veriest trifles capriciously carry meanings" (52). Nonetheless, Ishmael's own urgings that we try to "read the awful Chaldee of the sperm whale's brow" (79), the avowal that his method is "careful disorderliness" (82), and his confession that he finds "plain things the knottiest" (85) all push us to that monomaniacal exercise of interpretation. The book demands such activity of its readers, but can our response to such a book be any more sure than our response to the whale itself?

> This peaking of the whale's flukes is perhaps the grandest sight to be seen in all animated nature. Out of the bottomless profundities the gigantic tail seems spasmodically snatching at the highest heaven. So in dreams, have I seen majestic Satan thrusting forth his tormented colossal claw from the flame Baltic of Hell. But in gazing at such scenes, it is all what mood you are in; if in the Dantean, the devils will occur to you; if in that of Isaiah, the archangels.
>
> [86]

This undecidable split between the devils and archangels repeats the mystery that Carlyle and Melville felt within each individual and recalls the split within Carlyle's own writings that his most acute interpreters discovered.

In the overall movement of *Moby-Dick* the same difficulty emerges. How is one decisively to grasp a book that begins with the need to leave land for sea and pushes us off with the exhortation that "in landlessness resides the highest truth" (23) but by the middle looks back nostalgically to the "one insular Tahiti, full of peace and joy," the verdant land that "this appalling ocean surrounds" (58)? Melville's capacity to survey alternatives produces in *Moby-Dick* a whole poetic fiction of social motion, "not found in staying at home, nor yet in travelling, but in transitions from one to the other, which must therefore . . . present as much transitional surface as possible."[42] The "two poles" that structure both thought

42. *Representative Men*, in *Emerson's Complete Works*, 4:56.

and feeling appear in Melville as fully as Emerson found them in Plato. The tension in Plato's text between "transcendental distinctions" and everyday occupations marks also the meaning of particular experience and individual lives that Carlyle presented to Melville's eager and aching eyes through the hieroglyph that he sealed into his books. As an example for Melville in this crucial stage of his career, Carlyle offered an avenue of liberating escape from the stifling squabbles of provincialism trying to become nationalism onto the main stage of European literature; a compendious storehouse of the predominant types and attitudes of advanced art and thought; and a powerful model of writing as a career.[43]

43. I have attempted newly to define the relationship of Melville to Carlyle. The major compendium of references relating the two, the annotation to the edition of *Moby-Dick* by Luther S. Mansfield and Howard P. Vincent (New York: Hendricks House, 1952), primarily lists verbal similarities, while I am trying to define larger complexes of meaning or attitude. As far as I know, all the verbal similarities that I do highlight are new. For other comment (beyond items cited by G. B. Tennyson, "The Carlyles," in *Victorian Prose: A Guide to Research*, ed. David J. DeLaura [New York: Modern Language Association of America, 1973], pp. 67–68) see Matthiessen, *American Renaissance;* Howard, *Herman Melville;* Lawrance Thompson, *Melville's Quarrel with God* (Princeton: Princeton University Press, 1952); and Leo Marx, *The Machine in the Garden* (New York: Oxford University Press, 1964), for all of which consult index entries on Carlyle.

VIII

The Novelty of *Our Mutual Friend*

The power of writing that Carlyle brought to consciousness for the mid-nineteenth century, and that runs through *Bleak House* and *Moby-Dick*, took in the later careers of Dickens and Melville directions different from any that Carlyle had intended. The authors' engagements with their audiences and with their audiences' worlds became ever less direct and satisfying. The destructive power of writing turned against itself rends Melville's *Pierre* (1852) and ruins the confidence of *Moby-Dick* that "experience" and writing are compatible, even if only through heroic struggle. Once he becomes an author, Pierre discovers that the experience of writing is wholly cut off from the rest of life, and that his every attempt to bring life into his writing only makes his book more deadly, monstrous, and impossible to achieve. Life and art are at war, and they combine to lay waste the book that is their battlefield. In contrast to this disaster, the sterile fictionality of *The Confidence-Man* (1857) marks the clear triumph of literature. Its plotless "masquerade" glitters bafflingly, a disconnected sequence of surfaces cut off from any coherent experience of action or inwardness. Even if *Billy Budd* suggests a return to effective interaction between experience and writing, its acomplishment remains purely private, experience closed wholly within itself, for Melville died leaving it unpublished.

Though the public facts of Dickens's later career are less disastrous than Melville's, anger against his society marks Dickens's correspondence of the middle 1850s, and by the later 1850s he turned to a series of new experiments in life. Separating from his wife, he abandoned the possible intimacy of the family and attempted instead a paradoxical public intimacy, turning his readers into an audience for his public readings. Yet while he gave nostalgic voice to his earlier work, his current literary production grew increasingly private. In theme and practice alike, it moved away from the dual goal of revealing social connections in the fictional world and enacting such connection through the author's relation to the public world he shared with his audience. Throughout these years, Dickens continued to "conduct" the periodical he had founded in 1849 as *Household Words* and renamed *All the Year Round* after leaving his household. That organ remained closely in touch with the concrete public realities of the day. It seems that a segregation of orientations was breaking up Dickens's work. The affective orientation toward moving an audience was specialized into the readings; the mimetic orientation toward presenting the world was taken over by journalism, leaving novel writing to negotiate the relations of self and text, the expressive and formal orientations of literature.[1] The expansion of the novel's responsibility that we saw culminate in *Bleak House* now diminishes, isolating the practice of fiction. *Little Dorrit* begins to hollow out the accomplishment of *Bleak House,* and *Our Mutual Friend* thoroughly undoes it.

In his self-revision, however, Dickens does not wholly depart from his earlier forms. *Our Mutual Friend,* therefore, appears temptingly like the earlier comprehensive novels, and critics naturally wish to assimilate them to each other in order to define a stable "maturity" of Dickens, a "major phase" that can be taken whole. Critical vision no less than narrative vision may yearn for integration rather than fragmentation.

THE DISINTEGRATION OF PLOT AND DISSOLUTION OF LONDON

LET US BEGIN WITH A PASSAGE FROM *Our Mutual Friend* that Edmund Wilson has canonized as the key to "the real meaning of the dust-pile" that figures so prominently in the novel:[2] "My lords and gentlemen and honourable boards, when you in the course of your dust-shovelling and cinder-raking have piled up a mountain of pretentious failure, you must off with your honorable coats for the removal of it, and fall to the work with the power of all the queen's

1. On these four orientations see M. H. Abrams, *The Mirror and the Lamp* (New York: Oxford University Press, 1953), chap. 1.

2. Edmund Wilson, "Dickens: The Two Scrooges," in *The Wound and the Bow* (Cambridge: Houghton Mifflin, 1941), p. 76.

horses and all the queen's men, or it will come rushing down and bury us alive" (III, 8).

Such a passage echoes moments in Dickens like those I surveyed in Chapter IV and explored more closely in *Dombey and Son* and *Bleak House*. Like them it remarkably condenses concrete detail and abstract meaning, while joining widely various elements. This moment from *Our Mutual Friend* is part of the introduction to Betty Higden's death. The previous chapter ended with Wegg greedily watching the removal of Boffin's dust pile, and the literal dust pile immediately becomes Dickens's metaphor. He continues:

> Yes, verily, my lords and gentlemen and honourable boards, adapting your catechism to the occasion, and by God's help so you must. For when we have got things to the pass that with an enormous treasure at disposal to relieve the poor, the best of the poor detest our mercies, hide their heads from us, and shame us by starving to death in the midst of us, it is a pass impossible of prosperity, impossible of continuance. It may not be so written in the Gospel according to Podsnappery; you may not "find these words" for the text of a sermon, in the Returns of the Board of Trade, but they have been the truth since the foundations of the universe have been laid, and they will be the truth until the foundations of the universe have been shaken by the Builder.
>
> [III, 8]

The allusion to Podsnappery not only condemns Podsnap's irresponsibility in refusing to hear of people starving to death. It also explicitly connects the world of high society to the book's larger context of decay and death, dust and the river, as well as mediating, through the narrator's overview, between the book's world and the reader's world.

One significant element linking the book's world to that of the mid-nineteenth century is the mention of the Board of Trade. This administrative body had seemed to Burke in 1780 a clear instance of empty and abusive royal patronage when he proposed abolishing it: "We want no instructions from boards of trade, or from any other board."[3] But by the 1830s the industrial revolution had given

3. "Speech on . . . Economical Reformation," in *The Works of Edmund Burke* (Boston: Little, Brown, 1884), 2:342.

it new life, and its new statistical department provided the government with a growing array of facts from which economic policy could be determined. To Burke it seemed that commerce "flourishes most when left to itself,"[4] but half a century and more later, despite the energy directed against the Corn Laws and for Free Trade, it was clear that government had a place in business. By 1844 joint-stock companies no longer had to gain recognition through private acts of Parliament; they had merely to register with the Board of Trade. This new policy was devised in response to the huge increase in joint-stock incorporation fostered by the boom in railroads, which required far more capital than any other enterprise. Its effect was simultaneously to increase the ease and freedom of business (registration was faster and cheaper than private bills) and to bring business under government surveillance and potential control.[5]

Thus in referring to the Board of Trade, Dickens pointed to a crucial nexus of Victorian values and practice, and in condemning its inability to heed matters of dignity and decency in life and death, he hit at a grave flaw in his society, just as he had in *Bleak House*. But in *Our Mutual Friend* the tone of prophecy, the echo of the earlier social novels, whatever its resonance with the outer world, rings hollow within the book itself. For there are no actual connections among the Podsnaps, the dustheaps, and Betty comparable to those that move the earlier novels. Nor is there any social retribution within *Our Mutual Friend* large enough to justify the image of the falling dustheap. We have seen earlier the special function of plot in *Dombey and Son, Bleak House,* and even *Little Dorrit,* and the vision it projects of English society as intimately connected, in genealogical and historical relation, across the gulfs that separate classes. Plot provides a driving necessity to most of the relations between separated characters, not only making them meet but making their meetings significant for the book's action.

I would oppose this notion of plot to the techniques of simply telling a neat story without loose ends, or even to the technique in *Nicholas Nickleby* that reveals Smike at last as Ralph Nickleby's son. For such a shock is of thematic use but has only symbolic bearing on the action, because it surprises us. Inevitability is the characteristic of plot in the sense that I am using the term. The

4. Ibid., p. 341.
5. R. K. Webb, *Modern England* (New York: Dodd, Mead, 1968), p. 267.

plot is the ground from which the book's events spring and in which their roots can be traced. Such tracing-out, tracking-down, investigation is the narrative thrust of the earlier comprehensive novels, but even in *Little Dorrit* Dickens experiments with a relaxation of this mode. In his monthly number plan, one of the famous "mems," for the first number of *Little Dorrit,* he remarks on the disparate characters brought together in the first scene: *"Try this uncertainty and* THIS NOT-PUTTING OF THEM *together, as a new means of interest* [denotes *single* and DOUBLE underlining in original]."[6] We have analyzed in Chapter II the various figurative means of connection that already begin to conjoin these characters, but as we also noted there, the novel finally brings them together through plot as well. This "uncertainty" proves only a technique of suspense within the mystery framework rather than a challenge to that framework. *Our Mutual Friend,* however, significantly diverges from the old model.

The past that exercises its force in *Our Mutual Friend* is no buried secret that demands fearful glances backward; rather it is a very explicit will. The interrelations that do exist among the various social groups of the novel reveal character rather than advance the laying bare of mysterious corruption. The murder that sets the book going, that of Radfoot mistaken for John Harmon, is never solved. Harmon never even locates what he calls "the scene of my death": "the wall, the dark doorway, the flight of stairs, and the room" where "it was not I" for those incomprehensible moments before "a downward slide" brought "consciousness" and "it was I . . . struggling there alone in the water" (II, 13). The recovery of such original, criminal scenes had been crucial to the earlier books, but here it fades away.

Our Mutual Friend has an intricate story line, but it does not have a coherent plot like the earlier novels, nor is London used as a basis for coherence. As the area of Bradley Headstone's school is described, it reveals no more meaning than did the view from Todgers's in *Martin Chuzzlewit.* The neighborhood

> looked like a toy neighborhood taken in blocks out of a box by a child of particularly incoherent mind. . . . Here, one side of a new street; there, a large solitary public-house facing nowhere; here, another unfinished street already in ruins;

6. Paul D. Herring, "Dickens' Monthly Number Plans for *Little Dorrit,*" *Modern Philology* 64 (1966):23.

> there, a church; here, an immense new warehouse; there, a dilapidated old country villa; then, a medley of black ditch, sparkling cucumber-frame, rank field, richly cultivated kitchen-garden, brick viaduct, arch-spanned canal, and disorder of frowsiness and fog. As if the child had given the table a kick and gone to sleep.
>
> [II, 1]

The scene's incoherence breaks down the ordering power of the syntactic antitheses; the rhythmic alternation of "here" and "there" yields to a "medley" of listing and finally "disorder." Nonetheless, no sense of danger to the observer emerges here as it did at Todgers's. Indeed, the conceit of the child with his toys is repeated and laid to rest in the scene at the Children's Hospital where little Johnny Harmon dies: "Over most of the beds, the toys were yet grouped as the children had left them when they last laid themselves down, and in their innocent grotesqueness and incongruity, they might have stood for the children's dreams" (II, 9). Not that Dickens sees this as a good way to plan a city; but nothing is done to fill the scene with promise of revelation or to deliver on any such sense that may linger in our expectations from reading Dickens's earlier novels. We may perform extensive interpretation to align such a passage with Dickens's pre-Freudian sense of dreams and the unconscious in his analysis of civilization and its discontents, but there is no such activity by the narrator.

Such highly energized London scenes as the Podsnap or Veneering interiors—or the outdoors moments such as that when Eugene Wrayburn follows Rogue Riderhood down to the river one windy evening when "it seemed as if the streets were absorbed by the sky, and the night were all in the air" (I, 12)—provide "a world attuned" to the story line, but the connections must be made at the verbal level by the reader rather than by the narrator or author at the level of action.[7] London has become less a functional social system than a city of words. Critical scrutiny of the book's meetings between widely separated characters reveals how little such meetings build plot.

After inheriting the fortune derived from old John Harmon's dustheaps, Boffin hires Wegg for a servant—of sorts—and once we

7. On the "world attuned" see Percy Lubbock, *The Craft of Fiction* (1921; rpt. New York: Viking, 1957), pp. 214–215.

have met Wegg and Boffin, we follow Wegg to the shop of his friend Mr. Venus, and through the love of Mr. Venus for Pleasant Riderhood, this chain links the mounds to the riverside. It remains up to the reader, however, to make meaning from the analogies among the mounds, Venus's taxidermy, Pleasant's pawnship, and the body-fishing of Rogue and Gaffer Hexam.

Wegg's digging around in the dustheaps in search of a suppressed will hollowly echoes Dickens's old mystery plots. From the very first Dickens intended Wegg's game to be fruitless, as he introduces the "friendly move" in the "mem" for No. IV, "and establish[es] Wegg at the Bower . . . on a false scent."[8] Dickens has a note to himself about the wills in the "mem" for No. XIX-XX which resembles his note for the last number of *Little Dorrit* (see Chapter IV, above) in setting out an obscure issue that must be clarified. The explanation reveals, however, that there was no mystery, that Boffin has just been leading Wegg on: "Finding certain signs . . . that Wegg was poking about, and delving in the Mounds," Boffin "took . . . up again" the hidden will, safely out of Wegg's reach. The real importance of Wegg's poking and delving is to provide a concrete basis for meditation on the dustheaps, which without his continual presence, his wooden leg half-stuck in them, would become themselves a false scent, mere tokens of willed meaning.

Comparing Wegg with Krook suggests the difference between the construction of *Bleak House* and of *Our Mutual Friend.* Even as Wegg and the dust mounds mediate between the river and society through the language generated around them, so Krook mediates between Chesney Wold and Tom-all-Alone's in his role as "Lord Chancellor." Yet Krook actually harbors Hawdon, and his rummaging for secrets, although as disgusting and foolish as Wegg's, results in the papers that allow the Smallweeds to try to blackmail Lady Dedlock and start her on her journey to death. Along with Jo, Krook is at the plot's nerve center. Wegg, however, sets up waves of possible meaning, not of action. His long, vivid renditions of misers parallel and substantiate Boffin's performance as a miser, but they in no way make Boffin act like a miser. His pretended miserliness is part of an independent plan.

Boffin's new wealth brings him new acquaintances beyond Wegg.

8. Throughout this chapter I cite Dickens's "mems" from Ernest Boll, "The Plotting of *Our Mutual Friend,*" *Modern Philology* 42 (1944):102–122.

Wishing to fulfill charitable responsibilities, Boffin seeks out the Reverend Frank Milvey, and through Milvey a connection is made late in the book with Bradley Headstone. When Boffin and his associates are en route to the marriage of Eugene Wrayburn and Lizzie Hexam, Milvey recognizes Headstone moping about the railway station, tries to alleviate his evident distress, but only drives him to a fit when he reveals that Eugene is not dead but going to wed Lizzie. Although this chance meeting increases Bradley's torment, it leads to no action; Bradley does not move again until Riderhood begins his blackmail attempt. In his "mem" for No. XVIII, Dickens notes, "glimpse of Bradley in his misery." Evidently this loose construction, building from glimpses rather than causes, is fully in line with Dickens's own idea of the novel.

Further evidence for Dickens's plan in *Our Mutual Friend* comes from the connection with Betty Higden that Boffin makes through Milvey. We have already seen that the narrative rhetoric preparing for Betty Higden's death resembles that which in Dickens's earlier books signals a plot connection that brings retributive justice across wide social gulfs. Betty Higden, however, figures in no such action. Her death does not even act as a short circuit to connect Eugene Wrayburn with Lizzie Hexam. Shunning such coincidence, and the view of society that underlies it, Dickens leaves Eugene to locate Lizzie by bribing Jenny Wren's father. Betty's death does cause the meeting of Lizzie with Bella Wilfer, an important chance to display the characters of the two girls. Dickens's "mem" for No. XIII says, "LIZZIE TO WORK AN INFLUENCE ON BELLA'S CHARACTER, AT ITS WAVERING POINT [denotes DOUBLE underlining in original]." "Influence" becomes a matter of private personality, no longer "something in the air" of public circumstance. Furthermore, the scene also presents our only image of Lizzie's mind over the long period that she is separated from Eugene and provides the background for her crucial conversation with him that Bradley observes and after which he murderously attacks Eugene.

Boffin's new wealth also brings him into high society as well as into contact with poor people like Betty Higden and Wegg. The Veneerings call on him, and through them the Lammles meet the Boffins. The Lammles attempt to flatter Bella Wilfer (who has become the Boffins' protégée), weasel a prideful confession from her, and in their hour of need try to advance themselves by acting against Rokesmith. But they only precipitate a mock crisis, for Rokesmith is already in secret league with the Boffins. Although the Lammles are the pretext for Boffin's great show of rage, they are not a necessary cause. That is, their action moves the story sequence along but is not part of the plot. The real results of their scheme are a display of reassuringly good character on Boffin's part ("The Golden Dustman Rises a Little"), pathetic friendship from Miss Podsnap, and final decency from Mrs. Lammle.

John Harmon is also involved in a number of long-connecting chains of relations, but they too prove to have little plot significance. His accidental falling in with Radfoot projects him into the disguises that he maintains through most of the book, but these roles make only a temporary and unserious joining of himself to the lower classes. His voluntary choice of a new role is very different from the leveling bonds that activated the earlier novels. The murder of Radfoot is certainly sobering, but it does not make the disguise essentially more weighty, for Harmon retains the power to doff his disguise at any time. Nor do the further ramifications of Harmon's disguise create plot. The only fruit of Harmon's first alias as Handford is to create the rule of the game that Rokesmith (Harmon's later name) must avoid Lightwood and the inspector. A few mildly amusing but mostly embarrassing impasses arise from this, as Harmon reflects how droll it would be to be accused of his own murder. In his planning Dickens seems really to have cared for this aspect of Harmon's role. The "mem" for No. V notes "*Work on Detach the Secretary from Lightwood* [denotes *single* underlining in original]." The "mem" for the last number summarizes Rokesmith's role: "His supposed poverty. He seems under suspicion of murder. BELLA ALWAYS FAITHFUL [denotes DOUBLE underlining in original]." This twist of Rokesmith's activities, then, primarily puts Bella's character to yet one more test. Even where its success is small, Dickens's construction in *Our Mutual Friend* aims at revealing and testing character in a more concerted way than in any of the earlier social novels.

Harmon's meeting with Bradley Headstone is one of the most overdetermined episodes in the book. It arises from Betty Higden's leaving on her fatal journey, in order to free Sloppy from his responsibility to her. Harmon wants a tutor for Sloppy and hopes, for very vague reasons connected with his exoneration of Gaffer Hexam, to open "some channel altogether independent of Lightwood" to Lizzie Hexam (II, 14). So he contacts Bradley, who he knows is Charley Hexam's master. Harmon imprudently mentions Eugene Wrayburn and Lizzie Hexam in the same breath, and all that comes of the interview is another demonstration of Bradley's passion for Lizzie. Though in this book of the river we expect significance from the metaphor of "channel," we never even hear any more about a tutor for Sloppy; nor does Harmon's visit to Pleasant Riderhood lead through Venus back to the mounds in any new way.

In *Bleak House* Hawdon's work as a copyist for Jarndyce and Jarndyce is a crucial pivot in the plot, as is Snagsby's stationery store; and in *Little Dorrit* Amy serves Mrs. Clennam and arouses Arthur's conscience. Mr. Wilfer is a clerk for Veneering. It is thematically significant that money from the house enriches Veneering while his small wages cripple Mr. Wilfer's life, but the book never activates the connection. Once as dinner-table capital Veneering mentions that he employs the father of the murdered heir's intended. If poor do not affect rich, neither do the rich affect the poor. As opposed to the effect of Merdle's bankruptcy in *Little Dorrit,* Veneering's smash does not affect the lower orders at all, for Mr. Wilfer has already become secretary of the Harmon fortune by the time Veneering falls.

The most important relation between the classes in *Our Mutual Friend* is that between Lizzie Hexam and Eugene Wrayburn, and the most important fact about it is that it is determined by no past secrets or shames but grows from the activity of free wills in the present. Although the Harmon story creates the first opportunity for the meeting of the two, from a very early point it is of no further relevance. (We have already noted how Betty Higden's death is not allowed to bring Eugene to Lizzie.) Eugene lacks in all his other relations the ability to make decisions and act on them. His desire for Lizzie is the means of healing his will. His pursuit of Lizzie enables Eugene to discover in himself feelings of cruelty, power, and aggression during their riverside interview; and even after Bradley Headstone's assault nearly kills him, Eugene marries Lizzie and cuts himself loose from his father's wishes and "the voice of society." A note made by Dickens in the "mem" for No. IV reveals the importance he ascribed to the gradual development and revelation of Eugene's character, "BRING ON EUGENE. IMPLY [denotes TRIPLE underlining in original] some change between him and Lizzie Hexam."[9]

9. For the most interesting analysis of Eugene, see Taylor Stoehr, *Dickens: The Dreamer's Stance* (Ithaca: Cornell University Press, 1965), pp. 208–222; and for the most challenging evaluation of Dickens's suc-

The relaxation of plot in *Our Mutual Friend* allows a mixing of characters such as we associate with Thackeray.[10] Recall a characteristic moment from *Vanity Fair* that goes against the grain of Dickens's earlier social novels but is much like this one. Briggs and Becky meet on the street after a long separation, and the narrator squashes Briggs's "ejaculations of wonder" by commenting, "People meet other people every day, yet some there are who insist upon discovering miracles."[11] This everyday mixing encourages a free play of character at times reminiscent of George Eliot, but only for Lizzie, Eugene, and those involved in their story. The story line involving Harmon and Boffin does not work in the same way. Dickens's first conception of someone like Harmon emphasized the "singular view of life and character" imparted by his secret identity.[12] Harmon's view, however, is more hazy than rich and rewarding. The problem lies not even so much in the early series of aliases as in the later chapters, once he is finally and certainly revealed to us. At this point a clear and singular view does not establish itself, and we are still denied Harmon's candid consciousness because he is party to the Boffins's secret mousetrap play to cure Bella of her greed. Dickens's desire to trick the reader as well as Bella prevented him from realizing the full potential of his new mode.

Dickens's first thoughts for *Our Mutual Friend* involved three germinal ideas corresponding roughly to the Society, Harmon, and lower-class elements of the finished novel. Although as he began to write he saw "the one main line on which the story is to turn,"[13] his "mem" drawn up after No. X shows him still envisioning the novel in three distinct units: the "part of the story" concerning Lizzie Hexam and including Eugene Wrayburn, Jenny Wren, and Bradley Headstone; the "part of the story" concerning Harmon and

---

cess with him, see Robert Garis, *The Dickens Theatre* (Oxford: Clarendon, 1965), especially pp. 229–233.

10. Thus J. Hillis Miller likens the novel to a "slow dance," *Charles Dickens: The World of His Novels* (Cambridge: Harvard University Press, 1958), p. 287.

11. William Makepeace Thackeray, *Vanity Fair* (1847–1848), ed. Geoffrey and Kathleen Tillotson (Boston: Houghton Mifflin, 1963), chap. 40.

12. *The Letters of Charles Dickens,* ed. Walter Dexter (London: Nonesuch, 1938), 3:271.

13. Ibid., p. 364.

including Bella Wilfer, the Boffins, and Wegg; and the "chorus" of high society and their "Humbug, Social and Parliamentary."

If we work from Dickens's own plan and our analysis of interaction, we can distribute the book's characters in the three groupings, corresponding roughly to class, that Dickens has established:

	River group	Dustheap group	Social chorus
Daughters	Jenny Lizzie	Bella	Georgiana
Sons	Charley	Harmon	Eugene
Brutes	Rogue	Bradley	Lammle
Rascals		Wegg	Fledgeby
Homes	Hexams' Jenny's	Boffins' Wilfers'	Veneerings' Podsnaps'

Except for the defection of Eugene and Bradley to Lizzie, each action remains within its own column, but nonetheless, people in all three groups face broadly similar problems.

Violence and constraint are omnipresent. Just as much as Bella and Jenny, Georgiana Podsnap is driven to anger and aggressiveness in those relations that should be warmest: "'It's enough for me to see how loving you and your husband are. . . . I couldn't bear to have anything of that sort going on with myself. I should beg and pray to—to have the person taken away and trampled upon'" (II, 4). Sons are crushed by their fathers, John Harmon as well as Charley and Eugene, and the need to fight back if one is not to be annihilated can lead to the excessive selfishness and hardness that are ruining Charley Hexam. Even Harmon says: "'I repress myself and force myself to act a part. It is not in tameness of spirit that I submit. I have a settled purpose'" (III, 9). The doubling of Lizzie and Jenny—interestingly Dickens seems to refer to Lizzie as "Jenny" in his first "mem"—reflects the need to keep Lizzie free from violent traits; and the displacement of Eugene, whose clearest links are with Bradley and Rogue, seems similarly motivated. The rivalry of Fledgeby and Lammle is most simply the struggle between the whiskered brute and the beardless sneak. No systematic social view joins these individual violent characters into a totality; they remain an aggregate. They are all like each other, but no longer as in Dickens's earlier social novels do they link together in action as well as theme.

THE ESCAPE FROM SYNECDOCHE

IF WE TURN FROM THIS EXAMINATION of the world of *Our Mutual Friend* as specified by story and interaction and instead consider the three stories more broadly, we find large implications in Dickens's change from the tightly integrated mystery plot to the looser structure of *Our Mutual Friend.* In his treatment of the Veneering group, Dickens turned with his freedom in the opposite direction from psychology. As "experience" turns inward, the language of social representation becomes pure surface. The Veneering parties play a structural role in *Our Mutual Friend* different from that to which Dickens usually puts parties. The party based on no love or sociability, the antithesis of the famous "Dickensian" festivity, was a longstanding target of Dickens's scorn. Yet never before had he held it up as a thing in itself, pure emptiness and wilfully self-isolating smugness. The fantastic play of language and the grotesque physical circumstantiality of the scene reduce to insignificance the partygoers' claims to personality.

In the earlier comprehensive novels a social event is linked to its central character, who is in turn a focus of the book's action: "Mr. Dombey represented in himself the wind, the shade, and the autumn of the christening. He stood in his library to receive the company, as hard and cold as the weather; and when he looked out through the glass room, at the trees in the little garden, their brown and yellow leaves came fluttering down, as if he blighted them" (*DS* 5). The figure of representation, the synecdoche that relates part to whole, is, as we have seen, crucial to the technique and vision of Dickens at this point. In *Little Dorrit* the perfect reciprocity between Merdle and the society he represents also shows clearly: "Mr. Merdle's right hand was filled with the evening paper, and the evening paper was filled with Mr. Merdle" (*LD* II, 12). If such a man has a "complaint," it cannot be "solely his own affair" (I, 22).

The Merdle parties in *Little Dorrit* demonstrate Merdle's nullity —another version of the "nobody" trope that Dickens first thought to organize the book with—and thereby prefigure his bankruptcy and the failure of the society that has made him the measure of its value and values. In the portrait of a finance capitalist who seems literally to believe that every deal he makes to enrich himself and his suitors is a duty that he owes society, laissez-faire hypocrisy comes to absurdity, as does the synecdochic confusion between society—meaning everyone—and "Society," the world of fashion.

Yet, when he finally kills himself, a new synecdoche prevails, for the taint from his "carrion" (II, 25) ruins Arthur Clennam as well as impoverishing the Dorrits. Furthermore, Mrs. Merdle's son has married Fanny Dorrit and works in the Circumlocution Office, linking its ruinous "how not to do it" to Merdle's "how not to be" in both plot and point.

In *Our Mutual Friend*, however, the situation is different. If Dickens cites Podsnap as a "representative man" (I, 11) and calls a whole way of life "Podsnappery," he also ridicules such synecdoches through his treatment of Veneering. Veneering is declared a "representative man" in his turn and sent to Parliament (II, 3), but the mechanics of the election reveal the fraud: he does not represent his constituents. Veneering's attempt to define Twemlow's relation to the new baby reveals how empty yet problematic representation has become. Twemlow "stands in the proud position—I mean . . . proudly stands in the position—or I ought rather to say . . . places . . . myself in the proud position of himself standing in the simple position—of baby's godfather" (I, 10).[14]

The Veneerings themselves are even less than the surface that their name implies, for no one so much as notices them at the sumptuous dinners that they have bought for society, and they will vanish without a trace when Mr. Veneering's credit busts. In apparent opposition is the hideous solidity of the Podsnaps. Even Podsnap, however, is far removed from any reality. Although he is in marine insurance, the nearest he comes to the sea or a ship is when he inspires Veneering to coin the ship-of-state cliché in his election speech. His massive plate resembles nothing so much as the dustheaps in its lack of value for life. It suggests that the dustheaps' worst threat is not to fall down, but to remain standing. Harmon's money turns bright again as the dustheaps are removed, but Podsnap's plate and routine crush out life. Consequently Georgiana Podsnap is full of hostility and overeager to grasp at the Lammles' false friendship. The Lammles themselves are attempting to reproduce the same kind of loveless marriage they are trapped in, in order to make the money that their own union did not bring.

In contrast, John Harmon dreads being forced by his father's will to marry Bella Wilfer, thereby "perpetuating the fate" of evil that

14. On the relations between political and artistic representation, see Richard Bernheimer, *The Nature of Representation* (New York: New York University Press, 1961), chaps. 8–9.

the riches have brought (II, 13). In its bare outlines the Harmon story is the most boldly optimistic statement of Dickens's later phase. The successful purpose of the Boffins' and Harmon's ruse is to bring the old gold out from the dark and let it "sparkle in the sunlight" (IV, 13). Although Bella and John have their baby before they become wealthy, Dickens unquestionably includes the £100,000 as an important part of the happy ending. In his "mem" for the last part, he concludes his summary of Bella, "she is Mrs John Harmon, and comes into no end of money." Not since *Chuzzlewit,* the similar trickery of which we have noted, has a fortune been so emphasized or an ending been so happy.

Yet *Our Mutual Friend* goes beyond even *Martin Chuzzlewit* in the audacity of this resolution, for in the earlier novel, Old Martin's ruse had served only to test and expose Pecksniff for what he had been all along, but in this work the elaborate artifice of Boffin and Harmon actually converts Bella from the perspective acquired through long years of financial want at the extreme bottom edge of shabby gentility. Against the experience of her whole life as she has understood it, she comes to see "realities" in another context than that of "poverty and wealth" (II, 8).

Dickens had this device in mind from the time that the miserhood of Boffin first appears in No. XII, for in the "mem" he wrote, "Mr Boffin and Rokesmith and Mrs Boffin, having, unknown to the reader, arranged their plan, now strike in with it." Even earlier, however, Dickens seems to have aimed this way, for in a letter written at the time of the ninth number, he comments archly, "It amuses me to find that you don't see your way to a certain M. F. of ours. I have a horrible suspicion that you may begin to be fearfully knowing at somewhere about No. 12 or 13. But you shan't if I can help it." Since Harmon reveals the mysteries of his identity fully in the tenth number, Dickens must be referring to some other "M. F. of ours," and the reference to the twelfth number and the determination to preserve a secret from the reader suggest strongly that it must be Boffin. A second letter definitely alludes to this turn of the story, for Dickens congratulates himself, the month after No. XII, for "from the first tending to a purpose which you couldn't foresee."[15]

These two letters strongly suggest that this ruse was one of the elements in the book that gave Dickens most active pleasure in

15. *Letters of Charles Dickens,* 3:412, 422.

writing, for no other letters about the book have the same playful vigor in them; they tend rather to the gloomy or dogged in tone. More characteristically the letters speak about his feeling "dazed" at his return to the "large canvas" and "big brushes" of the *Pickwick* form and about the "pain" that comes even in this spacious form from the "throwing away" of interesting points in the service of composition. "Industry" he felt he had, but "invention" seemed wanting.[16] Yet in the Boffin ruse he invented a device to cancel the weight of the past, to segregate for the better a character from the circumstances of her life and the values of the society around her, to split a part off from the whole. This technique is at one with our general observation about the ways in which the various portions of society in *Our Mutual Friend* do not connect into a totality.

Bella's conversion comes through emotional and psychological means rather than intellectual and sociological ones. The ruse of Harmon and the Boffins to act out the selfishness they wish to cure in Bella typifies the nineteenth-century method of treating madness through "recognition by mirror": "It is not a question of dissipating error by the impressive spectacle of a truth . . . but of treating madness in its arrogance rather than its aberration."[17] The aberrant society can be disregarded, and the individual's arrogance treated through fiction. In no other of Dickens's later novels can such a change be so complete. Esther Summerson still bears her poxmarks, Amy Dorrit the prison's shadow, and Arthur Clennam the taint of Calvinism, but the dustheaps can be removed and bright gold remain. Bella's saving vision is not an overview that reveals interconnections but insight into an analogy. Metaphor replaces synecdoche as "the imagination's new beginning."

TOWARD A NEW ECONOMY OF WRITING

DICKENS'S CONCERN FOR SELF-RENOVATION in his writing projects itself thematically into the action of *Our Mutual Friend*. The hope for a fresh start is the powerful basis for both of the love stories. Harmon describes himself as having "now to begin life" when he first approaches Boffin as Rokesmith (I, 8), and Bella, after the apparent humiliation of Rokesmith has had its effect on her, de-

16. Ibid., pp. 378, 394.

17. Michel Foucault, *Madness and Civilization* (1961), trans. Richard Howard (New York: Random House, 1965), p. 264.

termines to leave the Boffins and "begin again entirely on [her] own account" (III, 15). Only on such a basis can they marry, and if Harmon comes into possession of the gold that was once his father's, it is nonetheless not "through any act of [his] father's" (IV, 14) but only because the Boffins have broken the old man's will and voluntarily given up their fortune to the child they had loved and pitied. Lizzie Hexam is "left free by [her] father's death" (II, 1), and in his love for her, Eugene Wrayburn breaks with his father and the life of Society that has made him indolent and worthless.

The book also explores the dangers of such innovation, from the "bran-new" Veneerings to the problems of Mortimer, who has "founded" his identity on Eugene (II, 6). Charley Hexam is perhaps the most straightforward negative instance of new beginnings. From the first, Lizzie sees that "it is a great work to have cut your way from father's life, and to have made a new and good beginning" (I, 3), but Charley's attempt to "seek his fortune" can also be defined as having "disowned his own father" (I, 6), and his father then disowns him in turn. His attempts to "cancel the past" (II, 15) lead to conflict with Lizzie that alienates him from her, and finally his determination to keep "going on to the end" (IV, 7) drives him to sever relations with his mentor and only friend, Bradley Headstone. Charley's quest is undercut when he defines his end as "perfect respectability" (IV, 7), but one cannot so easily avoid the issues raised by the radically antisocial pattern of his course, for his determinations echo Dickens's.

Bradley Headstone may seem at first determined by the "origin" that he wishes "forgotten" (II, 1), but he transforms himself through the "connexion" he wishes "voluntarily" to make with Lizzie, and he emphasizes that such a connection is much stronger than any that would follow merely from blood or social station (II, 1). His attempt to kill Eugene Wrayburn ultimately arises not from class antagonisms or money, dust piles, or misgovernment, but from anarchic personal passion. His struggles reach forward "towards" his crime (III, 11). His bizarre pursuits of Eugene are in order to witness, indeed to construct, the scene of Eugene and Lizzie intimately together, so as then to strike down Eugene. If, as we have seen, Harmon's traumatic scene of struggle by the river is never reconstructed, that scene disseminates and projects itself through the book into Bradley's scenes, first with Eugene and then with Rogue Riderhood, that finally culminate in the watery death that

Harmon escaped. Bradley's spying on Eugene is an inverse Nadgettry in a world where one may feel more guilt in detection than in crime itself (cf. I, 13).

If, through Bradley, Dickens undoes one pattern of detection important to his earlier work, through Wegg, Dickens reduces and criticizes the larger pattern of the authorial wish for omniscient overview. For years Wegg sets up his corner nut-and-ballad stand by a residence that he comes to call "Our House." Despite his having "no authority," Wegg gives names to the inhabitants "of his own invention" and exercises a similar "imaginary power" over their affairs and those of their household. Although he had never been inside, "this was no impediment to his arranging it according to a plan of his own," which it costs him great trouble to devise "so as to account for everything in its external appearance" (I, 5). This seller of stale treats and amusements performs with his house the same activity that a novelist like Dickens has done in making the great social fictions of his earlier years, making up unauthorized models of his own. A man in the entertainment business taking himself too seriously, he has no special power or warrant, no magic, just an outsider's will to appropriation and coherence. Only in the glee of his misguided imagination does Wegg have the possibility of becoming the "Evil Genius" of the house with "power to strip the roof off" (III, 7) in the gesture of detection that had once been so desired for the "good spirit" of *Dombey and Son.*

After the triumphant overview of *Bleak House, Little Dorrit* already begins to question that power. The omnipresent vision of the sun in the opening chapters emphasizes its oppressive force and becomes associated, as we saw in Chapter II, with the rigoristic need of Mrs. Clennam to put everything in its place through a self-serving fiction. In contrast, Arthur begins to liberate himself when as a dreamer he looks up and out from his window (*LD* I, 3), and his gesture is repeated by Amy Dorrit in the illustration that accompanies her self-allegorizing tale of the "Little Princess" (I, 24). In the opening number of Book II, her view over Venice melts away all the city's surfaces into "unreality" and returns her to the unchanging "realities" of her formative experiences in the Marshalsea (II, 3). This tendency within *Little Dorrit* to replace overview with inner view predominates in *Our Mutual Friend.* In this novel the vision from the rooftops is not a means of clairvoyantly seeing into the interrelations of English society, but a way of escaping that society with Jenny Wren, who invites us to "come up and be dead" with her: "You see the clouds rushing on above the narrow streets, not minding them, and you see the golden arrows pointing at the mountains in the sky from which the wind comes" (II, 5). The scene has the vitality that one felt in the view from Todgers's, but it points upward, not down into the street.

These reductions and displacements of the sort of overview that had once been in part the privilege of the detectives, and more fully of the narrator, are of a piece with the move away from a coherently organized action to reveal the meaning hidden in English life. By this time there was already too much of that. The plea of the "good spirit" for organized self-knowledge on the part of the English had been greatly answered. England as a whole was now literally mapped. The Ordnance Survey project, begun in the late eighteenth century and spurred by the threats of the Napoleonic Wars, finally reached completion in 1862.[18] The new technology of the telegraph, with its power to annihilate distance and render communication instantaneous, made Reuter's news service unparalleled. The telegraph had briefly struck Dickens as a device for connecting two separate sets of characters in the opening number of a novel, shortly before he conceived *Our Mutual Friend,* but he never developed this conceit.[19] The railroad industry, however, quickly exploited the telegraph, and it had been in use since the 1850s as an increasingly common and effective means of organizing railroad signaling. Crucially, it was used not just for information, but for control.[20] The network of its lines had the effect of an overview.

The willful, individual energy of the railroad had in *Dombey and Son* or *Moby-Dick* represented all that challenged the established order, but now it was harnessed technologically, as it had also been harnessed administratively through government surveillance. The massive capital requirements of the railroad made it the leading edge in the move from individual enterprise to joint-stock companies, and such large scale and anonymity entailed further augmentation in the apparatus of management. But the railroad is no longer an imaginative center in *Our Mutual Friend,* despite its historical significance. It is simply there, assimilated into the

18. E. J. Hobsbawm, *The Age of Capital* (New York: Charles Scribner's Sons, 1975), p. 52.

19. *Letters of Charles Dickens,* 3:302.

20. Henry Parris, *Government and the Railways in Nineteenth-Century Britain* (London: Routledge and Kegan Paul, 1965), p. 177.

book's world. Not even Dickens's own nearly fatal involvement in a rail disaster while writing the novel (see his postscript) energizes it beyond the routine. The railroad functions merely as an established part of ongoing modern life, which seems well—too well—under control.

As the novel indifferently takes in the railroad, so it does also the world of administration. The Registrar General, whose office had only been founded in 1836 and whose reports by the middle forties were crucial documents in the arguments over public health measures, had become so much a part of English life that he is mentioned in the characters' conversation in *Our Mutual Friend.* It is not just pernicious social policy but simply inaccurate by this time for Podsnap to cry, "Centralization. No. Never with my consent. Not English" (I, 11). In his speeches on behalf of public health around the time of *Bleak House,* Dickens had denounced fears of centralization and mocked the alternative of "vestrylization," and the view had prevailed that centralization was only a red herring to divert attention from the real issue of "irresponsibility."[21]

Nonetheless, as a writer Dickens is with Podsnap, for the novel as a whole is not centralized. What had once been the novelist's prophetic task is now safely in the hands of the constituted authorities, and literature as an institution must find another task for itself, another relation to its materials and its audience. The novelist steps away from complicity with the establishment by abandoning the position of overview that had been so hard won. Furthermore, in his view of a social world that gives value to, capitalizes on, makes profit out of, every scrap of life by recirculation, Dickens seems strangely to appeal to waste—a certain giving up—as the only way to real life. Just as the novelist had done in *Bleak House,* the taxidermist and "articulator" (I, 7) Mr. Venus has " 'the patience to fit together on wires the whole framework of society—I allude to the human skelinton' " (III, 6), and in *Bleak House* too the illumination needed to see the whole shape could only be achieved at the cost of death after death, each revealing a bit more of the whole. But we do not want to be in the grotesque shop of Venus, or out on the river with Gaffer, or stumping in the mounds, ready for a

21. *The Speeches of Charles Dickens,* ed. K. J. Fielding (Oxford: Clarendon, 1960), p. 130; Edwin Chadwick, *Report on the Sanitary Condition of the Labouring Population of Great Britain* (1842), ed. M. W. Flinn (Edinburgh: Edinburgh University Press, 1965), p. 394.

fall. We want to get away from this closed system of life and death.

By not using a plot based on buried mystery and by emphasizing voluntary association and a change of heart, Dickens has brought a hope of escape from social determinants into *Our Mutual Friend* and has opened interstices in the social web where free play is available apart from the whole. He has given up the system of overview and synecdoche that characterized the earlier social novels and offered instead a more dispersed world, one that follows the river rather than relying upon synoptic perspective. Like the river too is the unfixed circulation of figurative language in the book, moving like the shares of paper that pass from hand to hand in the market. The wild play of metaphor, the abundance of pure word games, as well as the endlessly interacting images, all point to a freedom in his writing that Dickens achieved in liberating himself from the constraints of the sociological plot and the commitment to usable meaning.

Dickens wrote in the process of composing *Our Mutual Friend:* "I have grown hard to satisfy, and write very slowly. And I have so much—not fiction—that *will* be thought of, when I don't want to think of it, that I am forced to take more care than I once took."[22] "Care" operates as a force of exclusion. Dickens must take care not to think of certain things in writing, to make sure that his page is kept clear of those things. Such a process produces the more open texture of the novel; there is space where things have been omitted. What must be kept out is what is "not fiction." The deliberate sense of writing fiction, something that is all fiction, a fiction made up of fiction, corresponds again to our sense of the book's newly specialized orientation.

It has been often noted that *Our Mutual Friend* is obsessively, recurrently concerned with the relation of life and death. In the years that *Our Mutual Friend* was being formed as a project by Dickens (1861–1863), nine people close to him died, including his mother, his son Walter, and his friend, contemporary, and rival Thackeray. In contrast to this erosion in time, something else was happening that seemed to deny that time had any such power. In 1847, before writing *David Copperfield,* Dickens had confided to Forster the famous autobiographical fragment describing his childhood history and its continuing significance for him. In 1862 Dickens writes with concern to Forster that in the last five years, with in-

22. *Letters of Charles Dickens,* 3:384.

creasing frequency, the "child" within him described in that narrative has been returning.[23] Disturbing as such an uncanny return may be, it also provides reassurance of one's continuing youthful vitality, despite what is happening to everyone else. By separating oneself from life in writing, by taking proper care, one may nourish that youthful ghost and find within it now, as had been possible at the time of *Copperfield* also, the possibility of self-renewal, a continuation exempt from the accidents of biological contingency. No one was to understand this strategy better in his own later years than Henry James, but it was James as a young reviewer who criticized most savagely the old Dickens for beginning to find his way to the haven that James would forty years later make his own and share with us in his prefaces to The New York Edition. James found *Our Mutual Friend* "dug out as with a spade and pickaxe" and rather than being "seen, known, or felt," it was above all "*written.*"[24]

23. Ibid., p. 297.

24. [Henry James], review in *The Nation,* 21 December 1865, rpt. in *Dickens: The Critical Heritage,* ed. Philip Collins (London: Routledge and Kegan Paul, 1971), pp. 469–470.

Conclusion

By the time Dickens wrote *Our Mutual Friend,* he had redrawn the "boundaries of fiction" that his earlier career established. The alliance with journalism, social theory and polemic, and history that had allowed his fiction its powerful engagement with the public world now yielded to a new specialization that would tend increasingly to restrict literature to the private realm. The "experience" that blended with theory in *Bleak House* and *The French Revolution* to compose a wholly accessible world of human action was already for Melville in *Moby-Dick* increasingly difficult to specify directly, and in *Our Mutual Friend* it has moved almost wholly inward. No longer does any major action link class to class to reveal the public shape of experience; no overview brings together all the private homes of the city into one whole. Balzac had taken as his ambition to be "secretary" to French society and thereby show it to itself.[1] John Harmon, however, in becoming Boffin's secretary is "one privy to a secret" (*OED*) that bears directly only upon himself and a few others, that of his own dissimulated identity. He alienates himself from this identity to become "one whose office it is to write for another" (*OED*), and he can fulfill himself only by abandoning this role and resuming the selfhood of John Harmon which gives continuity to his experience. Thus he withdraws from the public, documentary world, in which a "secretary" seems no more human than a "piece of furniture, mostly of mahogany" (*OMF* I, 15), just as in the overall construction of this work Dickens withdraws from that world into intimate enclosure.

1. *La Comédie humaine,* ed. Marcel Bouteron (Paris: Gallimard, 1950–1965), 1:7.

If the novelists of the mid-nineteenth century had to break across boundaries in order to achieve their characteristic forms and effects, so have I also had to cross boundaries within the discipline of literary studies. To analyze the making of the social novel, and especially its technique of overview and definition of the writer's "place," I have had to join the study of fiction to that of nonfictional prose and to break down the dichotomies that have marked off the study of American literature from that of English. The segregation of these areas has produced much valuable work; specialization is a disciplinary necessity. To gain new insight, however, has necessitated my overstepping, even at the cost of overlooking certain significant differences among the writers I study and affinities they share with writers I have ignored. I have myself taken something of an overview, drawing a new map in the hope of specifying fresh connections and relations.

In reading some of the work—published since I completed my own argument—that shares concern with my subject matter, I find across otherwise widely divergent positions a consensus opposed to the overview of nineteenth-century fiction. Terry Eagleton praises Dickens for his "scattering" effects that disrupt the "securely 'overviewing' eye of classical realism."[2] William C. Spengemann contrasts negatively the settled world of "domestic romance" (associated with England) to the strenuousness of the "adventurous muse" of American fiction. He therefore urges us to see the world "not as land looks on a map," but adventurously, "as a seaboard seen by men sailing."[3] John Romano praises Dickens for his allegiance to the perception that "reality defies formulation."[4] These critics make an important point. No one values literature for its complacency or stock forms. I have tried myself to show the extent to which the writers I have studied remained uneasy with the forms they achieved; that no one form lasted to be repeated.

Yet I must also insist upon the achievement of these writers. The

2. Terry Eagleton, *Criticism and Ideology* (London: NLB, 1976), pp. 126–127; see also Leo Bersani, "The Subject of Power," *Diacritics* 7, no. 3 (Fall 1977), pp. 2–21, especially pp. 16–17.

3. Ezra Pound, cited in William C. Spengemann, *The Adventurous Muse* (New Haven: Yale University Press, 1977), p. 7.

4. John Romano, *Dickens and Reality* (New York: Columbia University Press, 1978), p. 57.

"overviewing eye" was not already to hand for Dickens. It had to be fashioned as a technique. And this technique was in turn part of the great effort by which the people of the mid-nineteenth century tried to get a purchase on the chaotic mobility they felt lost in. A map may obscure much of the truth, but it has real use in pointing out some aspects of reality that may never be apprehensible as immediate experience. In contrast to the metaphysics of an ungraspable, "abiding primordial substratum" as reality,[5] we may appreciate the practical value of realized attempts to specify the world in fiction. We may therefore praise moments of coherence, as well as the moments of fading and failing that much recent criticism privileges. Recall that Emerson found poetic creativeness not "in staying at home, nor yet in travelling, but in transitions from one to the other."[6] Thus the movement toward making sense is no less valuable than that toward breaking sense. Rather than setting the fresh experience of protagonists against the "discursive, abstract language of generalizing narrators,"[7] we might better recognize that in Dickens, Carlyle, Melville, and Hawthorne narrative generalization is a crucial imaginative act. For all four of these writers it engages the richest linguistic resources they possess. Indeed, their narrative personae may be more significant creations than are any of their characters.

The current critical unease with overview, however, is more than literary. It is also political and must be confronted on this ground. Overview may simply seem elitist. Spengemann urges us with R. H. Dana "to come down from our heights . . . [to] the low places of life if we would learn truths."[8] Yet I hope I have shown that the overview itself provided a means of seeing and showing truths; that it raised many readers to an understanding of society that their place in it had previously denied them. There is no guarantee that ground-level experience reveals the truth. Fifty years beyond the writers I have studied, a similar problem arose for Theodore Dreiser. In his youth he "saw only the surface scene," even when "placed before a given series of facts," like a streetcar strike, that should have "given rise to at least some modest social speculation." But

5. Ibid, p. 62.

6. *Emerson's Complete Works,* Riverside Edition (Cambridge, Mass., 1883), 4:56.

7. Spengemann, *The Adventurous Muse,* p. 182.

8. Ibid., p. 7.

speculation requires distance, and only later could Dreiser move from the "stare" of experience to comprehend the larger picture, to "identify its true . . . social significance" and his "relationship" to it.[9] Norman Mailer has observed how much more powerful "outrage at injustice" becomes when it is joined to a "vision of society,"[10] and this formulation finely catches the progress of Dickens's career from *Oliver Twist* to *Bleak House*.

Overview may more complexly, yet still hostilely, be understood as part of a coercive, manipulative stance to the world that coincides with many of the economic and social relations of the nineteenth century most productive of misery for that time and ours. I have myself noted its link to the panopticon and factory organization, yet I do not think that in itself this connection condemns it. Many writers have not yet forgiven the English nineteenth century for giving us not a workers' revolution but instead the practical basis, both in government and industry, of modern management and bureaucracy. Yet even if the literature I have studied is part of the mid-nineteenth century "antipolitics" that saw also the rise of sociology and administration, nonetheless such new forms of intellectual and social organization made available great and significant new powers. Marx did not imagine that factory organization would be abolished, only that it would be transformed into new relations made possible by the energy released through the achievement of what they would then replace.

It betrays a laissez-faire timidity greater than the Victorians' to define "the reality of a thing" as "its freedom,"[11] when one means only freedom from constraint, form, knowledge; never freedom to make, shape, direct. For freedom as a value surely must include the power to produce as well as the power to resist. If one finds "fundamental at all times" in Dickens his "protest against . . . repression,"[12] it is only by ignoring the tendency in Dickens's career to construct ever more powerfully repressive forms, which only subsequently does he learn to undo. The "yes of the realist" authorizes powerful shapes of its own, which a "capital negation" may then

9. Theodore Dreiser, *Dawn* (New York: Liveright, 1931), p. 327.

10. Norman Mailer, *Cannibals and Christians* (New York: Dial, 1966), p. 98.

11. Romano, *Dickens and Reality*, p. 120.

12. Ibid., pp. 126–127.

molest.[13] Only through such interplay, such "transitions," does a world achieve its full freedom.

To find the techniques of overview evil in themselves is a strong metaphysical temptation, and to condemn all bureaucracy, administration, organization is an anarchist temptation almost irresistible in our society for the spirit that would be free. The fundamental historical issue, however, remains who is surveying whom and for what purposes. Dickens emphasizes the need for a "good spirit" to convert the powers that previously had seemed satanic when assumed by humans. Even the criticism of professional deformation and distance in *Bleak House* leaves room for the value of Woodcourt's professional, specialized function as a physician.[14] Yet, as we have noted, in life even public health meant government "crows' nests" for surveillance. Rather than wishing away a whole hard-won accomplishment of human energies, the task that remains for us is more fully to explore what the potentials of this literary and social form were and are, to try to recover what we have lost of them, and to bring to fruition the best possibilities of the systems of knowledge and power that still encompass us.

13. On molestation and authority see Edward W. Said, *Beginnings* (New York: Basic Books, 1975), pp. 83–84.

14. I draw here upon "*Bleak House* and the Politics of Laughter," a talk given to the Criticism Discussion Group at Princeton University in January 1978 by Bruce Robbins, now of Rutgers University.

Index

Index

A

B

F

G

H

I

J

K

L

N

O

P

R

S